The European Union and International Organizations

This volume seeks to explore the complex relationship between the European Union and international organizations, and to fill a remarkably wide gap in existing literature on the topic.

Analysing the way in which the EU engages in some of the most important international organizations, this book outlines a framework for analysis within this thriving subject of study. By demonstrating how the EU supports 'effective multilateralism' and global governance, as well as furthering developments within foreign policy, this volume adopts a novel perspective on the EU as an international player. Seeking to move the focus of study beyond the European Union as itself an international organization, contributors set out to demonstrate EU aspirations to act *within* international organizations. The volume's key features include:

- the first comprehensive study on this topic;
- eight case studies of the EU, including its role within the UN, WTO, NATO and the ICC;
- contributions from both internationally renowned political scientists and economists.

The European Union and International Organizations will be of vital interest to students and scholars of international relations, European politics, political science, and international organizations. It will also be of interest to a wider readership including policy-makers, diplomats and journalists.

Knud Erik Jørgensen is a Professor in the Department of Political Science at the University of Aarhus, Denmark. He has published widely on European international affairs. Currently he is preparing a textbook on IR theory and a monograph on European foreign policy.

Routledge/GARNET series: Europe in the World

Edited by Mary Farrell and Karoline Postel-Vinay
Centre for International Studies and Research (CERI), France.

Editorial Board: Dr Mary Farrell, *Sciences Po*, Paris, France; Dr Karoline Postel-Vinay, *CERI*, France; Professor Richard Higgott, *University of Warwick*, United Kingdom; Dr Christian Lequesne, *CERI*, France; and Professor Thomas Risse, *Free University Berlin*, Germany.

International Advisory Committee: Dr Salma Bava, *Jawaharlal Nehru University*, New Delhi, India; Professor Knud Erik Jørgensen, *University of Aarhus*, Denmark; Professor Sunil Khilnani, *SAIS, Johns Hopkins University*, USA; Dr Anne-Marie Legloannec, *CERI*, France; Dr Xiaobo Lu, *SIPA, Columbia University*, USA; Professor James Mittelman, *University of Washington*, USA; Dr Karen Smith, *London School of Economics*, UK; and Professor Elzbieta Stadtmuller, *University of Wroclaw*, Poland.

The Routledge/GARNET series, *Europe in the World*, provides a forum for innovative research and current debates emanating from the research community within the GARNET Network of Excellence. GARNET is a Europe-wide network of 43 research institutions and scholars working collectively on questions around the theme of 'Global Governance, Regionalisation and Regulation: The Role of the EU', and funded by the European Commission under the 6th Framework Programme for Research.

1. **EU Foreign Policy in a Globalized World**
   Normative power and social preferences
   Edited by Zaki Laïdi

2. **The Search for a European Identity**
   Values, policies and legitimacy of the European Union
   Edited by Furio Cerutti and Sonia Lucarelli

3. **The European Union and the Social Dimension of Globalization**
   How the EU influences the world
   Edited by Jan Orbie and Lisa Tortell

4. **Governance and the Depoliticisation of Development**
   Edited by Wil Hout and Richard Robison

5. **The European Union and International Organizations**
   Edited by Knud Erik Jørgensen

The European Union and International Organizations

**Edited by
Knud Erik Jørgensen**

LONDON AND NEW YORK

Transferred to digital printing 2010

First published 2009
by Routledge
2 Park Square, Milton Park, Abingdon, Oxon OX14 4RN

Simultaneously published in the USA and Canada
by Routledge
270 Madison Ave, New York, NY 10016

*Routledge is an imprint of the Taylor & Francis Group,
an informa business*

© 2009 Knud Erik Jørgensen selection and editorial matter; individual
contributors, their contributions

Typeset in Times New Roman by
Book Now Ltd, London

All rights reserved. No part of this book may be reprinted or reproduced
or utilised in any form or by any electronic, mechanical, or other
means, now known or hereafter invented, including photocopying and
recording, or in any information storage or retrieval system, without
permission in writing from the publishers.

British Library Cataloguing in Publication Data
A catalogue record for this book is available from the British Library

Library of Congress Cataloging in Publication Data
The European Union and international organizations/Knud
Erik Jørgensen [editor].
        p. cm.
Includes bibliographical references.
1. European Union. 2. International agencies. I. Jørgensen, Knud Erik.
JN30.J585 2008
341.242'2—dc22   2008027883

ISBN10: 0–415–46738–1 (hbk)
ISBN10: 0–415–59953–9 (pbk)
ISBN10: 0–203–88441–8 (ebk)

ISBN13: 978–0–415–46738–4 (hbk)
ISBN13: 978–0–415–59953–5 (pbk)
ISBN13: 978–0–203–88441–6 (ebk)

Contents

List of illustrations	vii
List of contributors	ix
Preface and acknowledgements	xiii

1 The European Union and international organizations: A framework for analysis — 1
KNUD ERIK JØRGENSEN

2 The accidental player: The European Union and the global economy — 21
JEAN PISANI-FERRY

3 Complex engagement: The EU and the UN system — 37
FRANZISKA BRANTNER AND RICHARD GOWAN

4 A single EU seat in the International Monetary Fund? — 61
LORENZO BINI SMAGHI

5 The World Trade Organization and the European Union — 80
JENS LADEFOGED MORTENSEN

6 The European Union and NATO: 'Shrewd interorganizationalism' in the making? — 101
JOHANNES VARWICK AND JOACHIM KOOPS

7 EU–OSCE relations: Partners or rivals in security? — 131
PETER VAN HAM

8 The European Union at the ILO's International Labour Conferences: A 'double' principal–agent analysis — 149
PETER NEDERGAARD

vi *Contents*

9 The European Union and the International Criminal Court: The politics of international criminal justice   167

MARTIJN GROENLEER AND DAVID RIJKS

10 Conclusion and perspectives   188

KNUD ERIK JØRGENSEN

Index   198

List of illustrations

Figures

2.1	Agriculture indicators for the EU-25	30
2.2	European MS voting weights in the EU and the IMF	33
5.1	Levels of EU trade diplomacy	82

Tables

2.1	Weight of the EU in international economic and financial institutions	23
2.2	Governance models in EU external economic relations	32
3.1	Distribution of seats on UN forums, by selected political groups, 1 August 2007	48
3.2	Assessed UN budget contributions by EU member states, 2005	49
4.1	EU constituencies in the IMF	63
4.2	Groupings' voting shares in the IMF	65
4.3	Financial support of major sponsors	70
4.4	EU-27 countries' quota and voting shares in the IMF	75
5.1	Overview of major changes in EC–GATT/EU–WTO relations	89
5.2	Combined top traders in world merchandise trade (2006)	90
5.3	Key quotes from Commission strategy paper, 2006	91
8.1	Components of coordination	150
8.2	Institutions and organs in the chapter	152

List of contributors

Franziska Brantner is a Research Associate at the European Studies Centre, Oxford University, UK, and is writing her PhD thesis with Professor Wolfgang Wessels (University of Cologne, Germany) on the role of the European Union in UN reform. She graduated in 2004 with a double diploma from the School of International and Public Affairs, Columbia University and of the Institut d'Etudes Politiques, Paris (Sciences Po), from which she graduated first out of her class.

Richard Gowan is a Research Associate and Associate Director for Policy in the Center on International Cooperation, New York University. He is responsible for developing CIC's outreach and profile, in addition to working on peacekeeping, multilateral security arrangements and the relationship between the UN and the European Union. He is also a Policy Fellow at the European Council on Foreign Relations. He has broadcast widely – including the BBC, CNN and the Lehrer News Hour – and frequently contributes to policy magazines and websites. He has worked with the OSCE Mission to Croatia, and published on the political philosophy of Raymond Aron.

Martijn Groenleer is an Assistant Professor in the Faculty of Technology, Policy and Management, Delft University, the Netherlands. His research interests include EU crisis and safety management, and bureaucratic politics in the European Union, particularly the creation of EU-level agencies. He has previously worked with the Task Force International Criminal Court of the Netherlands Ministry of Foreign Affairs.

Peter van Ham is Director of the Global Governance Programme at the Netherlands Institute of International Relations 'Clingendael', and Professor at the College of Europe in Bruges, Belgium. He is a member of the Advisory Council on International Affairs to the Dutch Government. His expertise includes transatlantic relations, European security and WMD proliferation, and he has published widely on these issues.

Knud Erik Jørgensen is Professor in the Department of Political Science, University of Aarhus, Denmark. He is editor or author of ten volumes on EU politics

x *List of contributors*

or international relations, most recently co-editor (with Mark Pollack and Ben Rosamond) of the *Handbook on European Union Politics* (Sage 2007) and (with Esra LaGro) *Turkey and the European Union: Prospects for a Difficult Encounter* (Palgrave 2007). In addition, he has published numerous articles in journals and chapters in edited volumes. Currently, he is preparing a monograph on EU foreign policy and a new introductory IR Theory textbook.

Joachim Koops is a PhD Candidate at the University of Kiel, Germany and an Analyst at the Oxford Council on Good Governance, UK. He holds a BA in Philosophy, Politics and Economics from the University of Oxford, an MSc in European Politics, Economics and Law from the University of Turku, Finland, and a Post-graduate Diploma in English Law from the University of Oxford, UK. His research focuses on the theory and practice of multilateralism and interorganizationalism, particularly in the field of crisis management.

Jens Ladefoged Mortensen, PhD, is an Associate Professor in the Department of Political Science, University of Copenhagen. He is a specialist on European trade policy and WTO relations. He has published WTO-related articles in various books and journals, including a contribution to *Political Economy and the Changing Global Order* (OUP 2006), and is currently completing a book entitled *WTO, Governance and the Limits to Law* (Routledge). His latest research project is concerned with trade-related EU climate politics and biofuels policy.

Peter Nedergaard, Professor, PhD, Department of Political Science, University of Copenhagan. He has published widely on EU politics and economics. Recently, he has published in journals like *Journal of Common Market Studies*, *Journal of European Integration*, *Public Choice*, *Cooperation & Conflict*, *Scandinavian Political Studies* and *Policy Studies*. For a number of years, he was Head of Division in the Danish Ministry of Employment.

Jean Pisani-Ferry is Director of BRUEGEL, a Brussels-based economic think-tank, and Professor at the Université Paris-Dauphine. He is a member of the European Commission's Group of Economic Policy Analysis and of the French Prime Minister's Council of Economic Analysis. He is also a Vice-President of the French economic association. In 2002–2003, he was a member of the Sapir Group appointed by the President of the European Commission.

David Rijks is a PhD Candidate at the Centre of International Studies, University of Cambridge, UK. His expertise includes EU foreign policy, and in particular diplomatic representation of the European Union and its member states. He is a fellow of the European Foreign and Security Policy Studies Programme, supported by the Riksbankens Jubileumsfond, the VolkswagenStiftung, and the Compagnia di San Paolo. He has previously worked with the Task Force International Criminal Court of the Netherlands Ministry of Foreign Affairs.

List of contributors xi

Lorenzo Bini Smaghi holds a PhD in Economics from the University of Chicago. He is a member of the Executive Board of the European Central Bank in Frankfurt. Previously, he has been Director General for International Financial Relations, Italian Ministry of the Economy and Finance. He has published extensively on monetary issues and recent publications include 'A Single European Seat in the IMF?', *Journal of Common Market Studies* (2004) and 'Powerless Europe: Why is the Euro Area Still a Political Dwarf?', *International Finance* (2006, 9(2): 1–19).

Johannes Varwick is Professor for European Integration and International Organizations in the Institute of Political Science, Christian-Albrechts University in Kiel, Germany. He is the author or (co-)editor of several books, including *Die Reform der Vereinten Nationen – Politikwissenschaftliche Perspektiven* (2006), *United Nations* (2005), and *Die Beziehungen zwischen NATO und EU* (2005).

Preface and acknowledgements

The purpose of this book is to analyse what the European Union is doing in international organizations, thus contributing to a comprehensive understanding of the functioning of the multilateral system at the beginning of the twenty-first century. To ask what the Union is doing implies most likely a dash of surprise and a certain degree of curiosity. The surprise may be caused by a traditional first impression image of the European Union, namely that it is often itself considered to be an international organization. First impressions are said to last and this one seems particularly long lived. However, the book is intended to question this movie 'take one' scene and to explain how we might conceptualize and explain the changing nature of EU relations with international organizations. This is a huge research agenda and, realizing that one book cannot possibly do everything, it has been designed to particularly explain change over time and variation across policy fields. This is where our professional curiosity comes into play, because the book aims at exploring what so far have been largely uncharted waters.

During the genesis of the book, some had to leave the project due to pregnancy or due to imperatives such as 'have to finish my PhD thesis'. Others joined the project along the road and I am most grateful for their decision to join. Whether present in the book or not, all are part of an increasingly flourishing community whose members are keen to understand the European Union's engagement in world politics in general and EU relations with international organizations in particular. The story is certainly to be continued.

Some draft chapters were discussed at a colloquium at the Institute of European Studies, Vrije Universiteit Brussel, in June 2006, and I am grateful to the academic director of the IES, Sebastian Oberthür, for hosting this colloquium. Other draft chapters were discussed at international conferences in Istanbul, Chicago and Turin. In this context, I would like to thank our panel chairs and discussants who generously contributed to improve the draft chapters. I am most grateful to the Routledge team, including the Garnet Series editors Mary Farrell and Karoline Postel-Vinay, Editorial Assistant Lucy Dunne and Senior Commissioning Editor Heidi Bagtazo. They have displayed all the deeds authors can wish for: encouragement, patience and engagement. I gratefully acknowledge Blackwell's permission to reprint Lorenzo Bini Smaghi's article 'A Single EU

xiv *Preface and acknowledgements*

Seat in the IMF?', originally published in the *Journal of Common Market Studies*, 42(2): 229–248. The article has been updated and slightly revised for publication in the present volume. Finally, I am most thankful to Nicole Meron, who language edited the manuscript and prepared the index, and to Anne-Grethe Gammelgaard, who prepared the final version of the manuscript.

Knud Erik Jørgensen
Aarhus, June 2008

1 The European Union and international organizations

A framework for analysis

Knud Erik Jørgensen

In his reflections on the future role of the European Union and the United States, the former US ambassador to the European Union, Rockwell A. Schnabel, points to a scenario outlined by the former EU Commissioner for external relations, Chris Patten: 'the US and the EU have two decades left to "shape the world" in the ways we deem best. After that, in his estimation, economic and demographic trends will force us to share that power with the two emerging Asian giants' (Schnabel 2005: 75; see also Patten 2005). Schnabel adds that Patten's deadline 'sounds all too realistic to me. Meaning that now is the Atlantic moment, the moment of America and Europe. Will we seize it?' (2005: 75; see also Daalder 2001). There are multiple ways and multiple arenas to shape the world, yet international organizations engaged in global governance constitute one such important arena and both the United States and the European Union have policies vis-à-vis international organizations.[1]

Whereas the relationship between the United States and multilateral institutions has been extensively examined in the literature, ranging from celebrative 'two cheers for multilateralism' to outright warnings against the 'false promise of international institutions' (Keohane and Nye 1985; Mearsheimer 1994), it is considerably less well known how (or whether) the European Union aims at shaping the world (of international organizations) in ways 'we deem best'. We do know that European diplomats during the first decade of the twenty-first century have discovered new aspects of European (multilateral) identity and interests. We also know, more specifically, that, according to numerous official statements and documents, the European Union has developed a strong belief in the value of effective multilateralism, 'with a strong United Nations at its heart. The UN, with its universal mandate and legitimacy, is uniquely placed to respond to our common challenges' (European Council 2003: 16).

Support of multilateralism is quite simply among those EU strategic objectives which most clearly have been spelled out in policy statements and numerous speeches. The risks of not supporting effective multilateralism have also been identified: 'Those who want pluralism and multilateralism to survive have a duty to make the United Nations effective (as the leaders of the democracies strikingly failed to do in the case of the League of Nations)' (Cooper 2003: 164, 168). These citations and several other indicators suggest that the relationship between the

2   Knud Erik Jørgensen

European Union and international organizations is crucially important for the future of both the European Union and international organizations. Unfortunately, this high degree of political importance has only to some extent been reflected in research. The field of study has for some time been in a rather unsatisfactory state of affairs. In other words, to the degree that there has been research on the topic, it has been more scattered and compartmentalized than comprehensive, systematic and integrated.

In light of this, the aim of this volume is to contribute to a comprehensive understanding of the relationship between the European Union and major international organizations, thereby contributing to fill a remarkably wide gap in the literature. In this fashion, we aim at a critical examination of the European Union's policy of supporting 'effective multilateralism' and, by outlining a framework for analysis, we also intend to 'try on for size' a number of potential factors explaining the changing relationship. In the following section, I describe the main trends in contemporary scholarship on the topic. Subsequently, I briefly outline the specific approach of this book, pointing to two main sources of inspiration and presenting three sets of potential factors of explanation – internal, external and constitutive factors – for why relations between the European Union and international organizations have changed the ways they have. In the final section, I summarize the chapter.

Five major trends

Five major strands of literature contribute to our understanding of the Union's multilateral engagements. First, there is a considerable amount of legal-institutional studies of the European Union's representation in international organizations (Brückner 1990; Eeckhout 2004; Govaere *et al.* 2004; Griller 2003; Wessel 1999, 2008). These studies explore the interplay between formal and informal rules regulating EU engagement and the dynamics and consequences of treaty reforms (EC/EU Treaty). Furthermore, these studies are characterized by inquiries concerning the legal competences of EU member states and the European Community/Union as well as debates about the legal personality of the European Union. Most of the studies remain limited in their scope in the sense that they either address the subject in a rather general fashion or address only selected international institutions in single case studies. Given that the European Union is deeply embedded in a legalistic administrative culture, it would not be wise to underestimate the role of the legal-institutional dimension. Furthermore, the European Union is keen to emphasize the positive role of international law. In short, the legal-institutional approach is in many ways promising and highly relevant. However, this volume seeks primarily to understand the *politics* of relations between the European Union and international organizations and the legal dimension will consequently play a less prominent role. At the same time, we do try to detect the implicit politics of legally framed arguments.

Second, a number of political scientists have conceptualized relations between the European Union and (other) international organizations as interorganizational networks (Jönsson 1993). Accordingly, the European Union is either itself regarded as an international organization (Keohane and Hoffmann 1990; Moravcsik 1998; Foot *et al.* 2003) or as being composed of organizational parts that are comparable to organizational entities in other international organizations. As a result, relations between the European Union and international organizations are primarily analysed as relationships between like-units that may be characterized as either cooperation, conflict or competition (Bierman, forthcoming; Haugevik 2007; Guigner 2006; Ojanen 2004; Stokke and Coffey 2006; Hofmann and Reynolds 2007). This strand of research contributes significantly to our understanding of the dynamics and driving forces of the relationship between the European Union and international organizations. However, it is less capable and does not pretend to analyse the European Union as an actor engaged in changing patterns of instrumental action. The issue of a possible changed nature of these relations is hardly addressed.

This leads us to the third perspective which is rooted in the literature on EU foreign policy and conceptualizes the European Union as an international actor (Bretherton and Vogler 2006; McCormick 2007). It is to be expected that aspects of identity, interests and policy characterize this literature, which by now has examined most of the European Union's major international relations (with states and regions) (cf. Hill and Smith 2005; Marsh and Mackenstein 2005). However, policies toward international organizations have constituted a rather neglected topic within the broader research agenda of this literature. To the degree that research has been done, scholars have paid attention to the European Union's role in the United Nations in particular, and prioritized General Assembly politics (Gregory and Stack 1983; Stadler 1993; Luif 2003; Johansson-Nogués 2004; see also Laatikainen and Smith 2006). This literature is highly relevant for the objectives of this book and it does not take more than some focused reflection to adapt analytical frameworks to the research agenda guiding this book. In many ways, this volume is a continuation of and complementary to Katie Laatikainen and Karen Smith's *Intersecting Multilateralisms* (2006) and Ole Elgstrøm and Michael Smith's *The European Union's Roles in International Politics* (2006).

The fourth cluster of perspectives focuses on the European Union's policy of supporting multilateral institutions. This literature is foremost concerned with contemporary policy issues and therefore addresses issues situated somewhere between policy analysis and policy implications (Biscop 2005; Cameron 2004; Eide *et al.* 2004; Ortega 2005). This priority necessarily has an impact on the analytical set-up, as studies often take their point of departure in the European Union's officially stated objective of supporting effective multilateralism, and proceed by means of examining what this might mean or the degree to which the political ends have been achieved. The time frame is usually short term and studies are naturally more concerned with policy than theoretical issues.

Fifth, the literature on global governance has produced insights that are most relevant for the exploration of the European Union's relations with international organizations. This type of research focuses on multilateral institutions as prime instruments of global governance and the European Union is sometimes analysed

4   *Knud Erik Jørgensen*

as an important feature of this framework (Jørgensen and Rosamond 2002; Rittberger and Zangl 2006; Hawkins *et al.* 2006; Barnett and Finnemore 2004; Barnett and Duvall 2005). More generally, it provides a general framework for analysing actor constellations as they relate to global governance efforts. These studies have produced important insights concerning the significance of specific institutional features as well as concerning the conditions for successful international cooperation (Goldstein *et al.* 2001; Finnemore and Toope 2001). In the major part of the global governance literature, the European Union has been assigned a role as international organization, whereas reflections on the European Union as an actor within international organizations are rather rare.

A framework for analysis

In this book we mainly take our point of departure in the European Union's aspiration to act *in* international organizations, not to *be* an international organization. In turn, this perspective explains why the extensive and analytically rich literature on the United States and the multilateral system can serve as a valuable source of inspiration (Karns and Mingst 1992; Ruggie 1993, 1998; Luck 1999; Patrick and Forman 2002; Foot *et al.* 2003).

In order to understand US policy towards multilateral institutions, Margaret Karns and Karen Mingst have developed a particularly useful framework for analysis. They focus on a two-way flow of influence and ask four main questions (1992: 1–3). If we with some care apply their analytical framework to the case of the European Union, the changing relationship between the European Union and international organizations can be thoroughly examined by asking the following four questions:

1   How has the use of international organizations as instruments of EU policy changed over time?
2   How have the constraints and influence of international organizations on the European Union changed over time?
3   Why have these changes occurred?
4   What are the policy implications for the European Union of these patterns of changing influence?

The following sections examine the analytical potentials and consequences of using these questions for structuring our explorations of the relationship between the European Union and international organizations.

Changing relations between the European Union and international organizations

Indicators of a changing relationship are legion, ranging from official documents to a considerable number of case studies. EU self-images of being a 'frontrunner' or a 'leading player' suggest that the times of being an international nobody and

The EU and international organizations   5

conducting reactive politics have been left behind, at least in some policy fields and in some international organizations (European Commission 2004). Well, such images could also suggest that a politics of aggrandizement is emerging. Yet, several case studies suggest that, whereas the European Union in the past may have been an organization in need of learning about international affairs, the European Union now seems to master several of the disciplines of international relations. Finally, it seems reasonable to assume that to some degree the changing relationship has been caused by the European Union's own transformation from being an international organization to becoming a player within international organizations. However, this transformation is far from being fully accomplished, implying that the Union has a split identity, being a Union but also a group of small or medium-sized countries, the latter identity paradoxically nurtured by the rather state-centric world of international organizations.

While questions and indicators are useful points of departure or pointers, they do not quite constitute a framework for analysis. Therefore, the following sections explicate the ramifications of asking the above questions. The context of such issues is not unimportant. Studies of the United States and multilateral institutions often lead to the conclusion that these institutions embody US interests, cf. the following statement, 'America's decisions to cooperate in multilateral forums will be determined predominantly by the extent to which any specific organization is perceived by important US domestic actors to be an effective and congenial vehicle for the promotion of America's objectives' (Foot *et al.* 2003: 14–19; see also Cowhey 1993). Such conclusions do not leave much room for manoeuvre for other actors, the European Union included. However, the question is whether such findings catch all important features of multilateral institutions or rather demonstrate some of the unintended consequences of focusing on just one (exceptional) state. The subsequent sections aim at addressing this issue by means of outlining a framework for analysis.

The European Union's instrumental use of international organizations

It is a widely held belief that US foreign policy practice is characterized by an 'instrumental' mind-set and EU foreign policy by a 'process' mind-set. In our reflections on these practices, we tend to reproduce the distinction. Hence, in studies of the United States and international organizations, it has been a regular key concern to analyse the degree to which the United States influences multilateral institutions, consistently analysed 'as instruments of American policies' (Karns and Mingst 1992: 6–8; see also Ruggie 1993; Foot *et al.* 2003: 14–19). By contrast, studies of EU policies towards multilateral institutions tend foremost to be consistent in terms of not asking about possible instrumental dimensions. It is well known that the 2003 European Security Strategy makes support of international organizations one of the European Union's key objectives. Such phrasing suggests a kind of disinterested global public service approach that is legion in EU documents and in speeches given by EU officials. However, analysts should

6   *Knud Erik Jørgensen*

not necessarily buy into such political discourse and should definitely not refrain from exploring the European Union's possible influence in, impact on, or instrumental use of international organizations.

Observers often quote two reasons for expecting considerable influence. First, the union consists of 27 states and, combined, they often have a significant share of membership of international organizations. Second, the EU/EU-27 provides major chunks of the financial contributions it takes to run international organizations. Given this uneven pattern of contributions, some are tempted to ask how much influence Euros possibly can buy. The following paragraphs address these issues of membership, budgets and impact.

In terms of formal membership, the EU-27 often has a significant share of membership in international organizations. Some critics even speak about European overrepresentation. A few illustrative examples explain why. The EU-27 has 27 members of the OSCE's total of 55 member states, that is, 49 per cent of all OSCE members can be found in the European Union. Having such a share of membership, one should perhaps expect a very considerable EU influence in determining the OSCE's general mission and operational missions. However, as Peter van Ham points out (Chapter 7), such an assumption is risky if not misleading. Furthermore, it is worthwhile emphasizing not only 'share of membership' but also form of 'representation'. The status of the European Community, represented by the European Commission, is particularly important. The European Community is a permanent observer in the UN and in some international organizations the European Union can be said to have 28 members because, in addition to European states, the European Community has been recognized as a full member. This applies to the FAO and the WTO. This significant variation in terms of membership and representation makes an important point of departure but we should not dwell for too long on the issue. Both Jean Pisani-Ferry and Lorenzo Bini Smaghi (Chapters 2 and 4) point out that formal membership, while important, is only one aspect of a longer and more complex story. Indeed both suggest that the European Union could gain significant influence by reducing formal (over)representation in international organizations. Yet such suggestions imply agonistic clashes between ceremonial and effective multilateral politics.

Concerning several of the European Union's relations with international organizations, the financial flow is very significant. The European Union (and its member states) is the biggest financial contributor to the general UN budget and many of the UN's specialized agencies. However, how can the European Union's capacity to translate financial means into political ends be characterized? Seemingly, the power that potentially could flow from this source evaporates in the hands of the European Union and its member states. Concerning international financial institutions, the European Union has for years aimed at strengthening its impact. These institutions are somehow special in the sense that both the IMF and the World Bank operate on the basis of weighed voting. While the United States is the single largest *state* contributor, the EU-27 collectively contributes about twice the amount of the United States and controls (collectively) more than one-third of all votes. However, as Pisani-Ferry and Bini Smaghi point out, the European Union's voting power is diluted amongst several constituencies that also include non-EU member states. Therefore, the financial input is far from being reflected in political impact. Instead, the institutional design, including governance structures of the international financial institutions as well as concrete policy-making, is grossly determined by the United States, and the launch of the Euro seems not to have changed this. The structural inability of the EU-27 to make use of their financial power is analytically intriguing and politically quite a challenge. However, with a few notable exceptions, the topic has not caught the attention of scholars (but see McNamara and Meunier 2002; Horng 2004; Pisani-Ferry 2008; Smaghi 2006).

Given the European Union's formal strong representation in many international organizations, one could perhaps expect a strong instrumental linkage between the European Union and specific organizations: what does the European Union want specific international organizations to be or to do? Put differently, according to the European Union, what is the function of a given international organization or what should the function be? Is the European Union happy with the performance of specific international organizations? Currently, several international organizations are in a process of institutional reform. We therefore have an interest in asking whether the European Union has clearly stated preferences as regards the reform process or the outcome. Which role does the European Union aim at playing in these reforms? Has the European Union proactively initiated reforms or rather responded to reforms initiated by non-EU states? As we know by now, the European Union was largely incapable of speaking with one voice in the case of UN Security Council reform (Ortega 2005). Instead we witnessed the old image of a European polyphony suggesting several and contradictory solutions. What does the case of the OSCE reform process tell us? Similarly, it is unlikely that the IMF and the World Bank will be governed in the same fashion for ever. In this context, it is worthwhile asking whether the informal US–EU condominium deal about 'balancing' directors/CEOs of the IMF/World Bank is sustainable. In the context of the WTO, the European Union has worked hard to put the Singapore issues on the agenda, yet so far without much success (Damro 2006).

Impact can be measured on four dimensions: (1) original or existing institutional design, (2) policy-making processes within the international organization, (3) activities of specific organizations and (4) institutional reform. These dimensions of impact will now be illustrated by means of taking the OSCE as an example. Given the EU-27 membership of the OSCE, the European Union's financial contribution to the budget of the OSCE, and the European Union's policy vis-à-vis the OSCE, the following questions are crucially important: Does the European Union have an impact on the OSCE as such, on agenda setting, policy-making, and on the activities of the OSCE? When the OSCE was created in 1995, did the European Union have an impact on the decision to institutionalize the CSCE process? Did the European Union have an impact on the 'tasking' of the OSCE? Did the European Union have an impact on the institutional design of the OSCE? Finally, does the European Union 'bifurcate' policy-making, in the sense of supporting the involvement of the OSCE, while in parallel being involved itself? How does such bifurcation work? On the one hand, the European

8 *Knud Erik Jørgensen*

Union supports the OSCE's involvement in the Caucasus. However, the European Union is, on the other hand, engaged in developing a neighbourhood policy vis-à-vis the eastern and southern arches of neighbours, the Caucasus included. Hence, some fear that the European Union pre-empts the role of the OSCE, slowly squeezing the organization out of business. In contrast, it is also possible to argue that the European Union demonstrates the type of 'double-layered' diplomacy – multilateral and bilateral strategies in parallel – that has characterized US foreign policy for years. In this perspective, there is nothing to deplore regarding bifurcation, except if one prefers an exclusive OSCE engagement or a neat and watertight division of labour between the European Union and the OSCE. In general, the above questions can be asked in relation to virtually all international organizations, though OSCE specifics obviously need to be translated into the specifics of other organizations. In a broader perspective, it is the significant variation of impact across policy fields that should attract our attention and analytical energy.

International organizations influencing EU policies and policy-making

While the European Union aims at influencing its external environment – international organizations included – EU institutions, policies and policy-making processes may also have been influenced by international organizations. This question is part of Margaret Karns and Karen Mingst's (1992) research agenda (and delivers most interesting findings). Similarly, Martha Finnemore (1996; see also Kelley 2004) has demonstrated how international organizations sometimes 'teach' states what they (really) want, and influence the definition of national interests or state preferences. Her cases include UNESCO, the International Red Cross and the World Bank, yet the book is otherwise fairly state-centric, which implies that the European Union is excluded from analysis. However, Finnemore's approach and general findings suggest that we should pay attention to the possibility of international organizations 'teaching' the European Union. In general, the perspective goes under the label of second image reversed explanations.

In several international policy fields, the European Union has been a rather inexperienced newcomer to the international arena, that is, an actor for whom teaching and nurturing is crucially important. Important examples include relations between the European Union and the WHO (Guigner 2006), the European Union and the WTO (de Burca and Scott 2000) and the fact that the European Union's politics of conditionality vis-à-vis East and Central Europe largely has been copied from the World Bank. Concerning the relationship between the WHO and European Union, the flow of influence has been reversed over time. Thus, it has for years been highly asymmetrical in favour of the WHO, yet the institutional balance of power seems to be changing (Guigner 2006). In other policy fields, the European Union has received advice on 'best practice' from international organizations. One such example is EU development policy which in

1998 was severely criticized by the OECD and subsequently thoroughly reformed. Similarly, the OECD regularly reviews the European Union's economic performance and provides policy prescriptions. An example in the field of security is NATO serving as a very experienced mentor, teaching the European Union a lesson or two on international security. The transfer of Javier Solana from NATO to the European Union has been highly instrumental in facilitating such processes of learning (de Witte 2004; Varwick 2005; see also Chapter 6).

The UN with its *global* outlook may have taught the *regional* institution – the European Union – some fundamentals about the global state of affairs. This is not to claim that the European Union does not have global dimensions in its foreign policy. After all, international trade and development have been constitutive parts of European foreign policy ever since the Rome Treaty was signed. However, despite these global perspectives, the main chunk of the European Union's existence has been predominantly regionally focused. Being taught by the UN is not unproblematic because the UN is not perfect either, displaying leanings towards somewhat uneven global outlooks. It should also be emphasized that lessons need not be only of the how-to-do-things category. Equally important is the how-not-to-do-things. Thus, during the first part of the 1990s Balkan crisis, EU reliance on the UN as a security operator (UNPROFOR) turned into the worst self-made foreign policy failure the European Union has ever experienced.

However, the flow of influence from international organizations is not unproblematic. When officials at DG Trade internationalize an issue by taking it to an international organization, they influence at the same time the domestic balance of power between promoters of and protectors against globalization. The method of making or taking an issue 'international' is well known in the literature on national foreign policy, yet hardly cultivated concerning EU foreign policy.

Contending explanations of change

Individual international organizations are not of equal importance to the European Union across time. The European Union's relations with the IAEA can serve as an example. On the one hand, the European Union has had a long relationship with the IAEA. However, since WMDs have been singled out as a main threat to European security, the IAEA has become an increasingly important international organization for the European Union. The diplomacy of the EU-3 vis-à-vis Iran since 2003 has also increased the instrumentality of the IAEA, that is, the fact that the European Union now finds the IAEA useful to do certain things. Second, the OSCE might serve as an example of declining instrumentality, that is, an organization whose importance to the European Union has been declining. It was useful as a bridge between Europe's Cold War environment and the European Union's increasingly important role in providing security in conflict-ridden regions such as the Western Balkans and the Caucasus. Finally, it is telling that the European Union has never made use of the exit strategy, that is, quitting an international organization. By contrast, the United States did (temporarily) quit UNESCO (cf. Coate 1992), and a number of US policy-makers are from time

10 *Knud Erik Jørgensen*

to time threatening to exit the UN ('if the UN does not reform, then we quit'). In the three following sections, EU-internal, EU-external and constitutive factors will be examined as potential factors capable of explaining changing relations between the European Union and international organizations.

EU-internal factors

In studies of American policy towards multilateral institutions, analysts consistently reach the conclusion that American policy predominantly is driven by domestic factors. Concerning changing patterns of US engagement, Foot *et al.* find that domestic factors determine policy towards international organizations, most notably American exceptionalism, 'when based on a definition that emphasizes US beliefs that its national values and practices are universally valid and its policy positions are moral and proper and not just expedient' (2003: 268; on American exceptionalism, see Ruggie 2003). Similarly, John Ruggie (1993) highlights the role of domestic values, images and principles as well as domestic institutions. Such a high degree of consensus is nothing but remarkable and it is perhaps tempting to assume that such conclusions also apply to the European Union. After all, the range and variety of EU-domestic factors is impressive. Several of these factors are well known in the literature on European integration and governance and thus standard components in many studies of EU policy-making; other factors have been less widespread, for instance power.

Interest groups and private companies constitute a factor that should not be underestimated – indeed many analysts find that the influence of interest groups is considerable. In the present context, it is sufficient to illustrate how this factor works. NGOs were part of the different policy networks which produced the International Criminal Court and the international ban on land-mines. Several NGOs have a direct interest in the European Union's promotion of democracy, development and human rights. Furthermore, several industries have a direct interest in EU regulations and regimes concerning commodities, ranging from wine and tobacco to bananas and shoes. They or their lobbyists consequently try to influence the European Union's position in international negotiations. Similarly, the European Union's so-called social partners are present in the ILO, protecting their interests and promoting their objectives, yet also having a keen interest in how member states coordinate their positions in this international organization (see Chapter 8). Finally, European farmers have high stakes in the European Union's positions within the WTO and the European defence industry has a natural interest in defence policy. In short, there are many good reasons to expect that interest groups and industries aim at having an impact on the European Union's relations with international organizations. But how important is this factor relative to other internal factors?

Traditionally, the political and institutional features of an international player have been among the most popular factors explaining foreign policy. In parts of the literature, the factor goes under the label 'second image'. How would this apply to the EU case? It is well known that the European Union's political system is notoriously complex and characterized by distinct dynamics (Hix 1999). Furthermore, the EU polity is itself characterized by elements of multilateralism. This home-grown multilateralism is a convenient feature, not least when policy-makers present reasons for political action, and not least when such political action consists of supporting the UN and other multilateral institutions. It is equally suitable when self-images are contrasted to images of others. European diplomats then emphasize that Europe supports the UN because Europeans have multilateral genetic codes or important experiences with multilateral processes. However, reasons for political action are not necessarily causes of action and, in the present context, we are into causal explanation. It is well known that it is common to project domestic institutions and practices internationally. With respect to the United States and multilateralism, it has been argued that the multilateral trade system launched after the Second World War was modelled on US domestic institutions (Goldstein 1993). Similarly, the European Union has consistently been presented as a model for other regional groupings. From time to time and increasingly so, the European Union has also been presented as a model for the emerging world polity and for global governance institutions (see Jørgensen and Rosamond 2002).

Divisions within the executive branch are pronounced, not least because the executive branch in Europe is bifurcated or more. That is, apart from the EU institutions characterized by their internal divisions, the European Union has currently 27 ministries of foreign affairs, 27 ministries of defence and 27 prime ministers/heads of state. Because of this complex executive, it is necessary in most cases to ask, who represents the European Union in international organizations? In the context of international monetary matters and defence, the three larger member states have a very significant say, a de facto monopoly. Yet, in some issue areas, the ECB single handed represents Eurozone countries. In some policy fields, the European Commission functions as the executive branch, whereas in other fields the role is played by the country holding the rotating Council Presidency. At the same time, the multilateral system is in essence a state-centric institution, created by and for states. From time to time most EU member states, some more than others, completely forget about their multilateral genetic codes and enjoy the power, pride and prestige resulting from being an international actor. When this happens, the 'divisions-within-the-executive-branch' factor turns into a euphemism.

Political culture appears intuitively to be a relevant factor, yet is notoriously difficult to pin down. Nonetheless, let us focus on two different yet overlapping aspects. When Robert Cooper points out that multilateralism has 'intrinsic value', and Javier Solana claims that European values inform the making of European foreign policy, both illustrate perfectly well how values, images and principles have a function in reasons for political action (Lucarelli and Manners 2005). Furthermore, they illustrate how discursive structures play a role as an explanatory factor. Discourses about the UN and international organizations are relatively stable structures determining legitimate and illegitimate political speech acts. In Europe, the UN is part of a discursive structure on international cooperation and development connoting something positive. Similarly, international law and treaties are regarded as constitutive components of international society. Global

12 Knud Erik Jørgensen

responsibility and obligations should not be questioned because they are owed to both Europe's self and to others. Such factors play a key role in European discourse, and part of the multilateral system is seen as instrumental for achieving the objective of international development. In summary, both values and principles as well as discourses seem to have important things to say about the relationship between domestic politics and EU behaviour towards international organizations.

Patrick and Forman (2002) aim at explaining why the United States has an ambivalent attitude to multilateral cooperation, and they want to assess the costs and benefits to the United States of this ambivalent engagement. Basically, they address the multilateralism–bilateralism–unilateralism trilemma in the making of American foreign policy. While there seem to be good reasons to ask such questions concerning contemporary US politics, we have an interest in asking whether it is equally relevant concerning the European Union and international organizations. Perhaps ambivalent engagement is not an exclusive American feature. Though the European Union professes to support the multilateral system, inhabited by numerous international organizations, the European Union does cultivate both multilateral and bilateral relationships and does occasionally act unilaterally. Hence, while focusing on multilateralism we should keep an eye on alternative foreign policy strategies and possible slides from one strategy to the other. For instance, the European Union's strong preference for multilateral trade agreements did not obstruct – as Mortensen demonstrates (Chapter 5) – bilateral agreements during a period when the multilateral Doha Round had been (temporarily) blocked.

EU-external factors

Studies of the United States and multilateral institutions conclude consistently that domestic factors are among the strongest explanatory factors that can be identified. However, this remarkable consensus conclusion should not dissuade us from including external factors in our 'factor portfolio', especially because the EU case might lead to different conclusions – perhaps being more sensitive to the external influence than the United States. The following external factors will be examined: international distribution of power, international interaction and social structures, the influence of other governments (and organizations) and, finally, the international cultural environment. In the following, each of these factors will be further described and characterized by means of illustrative examples.

The international distribution of power belongs to the traditional explanatory factors. In neorealist explanations of state behaviour, the change from Cold War bipolarity to an emerging post-Cold War multipolarity plays an important role (Waltz 2000). Though neorealism is a state-centric approach par excellence, it may nonetheless be possible to factor in the European Union, for instance, by asking whether or not the end of the Cold War constitutes the permissive variable that allows the European Union to significantly upgrade its international engagement, including the engagement in international organizations (Carlsnaes *et al.* 2004). At least it is remarkable that the end of the Cold War mirrors the European Union's increasingly important international commitments. Second, when analysing the importance of the international distribution of power, we do not need to confine ourselves to neorealist

The EU and international organizations   13

perspectives. Balance of power studies can be differentiated across policy fields. Thus, the WTO can be seen as a multilateral framework which incorporates an essentially bipolar EU–US relationship. Hence, EU (and US) positions on (and within) the WTO are expected to reflect this bipolar trade system. Similarly, NATO consists of the world's no. 1 (the United States) and no. 2 (EU-27) in terms of defence spending. This structural fact is likely to shape policy positions, including those of European members of NATO. Third, according to John Ikenberry, the United States 'has systematically used multilateral agreements as tools of grand strategy and world order building' (Ikenberry 2002: 122). Could it be that the European Union has similar reasons to support international organizations in general and the United Nations in particular? In any case, it might be misleading to separate issues of grand strategy from issues related to international organizations.

It is often claimed that the European Union's embrace of effective multilateralism is caused by the Union's own genetic codes. In other words, a multilateral being at home causes preferences for a multilateral environment abroad. However, the Bush administration's preference for selective multilateralism or multilateralism à la carte might have been instrumental in activating these codes and building a consensus position concerning conceptions of multilateralism (Aggestam 2004; Patten 2005; Jørgensen 2006a, 2006b). Furthermore, the war over Iraq and many other cases demonstrate that US pressure on Europe does not always breed European unity. It remains to be seen how the European Union will react to consistent efforts by the OIC to define human rights within the UN Human Rights Council (Smith 2008). Hence, it is an important general analytical objective to determine under what circumstances the European Union opts for unity and diversity, respectively, when feeling the diplomatic efforts of other governments or organizations.

Alexander Wendt (1999) highlights the importance of international social structures in his explanation of state behaviour. The theory leads one to expect that international interaction during the last decade has prompted the European Union to make a priority of the multilateral system. It is in this context significant that 'multilateralism' has become a contested concept, in particular because it indicates that the United States and the European Union have different visions of world order and consequently different ideas concerning which means to apply in order to achieve desirable political ends (Kupchan 2002; van Oudenaren 2003; Eide *et al.* 2004; Koops 2004). The 2003 European Security Strategy illustrates well the deeply embedded differences between US and EU conceptions of multilateralism. In other words, the argument is that, had the United States not been ambivalent or excessively instrumentally minded, the European Union would not have launched its high-profile endeavour in support of multilateralism. In general, the international interaction factor allows for mutual influence, sometimes even co-constitutive relations.

In studies on the United States, the possible influence of other governments on US behaviour towards multilateral organizations is examined (Foot *et al.* 2003). In explanations of changing EU multilateral strategies, the external factor, 'other governments', seems highly relevant. Among other governments, the United States can be singled out as particularly important, though the Russian, Chinese

14   *Knud Erik Jørgensen*

or Middle Eastern governments should not be neglected. The possible influence of other governments might change across time and space. Essentially, this is an empirical question that we need not further elaborate in the present context of outlining a framework for analysis. Furthermore, we may also want to include 'other organizations', as in ASEAN's efforts to influence EU multilateral policy on, for instance, Myanmar, AU efforts to influence EU policy on the Darfur crisis, or OIC efforts to influence EU policy on human rights.

The possible impact of the international cultural environment is not among the most often quoted external factors. However, Ronald Jepperson, Alexander Wendt and Peter Katzenstein (1996) have persuasively argued for the existence of an important impact causally flowing from the international cultural environment to identity and, in turn, to interest and policy. An application of their theory in the case of EU policy vis-à-vis international organizations might well produce interesting findings; their causal sequence of global culture, actor identity, interest and policy seems particularly promising.

Constitutive factors

The European Union shapes and is shaped by international society. EU member states are states, yet also constituent parts of a Union. The two examples demonstrate that some causal flows do not quite fit the external–internal dichotomy. They are both internal and external at the same time, and it takes considerable analytical violence to squeeze them into one or the other category. While obviously it can be done – actually, it is a standard operating procedure in several theoretical orientations – perhaps we should pause and ask whether such a squeeze is necessary. It is telling that Foot *et al.* regard the performance of multilateral institutions to be as much an internal as an external factor to the United States (2003: 13). While performance as such is a factor that is external to the United States, American perceptions of performance constitute an internal factor. This solution raises two important issues. Is it possible to analyse performance as such? And, is it possible or desirable to factor out a constituent member of an institution, for instance the United States, when analysing the performance of the institution as an external factor?

As mentioned, our search for explanatory factors has so far been structured by the inside/outside dichotomy. The distinction may still be relevant and it may also be applicable when analysing EU behaviour towards international organizations. However, if there is anything to studies of globalization and Europeanization or any value in structuration theory, then the distinction should be questioned and the search for complementary perspectives should begin. At an abstract level, Alexander Wendt and Raymond Duvall have made a plea for constitutive structuration approaches in studies of relations between international institutions and states. Instead of beginning with the 'interest, powers, and choices of already constituted state actors', they suggest integrating agent-centric and institution-centric approaches, preferably by means of bracketing (Duvall and Wendt 1989). Why not translate this abstract reasoning into a concrete research agenda that is capable of conceptualizing the European Union as actor, institution and arena?

Furthermore, there are several examples of EU member states taking an issue international only to see, in turn, the European Union adapting to decisions taken in some international forum. Thus, when the EU-3 have reached what they deem to be an impasse in talks with Iran, they put forward resolutions at the UN Security Council. Once these resolutions need to be implemented, the European Union is the context in which EU member states do this. Similarly, Pisani-Ferry (Chapter 2) points out that there is an intricate relationship between inside and outside dimensions of European governance: 'The main difficulty the European Union has to solve is the internal redistribution of power that will follow a redefinition of its external representation' (see Chapter 2). In general, we can ask, what is a European Union? Is it a collective of states, a union or both? All three options make sense and each option triggers different conceptions of the Union as an international actor, not least when we analyse the state-centric multilateral system, created by and serving state interests. How fortunate we are in the social sciences that a phenomenon under observation can change status by means of changing our perspectives.

In conclusion, we should take note of the serious problems and challenges that flow from attempts at assessing multilateral institutions from a constituent actor perspective. Most scholars in their effort to evaluate the effectiveness or influence of a particular actor tend to dichotomize the international organization and the actor whose influence they want to explore. Yet, international organizations are constituted by these very member states. When we analytically split off constituent parts from the organizations, we are in some sense erasing an important, fundamental part of any international organization. These problems are even further complicated when we begin analysing the European Union's multilateral engagements. On the one hand, the European Union is most often not formally a constituent part of most international organizations. On the other hand, the European Union can in practice be regarded as a de facto constituent member of several international organizations and has been recognized as such by both EU member states and other members of the international organizations.

Conclusion

The purpose of this introductory chapter is to introduce the topic, set the scene and outline a framework for analysis. The topic is politically important, not least because the current crisis of multilateralism requires reconsideration and an upgraded engagement by top politicians. The topic is intellectually a challenge – after all, it is some 20 years ago the issue of suitable approaches to the study of international institutions triggered what has become known as the constructivist-rationale debate. Furthermore, the topic concerns one of the classic issues in the study of world politics, namely relations between power and norms. Finally, the topic concerns another key distinction, that is, the one between instrumental and milieu-goal determined political action.

The scene is the phase in world politics during which the multilateral system is undergoing profound change, and international organizations face challenges each in their own distinct ways. In Europe, multilateralism and international organizations trigger predominantly positive connotations and are related to images of international cooperation and world order. The existence of international society is considered a fact of life and European policies towards multilateral international organizations reflect these perceptions of existing or desired international order. This is why the European Union is bound to lead initiatives identifying common solutions to global common problems.

Concerning the analytical framework, the primary source of inspiration has been neither studies of global governance nor the European Union's legal-institutional characteristics, the simple reason being that these approaches have severe difficulties in delivering answers to the kind of questions that originally triggered our interest in the project. In the first part of the chapter, I focused on changing relations between the European Union and international organizations. Being open for suggestions about a possible two-way flow of influence, I first examined how and why the European Union might influence international organizations and, subsequently, analysed how international organizations can influence the European Union.

In the second part of the chapter, I outlined a range of analytical options by means of identifying potential explanatory factors. Among EU-internal factors, I focused on six promising factors (interest groups, the political system, the executive, political culture, military weakness and diversity of preferences).

External context usually matters and perhaps more so for the European Union than for other international players. Basically, we do not know how much it matters until we have analysed the possible role of context. Among EU-external factors, the chapter focuses on four potential factors: distribution of power, other governments, international interaction and international organizations. Whereas the first factor has been dismissed as largely irrelevant to our understanding of changing US policies to multilateral institutions, we have to explore the degree to which the global distribution of power influences EU policies. At least, it is intriguing that the rise of EU involvement in international organizations has taken place after the end of the bipolar system and the Cold War. In a similar fashion it seems in terms of international interaction to be more than a coincidence that the European Union's strong commitment to effective multilateralism was declared in parallel to the Bush administration's somewhat dismissive approach to aspects of global governance, international law and some multilateral institutions. In order to possibly escape the inside/outside dichotomy, I included a section on so-called constitutive factors which potentially contribute to a more nuanced understanding.

In summary, the argument is not that all these factors are important in order to understand changing relations between the European Union and international organizations. Rather, the argument is that it seems worthwhile to examine their relative importance by means of empirical studies. Once such an examination has been conducted in a systematic fashion, it becomes possible to identify patterns and general trends. It is obviously beyond the purpose of this chapter to conclude which factors best explain change. The factors have to be closely examined in rich empirical studies and the following chapters have been designed to do precisely that.

Note

1 The chapter is a continuation of and slightly overlapping with my previous work on multilateralism (see Jørgensen 2006a, 2006b).

References

Aggestam, Lisbeth (2004) *A European Foreign Policy?* PhD thesis, Stockholm: Department of Political Science.

Barnett, M. and Duvall, R. (eds) (2005) *Power in Global Governance*, Cambridge: Cambridge University Press.

Barnett, M. and Finnemore, M. (2004) *Rules for the World. International Organizations in Global Politics*, Cornell: Cornell University Press.

Bierman, R. (forthcoming) 'Towards a Theory of Inter-Organizational Networking. The Euro-Atlantic Security Institutions Interacting', *Review of International Organizations*.

Biscop, S. (2005) *The European Security Strategy*, London: Ashgate.

Bretherton, C. and Vogler, J. (2006) *The European Union as a Global Actor*, London: Routledge.

Brückner, P. (1990) 'The European Community and the United Nations', *European Journal of International Law*, 1: 174–192.

Cameron, F. (2004) 'After Iraq: The EU and Global Governance', *Global Governance*, 10(2): 157–163.

Carlsnaes, W., Sjursen, H. and White, B. (eds) (2004) *Contemporary European Foreign Policy*, London: Sage Publications.

Coate, R.A. (1992) 'Changing Patterns of Conflict: The United States and UNESCO', in M.P. Karns and K.A. Mingst (eds) *The United States and Multilateral Institutions*, London: Routledge, pp. 231–260.

Cooper, R. (2003) *The Breaking of Nations. Order and Chaos in the Twentieth Century*, London: Atlantic Books.

Cowhey, P.F. (1993) 'Elect Locally – Order Globally: Domestic Politics and Multilateral Cooperation', in J. Ruggie (ed.) *Multilateralism Matters: The Theory and Praxis of an Institutional Form*, New York: Columbia University Press, pp. 157–200.

Daalder, I.H. (2001) 'The United States and Europe: From Primacy to Partnership?', in R. Lieber (ed.) *Eagle Rules? Foreign Policy and American Primacy in the 21st Century*, New York: Prentice Hall, pp. 70–96.

Damro, C. (2006) 'Institutions, Ideas and a Leadership Gap: The EU's Role in Multilateral Competition Policy', in O. Elgström and M. Smith (eds) *The European Union's Roles in International Politics: Concepts and Analysis*, London: Routledge, pp. 208–224.

de Burca, G. and Scott, J. (2000) *The Impact of the WTO on EU Decision-Making*, Jean Monnet Working Paper, Harvard Law School.

de Witte, P. (2004) 'Partnership or Rivalry? A View from Practice', paper prepared for the Kiel Conference: Die Beziehungen Zwischen NATO und EU: Partnership, Konkurrenz, Rivalität, 20–21 September.

Duvall, R. and Wendt, A. (1989) 'Institutions and International Order', in E.-O. Czempiel and J. Rosenau (eds) *Global Changes and Theoretical Challenges*, Lexington: Lexington Books, pp. 51–73.

Eeckhout, P. (2004) *External Relations of the European Union: Legal and Constitutional Foundations*, Oxford: Oxford University Press.

Eide, E. Barth (ed.) (2004) *'Effective Multilateralism': Europe, Regional Security and a Revitalised UN*, London: The Foreign Policy Centre.

18 Knud Erik Jørgensen

Elgstrøm, O. and Smith, M. (eds) (2006) *The European Union's Roles in International Politics*, London: Routledge.

European Commission (2004) *A World Player. The European Union's External Relations*, Brussels: DG Press and Communication.

European Council (2003) *A Secure Europe in a Better World*, Brussels: The Council Secretariat.

Finnemore, M. (1996) *National Interests in International Society*, Ithaca: Cornell University Press.

Finnemore, M. and Toope, S. (2001) Alternatives to 'legalization': richer views of law and politics, *International Organization*, 55: 743–758.

Foot, R., MacFarlane, S.N. and Mastanduno, M. (eds) (2003) *US Hegemony and International Organizations*, Oxford: Oxford University Press.

Goldstein, J.L. *et al.* (1993) 'Creating the GATT Rules: Politics, Institutions, and American Policy', in J. Ruggie (ed.) *Multilateralism Matters: The Theory and Praxis of an Institutional Form*, New York: Columbia University Press, pp. 201–232.

Goldstein, J.L., Kahler, M., Keohane, R.O. and Slaughter, A.-M. (2001) *Legalization and World Politics*, Boston: MIT Press.

Govaere, I., Capiau, J. and Vermeersch, A. (2004) 'In-between Seats: The Participation of the European Union in International Organizations', *European Foreign Affairs Review*, 9: 155–187.

Gregory, F. and Stack, F. (1983) 'The European Community and International Institutions', in J. Lodge (ed.) *Institutions and Policies of the European Community*, London: Pinter, pp. 240–251.

Griller, S. (2003) 'External Relations', in B. de Witte (ed.), *Ten Reflections on the Constitutional Treaty for Europe*. EUI, E-book, April 2003, pp. 133–157. Online. Available HTTP: http://www.iue.it/RSCAS/Research/Institutions/EuropeanTreaties.shtml (accessed 11 September 2008).

Guigner, S. (2006) 'The EU's Roles in Public Health within a Saturated Space of International Organizations: The Interdependence of Roles', in O. Elgstrøm and M. Smith (eds) *The European Union's Roles in International Politics*, London: Routledge, pp. 225–244.

Haugevik, K.M. (2007) 'New Partners, New Possibilities: Inter-institutional Security Cooperation in International Peace Operations', paper prepared for the 6th Pan-European Conference on International Relations, Turin, 12–15 September.

Hawkins, D.G., Lake, D.A., Nielson, D.L. and Tierney, M.J. (2006) *Delegation and Agency in International Organizations*, Cambridge: Cambridge University Press.

Hill, C. and Smith, M. (2005) *International Relations and the European Union*, Oxford: Oxford University Press.

Hix, S. (1999) *The Political System of the European Union*, Basingstoke: Palgrave.

Hofmann, S. and Reynolds, C. (2007) 'EU–NATO Relations: Time to Thaw the "Frozen Conflict"', *SWP Comments* 2007/C, June.

Horng, Der-Chin (2004) 'The European Central Bank's External Relations with Third Countries and the IMF', *European Foreign Affairs Review*, 9: 323–346.

Ikenberry, G.J. (2002) 'Multilateralism and U.S. Grand Strategy', in S. Patrick and S. Forman (eds) *Multilateralism and U.S. Foreign Policy. Ambivalent Engagement*, Boulder, CO: Lynne Rienner, pp. 121–140.

Jepperson, R., Wendt, A. and Katzenstein, P. (1996) 'Norms, Identity, and Culture in National Security', in P. Katzenstein (ed.) *The Culture of National Security*, New York: Columbia University Press, pp. 121–140.

Johansson-Nogués, E. (2004) 'The Fifteen and the Accession States in the UN General Assembly: What Future for European Foreign Policy in the Coming Together of the "Old" and "New" Europe?', *European Foreign Affairs Review*, 9: 67–92.

Jönsson, C. (1993) 'International Organization and Co-operation: An Interorganizational Perspective', *International Social Science Journal*, 138: 463–477.

Jørgensen, K.E. (2006a) 'A Multilateralist Role for the EU?', in O. Elgstrøm and M. Smith (eds) *The European Union's Roles in International Politics*, London: Routledge, pp. 30–46.

Jørgensen, K. E. (2006b) 'Intersecting Multilateralisms: The European Union and Multilateral Institutions', in K. Laatikainen and K.E. Smith (eds) *Intersecting Multilateralisms: The European Union at the United Nations*, Basingstoke: Palgrave, pp. 195–211.

Jørgensen, K.E. and Rosamond, B. (2002) 'Europe: Regional Laboratory for a Global Polity?', in M. Ougaard and R. Higgott (eds) *Towards a World Polity*, London: Routledge, pp. 189–200.

Karns, M.P. and Mingst, K.A. (1992) *The United States and Multilateral Institutions*, London: Routledge.

Kelley, J. (2004) 'International Actors on the Domestic Scene: Membership Conditionality and Socialization by International Institutions', *International Organization*, 58(3): 425–457.

Keohane, R.O. and Hoffmann, S. (1990) 'European Community Politics and Institutional Change', in W. Wallace, *Dynamics of European Integration*, London: Pinter, pp. 276–300.

Keohane, R.O. and Nye, J.S., Jr. (1985) 'Two Cheers for Multilateralism', *Foreign Policy*, 60: 148–167.

Koops, J.A. (2004) '"Effective Multilateralism": The Future of the EU's External Identity in a System of Trilateral Security Governance', paper presented at the Conference 'New Europe 2020: Visions and Strategies for a Wider Europe', Turku, Finland, 27 August 2004.

Kupchan, C. (2002) 'The End of the West', *The Atlantic*, November.

Laatikainen, K. and Smith, K.E. (eds) (2006) *Intersecting Multilateralisms: The European Union at the United Nations*, Basingstoke: Palgrave.

Lucarelli, S. and Manners, I. (eds) (2005) *Values, Images and Principles in EU Foreign Policy*, London: Routledge.

Luck, E.C. (1999) *Mixed Messages: American Politics and International Organization 1919–1999*, Washington, DC: Brookings Institution.

Luif, P. (2003) 'EU Cohesion in the UN General Assembly', *EU-ISS Occasional Paper*, 49: December.

Marsh, S. and Mackenstein, H. (2005) *The International Relations of the European Union*, London: Pearson/Longman.

McCormick, J. (2007) *The European Superpower*, Basingstoke: Palgrave.

McNamara, K. and Meunier, S. (2002) 'Between National Sovereignty and International Power: What External Voice for the Euro?', *International Affairs*, 78: 849–868.

Mearsheimer, J. (1994) 'The False Promise of International Institutions', *International Security*, 19: 5–49.

Moravcsik, A. (1998) *The Choice for Europe*, London: UCL Press.

Ojanen, H. (2004) 'Inter-organisational Relations as a Factor Shaping the EU's External Identity', *UPI Working Paper 49*, Helsinki: Finnish Institute of International Affairs.

Ortega, M. (ed.) (2005) 'The European Union and the United Nations – Partners in Effective Multilateralism', *Chaillot Paper*, 78.

20   Knud Erik Jørgensen

Patrick, S. and Forman, S. (eds) (2002) *Multilateralism and US Foreign Policy: Ambivalent Engagement*, Boulder, CO: Lynne Rienner.

Patten, C. (2005) *Not Quite the Diplomat. Home Truths about World Affairs*, London: Allen Lane.

Pisani-Ferry, J. (2008) *The End of Europe's Long-Standing Indifference to the Renminbi*, Bruegel Notes, January.

Rittberger, V. and Zangl, B. (2006) *International Organization. Polity, Politics and Policies*, Houndmills: Palgrave.

Ruggie, J.G. (ed.) (1993) *Multilateralism Matters: The Theory and Praxis of an Institutional Form*, New York: Columbia University Press.

Ruggie, J.G. (1998) *Constructing the World Polity: Essays on International Institutionalization*, London: Routledge.

Ruggie, J.G. (2003) 'American Exceptionalism, Exemptionalism and Global Governance', outline of a chapter for M. Ignatieff (ed.) *American Exceptionalism and Human Rights*, Princeton: Princeton University Press.

Schnabel, Rockwell A. (2005) *The Next Superpower? The Rise of Europe and Its Challenge to the United States*, Lanham: Rowman & Littlefield Publishers.

Smaghi, L. Bini (2006) 'A Single EU Seat in the IMF?', *Journal of Common Market Studies*, 42(2): 229–248.

Smith, K. (2008) 'Speaking with One Voice but Having Little Impact: The EU at the UN's Human Rights Council', paper presented at the ISA Convention, San Francisco, March.

Stadler, K.-D. (1993) *Die Europäische Gemeinschaft in der Vereinten Nationen: Die Rolle der EG im Entscheidungsprocess der UN-Hauptorgan am Beispile der Generalversammlung*, Baden Baden: Nomos.

Stokke, O. Schram and Coffey, C. (2006) 'Institutional Interplay and Responsible Fisheries: Combating Subsidies, Developing Precaution', in S. Oberthür and T. Gehring (eds) *Institutional Interaction in Global Environmental Governance: Synergy and Conflict among International and EU Policies*, Cambridge, MA: MIT Press, pp. 127–150.

van Oudenaren, J. (2003) 'What is Multilateral?', *Policy Review*, No. 117, February.

Varwick, J. (2005) *Die Beziehungen zwischen NATO und EU. Partnerschaft, Konkurrenz, Rivalität?*, Opladen/Farmington Hills: Budrich-Verlag.

Waltz, K. (2000) 'Structural Realism after the Cold War', *International Security*, 25: 5–41.

Wendt, A. (1999) *Social Theory of International Politics*, Cambridge: Cambridge University Press.

Wessel, R. (1999) *The European Union's Foreign and Security Policy: A Legal Institutional Perspective*, Den Haag: Kluwer Law International.

Wessel, Ramses A. (2008) 'The European Union as a Party to International Agreements: Shared Competences, Mixed Responsibilities', in A. Dashwood and M. Maresceau (eds) *Law and Practice of EU External Relations – Salient Features of a Changing Landscape*, Cambridge: Cambridge University Press, pp. 145–180.

2 The accidental player
The European Union and the global economy

Jean Pisani-Ferry

Arvind Virmani (2004), a distinguished Indian scholar, envisages for 2050 a tripolar world in which the three powers would be the United States, China and India. In a very short paragraph, he dismisses the perspective that the European Union would become one of the poles in such a world, saying that (a) its population is on a declining trend, and (b) that it would require the unlikely formation of a 'virtual state' in which nation-states would surrender power to a European government. Consistent with this view, his entire analysis is conducted on the basis of comparisons between states, and the European Union as such is entirely ignored.

Such views are frequent among non-European observers. For EU citizens, they are shocking. They know that you cannot beat demography and are used to hearing dismissive views on their growth perspectives (in fact, they themselves supply quite a lot of them), but they pretend to some form of existence and are not happy to be altogether ignored. Even the most fiercely Eurosceptic concedes the European Union has achieved something – if only to claim it should be undone.

However, challenges have virtues. They force us to re-examine things and to question what has been taken for granted. I therefore wish to reflect on the international economic role of the European Union: its representation in international economic organizations, the way it uses the power it has, the involvement of the member states and the Union as such in this external representation, and the choices it faces.

This will give me the opportunity to address an issue of current relevance. In the early 2000s, political pressure started to rise in favour of a reduction of Europe's weight in international organizations. In the G20 meeting of October 2005, finance ministers agreed 'that the governance structure of the Bretton Woods institutions – both quotas and representation – should reflect changes in economic weight' – meaning, the European Union's weight should be reduced. A few days before, the US Treasury lent support to a rebalancing of quotas in favour of emerging market economies and indicated that a consolidation of European chairs would 'help to increase the relative voice of emerging markets and developing country members' (Adams 2006). In April 2008, members in the International Monetary Fund (IMF) agreed on a reform of quota and voice that reduces the weight of Europe – but keeps the number of seats constant. In May 2008, the European Commission called for a

22   *Jean Pisani-Ferry*

consolidated euro area representation in the IMF. The system of external representation, and its relationship to policies, has thus become a concrete policy issue.

Focus on this topic will not allow me to address a more fundamental critique, namely that the European Union as an entity is in fact irrelevant. Coming from a country whose citizens rejected in 2005 a proposal for an EU constitutional treaty, I am not inclined to underestimate the problems it is facing. Nevertheless, I think the degree of economic and political integration that has been achieved is considerable: all border controls are past memory; EU law has precedence over national law; most of the economic legislation in force in our countries is now EU legislation; states are routinely fined in cases of non-compliance; competition policy cases are decided in Brussels; the euro, which has replaced the national currencies of fifteen countries, is run by a federal central bank; there is a parliament and a sort of government. 'Surrender of national power' has therefore taken place already to a considerable extent.

In what follows, I start by looking at Europe's share in the distribution of power in international economic and financial institutions and discuss whether and where Europe is making use of this power to set the international agenda. Then I turn to discussing reasons why the European Union refrains from using the power it has and examine whether that can be ascribed to preferences or to governance structures. Finally, I offer some policy implications.

The paradoxes of European power

How well is the European Union represented in international organizations?

Assume for a moment that an inhabitant of planet Mars is aiming to assess the distribution of power in international economic institutions on planet Earth. An informed and intelligent Martian would probably come up with something like Table 2.1.

He would then note two basic facts. First, that several international institutions – the Group of Eight, as well as the OECD and the International Energy Agency – have a very Eurocentric membership. Thanks in part to the small average size of EU countries, European membership within these institutions accounts for far more than the share of the European Union in total GDP or population. Looking at the details, the Martian observer would probably be astonished to learn that, in G7 finance meetings, the EU commissioner for economic and financial affairs and the finance minister of the country holding the EU presidency participate in part, in addition to the ministers of finance of the four European members (France, Germany, Italy and the United Kingdom), and that the president of the European Central Bank replaces the three governors from the euro area countries for discussions on multilateral surveillance. He would also note that another European country, Russia, has been slowly making its way towards becoming a full member of the G7 – and conclude that Europe should be playing the key role in the G7/G8.

Our Martian would note that an exception to this Eurocentric pattern is the Group of Twenty[1] (an informal forum created in 2000 that includes the ministers

Table 2.1 Weight of the EU in international economic and financial institutions

Institution	No. of members		Current $ GDP 2005 (billions)		PPP-based GDP 2005		Population (millions)	
	EU	Total	EU	Total	EU	Total	EU	Total
WTO	28	150	13,426	42,289	12,892	56,150	489	5,767
Share (%)	19	100	32	100	23	100	8	100
IMF/World Bank*	27	184	13,426	43,862	12,892	60,253	489	6,351
Share (%)								
Membership	15	100	31	100	21	100	8	100
Quotas	32							
Control	33							
Seats	30							
G8	4	8	8,808	27,648	7,842	26,816	261	861
Share (%)	50	100	32	100	29	100	30	100
G20**	5	20	8,808	35,096	7,842	46,522	261	4,020
Share (%)	25	100	25	100	17	100	6	100
Memo:								
UN	27	192	13,426	43,943	12,982	60,340	489	6,385
Share (%)	14	100	31	100	21	100	8	100

Source: Ahearne *et al.* (2006), Bruegel calculations. The sources for GDP and population data are the World Development Indicators database of the World Bank and CIA's World Factbook. Data for Myanmar are missing. PPP-based GDP does not take into account the 2008 revision. IMF quotas and votes are those of 2007.

* For IMF and WB, 'membership' gives the proportion of EU-27 countries in total member countries, 'quotas' their share in the total quota-based votes 'control' the proportion of votes they control, assuming a country holding the chair controls the vote of its constituency, and 'seats' the proportion of seats held by EU member countries in the Executive Board.
** The G20 has 19 members, plus the European Union as an institutional member. In the WTO, the 'European Communities' are counted as a separate member.

Source for GDP and population: World Development Indicators database, World Bank, 15 July 2005.

of finance of the G7 members, Australia and eleven emerging countries, plus the European Union), but as he might learn, this grouping was created precisely to correct the prevailing bias in the G7 and to engage the major emerging countries in an informal economic dialogue. Nevertheless, with four country members and a representation as an entity, the European Union is well represented in the G20.

Second, turning to global institutions like the World Trade Organization (WTO) or the Bretton Woods institutions (IMF and World Bank [WB]), our Martian could observe that the European Union accounts for a significant share of their membership: 28 (the 27 member states plus the European Union as a separate entity) out of 150 WTO members[2] and 27 out of 184 IMF/WB members.

There is no weighting of votes (as there are no votes) in the WTO but there is one in the Bretton Woods institutions. Our Martian would thus devote some efforts to assessing the weight of the European Union in those institutions as there are several ways to measure it, but having understood their intricate governance structure, he would conclude that they converge to assess the voting weight of the

24 *Jean Pisani-Ferry*

European Union at about 30 per cent. This is, he would note, in line with the share of the European Union in the current-dollar world GDP but significantly more than its share in PPP-based world GDP or population. It is also far above the 17 per cent quota of the United States and the 15 per cent blocking minority.

Martians have a reputation for being good mathematicians. With some maths and the help of a computer, our observer could compute the true power of the European Union: its Banzhaf voting power index – that is, the frequency with which it is the swing voter when behaving as a block. He would then conclude, as did Lorenzo Bini Smaghi (2005; see Chapter 4), that the potential power of the EU-27 in the IMF is about 50 per cent higher than its voting weight. If they were to form a coalition, the EU countries would by far be the dominant power in the IMF with a voting power index of 48 per cent – the next one being the United States with 7 per cent.

Talking to insiders, the Martian would learn a few additional facts: first, that being by tradition a European, the Managing Director of the IMF is in fact designated by the European Union;[3] second, that the G7 routinely behaves as a caucus within the International Financial Institutions and that, since it represents almost half of the vote in those institutions, its positions hold considerable clout. From that, he would certainly deduce that the power of the European Union goes beyond its formal voting power.

Our Martian would presumably conclude that the European Union is the clear winner in the distribution of international institutional power. In fact, this observation has not escaped some inhabitants of planet Earth. For example, Vijay Kelkar and co-authors (2005) noted that in the early 2000s the combined votes of Brazil, China and India in the Bretton Woods institutions were about 20 per cent below those of Italy, Belgium and the Netherlands, while their combined GDPs at market exchange rates were 23 per cent higher, their combined GDPs at PPP exchange rates four times higher and their populations 29 times higher.[4] This astonishing disproportion – that remains after the 2008 quota revision – may explain why the Asian countries feel so little ownership in the Bretton Woods institutions.

Assuming he had some kind of Marxist background, our Martian would carry on his investigation and look at the power of money. He would then note that the EU member states provide between 30 and 40 per cent of the financing of international institutions. He would also look at the financing of development and observe that in 2004 the members of the European Union provided 64 billion US dollars in official development assistance out of a total of 104 billion.[5] He would also observe that, in addition to having two development banks of their own (the European Investment Bank and the European Bank for Reconstruction and Development), they participate in the African, Asian and Latin American regional development banks.

Having observed that the European Union combines the power of number, the voting power and the power of money, our Martian would presumably conclude that it is the dominant player in the international economic and financial game – meaning, that it holds the agenda-setting power and is in a position to assemble majorities that support its views. The next question our Martian would ask himself is whether the European Union makes use of its institutional power to set, or at least to shape, the architecture of the multilateral system, to determine the agenda of the discussions, to broker deals that correspond to its objectives, and to influence decisions. Answering that question is however much more difficult as it implies relying on case-by-case observations and on the testimonies of the inhabitants of planet Earth.

Is the European Union an agenda setter?

To hold voting power in international organizations does not necessarily mean being an effective power. Indeed, three years ago, the Europeans were shocked by the publication of a paper by Robert Kagan (2002) entitled 'Power and Weakness'. Kagan's main thesis was that it was time to realize that Europeans and Americans did not share a common view of the world. Europe, he said, 'is turning away from power, [...] it is moving beyond power into a self-contained world of laws and rules and transnational negotiation and cooperation'.

The Europeans, however, were quick to take some comfort from a book by another US foreign policy scholar, Joseph Nye (2002), whose thesis was rather that the world is moving in Europe's direction. International power, he said, does not need to rest on force and be discretionary. It can be based on, and draw legitimacy from, commonly agreed rules. In short, there can be something called *soft power*.

This was exactly what the Europeans wanted to hear. Being a soft power could reconcile the aspiration to play a world role and the aversion to force. The competition commissioner Mario Monti – who, while playing by the rules, was able to block the merger of US giants GE and Honeywell – and the trade commissioner Pascal Lamy became the incarnations of this new kind of civilized international power.

There is considerable truth in this characterization. In international economics as elsewhere, the European Union is the champion of rules (Laïdi 2005). The reason for that is straightforward: it is itself based on rules. The entire history of European integration can be looked at as a patient, yet consistent attempt at rebuilding intra-European relations on the basis of a system of law, rules and decision-making procedures. It is therefore quite natural for it to envisage international relations in the same way and to champion global governance. Hence, for example, the European Union's active role in the creation of the International Criminal Court, the WTO, or the Kyoto protocol on global warming. The United States, by contrast, remains suspicious of any international constraint that would bind the exercise of discretionary power. In the words of George W. Bush, it does not accept having to ask for a 'permission slip' before taking decisions.

But is the European Union *really* a soft power? Does it have a vision of the world and an agenda? Does it play the power game within institutions? Or does it only take comfort in an oxymoronic characterization of what it pretends to be?

To answer these questions and assess the role the European Union has been able to play, topics have to be taken one by one. Providing a comprehensive and systematic assessment would require very substantial research.[6] Here, I will only survey three domains in a fairly brief fashion: international trade, exchange rates and macroeconomic surveillance, and international finance.

26   *Jean Pisani-Ferry*

Trade

The European Union is without any doubt a major player in international trade negotiations. It has clearly stated priorities – including, you may think, disputable ones – and the ability to push them through. Together with the United States, it has in fact steered the successive international discussions on multilateral trade liberalization.

In the 'legacy' paper he posted at the end of his mandate as trade commissioner, Pascal Lamy claimed that

> The lesson to be taken from the experience of the past five years is that, when it chooses to pursue a truly federal policy, the EU can play a decisive role on the world stage. Together, we have a far greater 'weight' than the sum of the Member States. We have the ability, not only to resist initiatives that we do not support […], but also to set the international agenda. The priority given to development in the Doha Agenda, or the agreement on medicines, are evidence of this pivotal European role.
>
> (Lamy 2004)

There is perhaps a degree of exaggeration in this self-assessment. The failure of the Cancun ministerial conference and the European Union's inability to make the Singapore issues an essential part of the Doha round are useful reminders of the limits to European power. Nevertheless, Europe is a strong player and, interestingly, its power seems able to survive changes in negotiation arrangements. The failure of Cancun was widely attributed to an underestimation by the incumbents (the industrialized countries) of the rising weight of emerging countries. Having reached a bilateral deal on agriculture, the United States and the European Union had not properly assessed the difficulty of reaching an agreement with the other players.

However, the Lamy legacy paper notes that the 'Quad' – the informal group formed by the United States, the European Union, Japan and Canada that had been playing a steering role in the previous trade rounds – met for 20 minutes only during the 1999–2004 stint of the Prodi commission. In lieu of this has come what the paper describes as 'a flexible feast of mini and micro Ministerials, ad hoc small groupings, always with EU, US, Brazil and India at the core' (Lamy 2004). In other words, the rise of emerging countries has not led to a diminished EU role but rather to a de facto replacement of Japan and Canada by Brazil and India.

Turning to substance, today's international trade architecture owes a lot to the European Union. As already mentioned, the creation of the WTO was the crowning achievement of its sustained effort to strengthen the multilateral system. However, and somewhat paradoxically, the European Union is also the inventor of trade regionalism. It is itself a regional block and has actively promoted the creation of regional trade arrangements. Trade scholars are thus generally struck by the complexity of its actual policy, especially by its combination of regional and multilateral approaches. Why, for example, does the European Union have

The accidental player   27

preferential trade agreements with virtually all countries in the world? What is the rationale for having special trade agreements with both close neighbours and distant partners, rich and poor countries, competitors and protégés? How does that relate to its stated support for multilateralism? Why does it oscillate between multilateralism and regionalism?

The lack of clear answers to those questions is an indication of the limits to the European Union's ability to develop a consistent strategy. But here again, the European Union has for better or worse been providing leadership.

International macroeconomics

There are many reasons why the European Union should be a key player in international macroeconomic and exchange rate affairs.

First of all, Europe has made a major economic and institutional investment in the creation of a common currency and the setting up of supporting institutions. While the motivations for the creation of the euro were in large part internal, the expectation that it would become a major international currency also played its role – I suspect even a prominent one in the case of some of the proponents of the European currency.

Second, having a common currency has strong implications for policy-making. It implies that the balance of payments and the exchange rate become collective goods and must therefore be managed jointly – if at all managed.

Third, the European Union still accounts for one-third of world GDP at current exchange rates and one-fifth at PPP exchange rates. Its main currencies, the euro and the pound sterling, rank number two and four in international currency transactions. The European Union also holds very significant external assets and liabilities. According to Philip Lane and Gian Maria Milesi-Ferretti (2004), in the period since the creation of the euro, gross capital flows from and to the euro area have actually been higher than for the United States – 7.2 trillion US dollars in 1999–2003 against 6.1 trillion for the United States.

Therefore, the European Union and/or the euro area have undoubtedly a major stake in the international monetary system. However, since the launch of the euro, neither the European Union as a whole nor the euro area has expressed a strong intention to build on it to enhance their international role.

On the institutional side, there has been no major reshuffle in the external representation of the euro area after 1999 – in spite of numerous and long-standing proposals from academic circles and obviously from the European Commission. There is increased coordination and visibility of the euro area internationally, but no outright delegation of representation.

On substance, the Europeans have often remained soft spoken or even silent on global issues. In stark contrast to the United States, they have for long refrained from not expressing views on issues such as the unwinding of current account imbalances or the Chinese exchange rate. On the euro–dollar exchange rate, several mutually inconsistent opinions have frequently been expressed by the ministers of finance and central bank governors. On the nature and speed of the US

28 *Jean Pisani-Ferry*

current account adjustment, Europeans have more than once given the impression that their best hope was for a preservation of the exchange rate status quo – while routinely exhorting the United States to fiscal discipline and a correction of the external deficit. On the Chinese exchange rates, they waited until late 2007 to start making their views known – although their interest may differ substantially from that of the United States (Pisani-Ferry 2008). In short, European policy-makers seem to have de facto refrained from drawing the conclusions from the world status of their currency.

International finance

The IMF and WB boards very rarely go to vote. Rather, the chair proposes con-clusions based on its reading of the majority view, and decisions are then adopted by consensus. No formal analysis of the votes is therefore possible and one must draw on the analysis of episodes and actual decisions.

The years since the 1994 Mexican crisis – and even more since the 1997–1998 Asian crisis – have been characterized by an intense discussion on the reform of the international financial architecture. Although the frequency and intensity of crises have abated since the Argentine meltdown of 2002, the discussion is not over, as illustrated by the strategic review of the IMF. Major issues have been and are still on the agenda such as the resolution of financial crises, the role of the IMF and the WB, or the scope for regional arrangements, especially in Asia.

The Europeans have certainly been part of the discussion within the G7, the G20, the Bretton Woods institutions and in public forums, and they may claim some successes such as the partial reform of IMF governance through the cre-ation of the International Monetary and Financial Committee or the so-called involvement of the private sector in crisis resolution.

However, careful analysis of the discussion shows that they have rarely set the agenda. They have often responded to new developments in a reactive mode, slowly adapting to events and adjusting to new (frequently US) proposals, and have almost never pushed for radical new ideas. In a paper I wrote in 2000 with Benoît Coeuré, our conclusion was that the United States had behaved through-out the financial crises as the (mostly, but not exclusively benevolent) hegemon of international finance, and that Europe had not behaved as the world monetary and financial power it could be and sometimes pretended to be. Developments since that paper was written do not lead me to change this conclusion.

Riccardo Faini, a former Executive Director with the IMF, and Enzo Grilli (2004) have attempted to measure quantitatively the influence of the United States, the European Union and Japan in the IMF and WB decisions by assessing whether the geographical lending pattern of those institutions reflects their respective bilateral trade of financial relation patterns. Their results suggest that the United States and the European Union are both influential, but the former more than the latter. They especially contrast the importance of both trade and financial links for the United States with the absence of any discernible influence of the European Union's financial links. This is an admittedly rather indirect measure that is subject to technical discussion, but it corresponds well to the casual observation that the US financial community is much more concerned by, and vocal on, IMF issues than the European one.

Here again, the European Union's effective role does not seem to be commensurate with the potential role its representation in the Bretton Woods organizations could allow it to play. Summing up, there is a striking contrast between Europe's formal power in international organizations and forums and the less prominent role it plays in substantive international discussions – with the exception of trade matters. The question, thus, is why Europe does not really make use of the institutional power it has.

Why does Europe refrain from using its power?

Hypotheses

The first potential explanations for this contrast are *disinterest* and *distraction*. Europeans are perhaps happy not to be excessively involved in world governance and to free ride on a presumably benevolent US hegemony. Or they may be occupied by domestic and regional affairs.

There is certainly some truth in those hypotheses. The median voter in the EU-27 member country is a small open economy that is used to taking the state of the world as given instead of trying to change it according to its preference or its interest. It is also undisputable that, since the launch of the Single Market programme in the mid-1980s, the European Union has been busy dealing with its twin processes of deepening and widening as well as with the corresponding reforms of its institutions and governance – not to speak of the domestic economic reforms. Most of the senior policy-makers' energy has in fact been devoted to this internal agenda, with the consequence that global changes have sometimes been overlooked in the process.

However, it is hard to be fully convinced by such explanations. To begin with, not all member states share the small-country culture and the European Union as a whole is without doubt a very large entity. As to the distraction hypothesis, it may have played a role temporarily but it cannot account for a permanent behaviour. At any rate, if this were the main explanation for Europe's intermittent international presence, the European Union can be expected to become more assertive on the external front if or when it solves its internal difficulties.

A related possibility is that the European Union is not equipped with the same intellectual firepower as the United States. Benoît Coeuré and I have observed that, in the discussion on the reform of the international financial architecture of the late 1990s and early 2000s, the US authorities had constantly drawn on new ideas and proposals emanating from the research community. A similar pattern has emerged on issues such as the global current account imbalances or China's exchange rate regime, which have become, more frequently than in Europe, the topic of policy-oriented academic research. However, the supply of policy research cannot be regarded as exogenous. A major reason why the field is less

30   *Jean Pisani-Ferry*

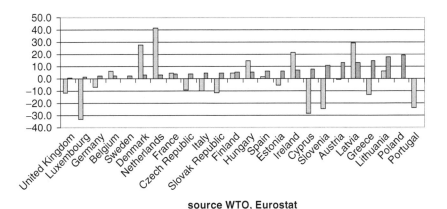

Figure 2.1 Agriculture indicators for the EU-25. Trade balance (per cent of GDP) and share in employment (per thousand).

active in Europe is that there is much less demand from, and interaction with, the community of policy-makers.[7]

This leaves us with two main hypotheses. One is that the European Union is divided because preferences differ among its constituent member states. The other is dysfunctional governance.

The preference heterogeneity argument has weight. Within an increasingly diverse European Union, there are many reasons why preferences should differ and there is none to believe that this diversity does not affect international economic relations. From intellectual and policy traditions to degrees of openness and patterns of trade and financial integration of the world economy, several factors can explain why the EU countries can have difficulties reaching common ground on global matters.

However, this is also true for international trade – and even more so. From development levels and specialization patterns to the functioning of labour markets and to domestic political institutions, there is every reason to consider that the economics and the political economy of trade liberalization differ widely within the European Union. The case of agriculture is especially striking (Figure 2.1): the European Union includes all varieties of situations – and therefore all kinds of preferences – but it *does* have a common policy for agricultural trade.

The same is actually true in the United States. A well-known stylized fact is that the regional specialization is more pronounced within the United States than within the European Union. Hence, from a political economy standpoint one can suspect a higher degree of trade preference heterogeneity among US states than among EU countries.

This leads to the *dysfunctional governance* hypothesis. The European Union has put in place very complex and diverse arrangements for organizing its international economic and financial relations with the rest of the world. In some fields, policy responsibility is fully delegated to an EU institution – in practice, the Commission or the European Central Bank – which has been given a clear mandate to act. In others, responsibility is divided between member states and they only endeavour to coordinate their views. It could thus be the inefficiency of some of its governance mechanisms that prevents the European Union from playing the role it could play.

This is clearly the interpretation suggested by Pascal Lamy when speaking of the European Union's ability to play the role of an agenda setter. This is also the one proposed by Lorenzo Bini Smaghi, who prior to his appointment to the board of the European Central Bank played a key role in the coordination of European positions in international monetary and financial affairs. He said: 'If EU countries wish to improve their collective influence in international issues and the IMF, some institutional changes in the way European interests are represented and promulgated may be necessary' (Bini Smaghi 2004, p. 247; see also Bini Smaghi 2006 and Chapter 4 of this volume). If this is the right explanation, the European Union first and foremost needs to reform its external representation in the fields where it is not effective.

This is where Arvind Virmani strikes back. The reason why the European Union is not a full power may have to do with the degree to which member states of the European Union stand ready to accept a federalization of international economic policy. A closer look at the governance of international relations in the European Union is therefore required.

Alternative models of governance

As already indicated, the European Union does not rely on a single template for organizing its external economic relations. On the contrary, depending on the field, responsibility for them can be assigned to the European Union, to the member states or jointly to both levels. However, there is a limited number of underlying models. Table 2.2, from Coeuré and Pisani-Ferry (2007, p. 31), provides a rationalization for the existing arrangements. We can distinguish between:

- an *unconditional delegation* model, in which the member states fully and unconditionally delegate a policy responsibility to an EU institution;
- a *supervised delegation* model, in which they delegate representation and negotiation authority while retaining control rights (the EU body can then be considered an agent and the member states multiple principals). The standard case here is trade, where the Commission has delegation but is given a mandate by, and is accountable to, a committee formed by representatives of the member states;
- a *coordination model*, in which member states simply commit to coordination while retaining their prerogatives. This is the model in use for the G7 and the international financial institutions.

As a matter of principle, none of the three models is intrinsically superior. Federalists have a preference for unconditional delegation, but it raises issues of accountability, especially when the mandate is broad and the performance not easily observable.

32   *Jean Pisani-Ferry*

Table 2.2 Governance models in EU external economic relations

Model	Main features	Examples
Unconditional delegation	Policy responsibility delegated to EU institution; monitoring by MS, if any, not binding on decisions by EU institution	Competition policy (no monitoring)
Supervised delegation	External representation and negotiation authority delegated to EU institution; Council exercises supervision through issuing guidelines and monitoring implementation	Trade in goods (supervision by committee) Environment (supervision committee)
Coordination	No delegation of external representation to EU institution. Member states coordinate among themselves and with EU institutions, may or may not commit to follow guidelines	Representation in IMF Board (ex ante coordination within sub-committee of EFC)

Supervised delegation is a compromise that combines accountability to the principals and centralization in implementation. Coordination has virtues when externalities are limited or depend on the issue that is being addressed.

A good way to assess these models is to look at them through the lenses of the theory of contracts – with the EU states playing the role of multi-principals and the body in charge of common policy that of an agent. This leads us to the conclusion that the choice for a particular one depends on externalities, preferences, the cost of acquiring decision-relevant information and the ability of the principals to monitor the agent, as well as on the distributional risks involved in majority voting.[8]

From this perspective, supervised and unconditional delegation each have virtues – as for the choice between decision by elected politicians and delegation to an independent agency. But few arguments prefer coordination to supervised delegation in the field of external economic and financial relations, where externalities are large and economies of scale significant. Quite apart from the power game in international institutions, independent participation in global governance accompanied by a loose intra-EU coordination mechanism discourages national governments from investing in the acquisition of relevant information, from trading-off short-term benefits for long-term gains and from resisting special interest groups. It encourages cajoling special interests and popular beliefs at home, or investing political energy on narrow issues, while free-riding on the more important ones. Those are in fact behaviours that can be observed in this field.

The advantage of supervised delegation over coordination is that it allows the member states to internalize externalities while retaining control of the mandate given to their agent in international institutions. It is a flexible mechanism that does not lead to transferring complete control to the EU level and retains a steering role for the member states. Summing up, the choice for the European Union is

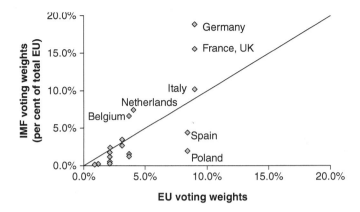

Figure 2.2 European MS voting weights in the EU and the IMF.

not between complete centralization and complete decentralization. Supervised delegation is a workable model that has been used for a long time in the trade field and provides a reasonable compromise between accountability and efficiency.

The question is, then, why has the European Union not adopted this model across the board? The reason is quite straightforward: moving towards supervised delegation does raise a significant difficulty as it affects the balance of power within the European Union.

In the field of international macroeconomics, the bigger member states – those who belong to the G7 – hold a de facto monopoly on external representation. They are not keen on surrendering it, as it would not only imply delegating power to the European Union but also sharing supervision with the smaller member states, which have virtually no say at present. Furthermore, the G7 is a flexible forum without a predetermined mandate that can address a very wide range of issues. This does not fit well with the governance model of the European Union, which assigns specific responsibilities at the EU level.

As for the Bretton Woods institutions and the field of international finance, Figure 2.2 gives relative voting weights within the European Union (according to the Nice voting system) and the IMF. It suggests that the major losers in the adoption of a supervised delegation model would again be the bigger countries, Germany, the United Kingdom and France, whose current weights within the EU representation at the IMF significantly exceed their weights within the European Union.

Other potential losers are the Netherlands and Belgium, which both are significantly overweighed and both hold a chair at the Executive Board of the IMF. In fact, the prestige attached to chairing a constituency is a further obstacle to a consolidated EU representation. This helps explain why the situation has remained unchanged until now. Summing up, the transfer of international representation to the European Union would involve an internal redistribution of power, not only from the states to the EU level – this could be lessened through an appropriate

34 *Jean Pisani-Ferry*

supervision mechanism that would leave control rights in the hands of the member states – but among the member states. This internal dimension of the power game certainly plays a significant role in the maintenance of the status quo.

Policy implications

Let me now turn to the policy implications of this analysis. The situation I have described is one of overrepresentation and under-effectiveness of the European Union in international economic relations. I think that this combination is increasingly unsustainable and that calls for a change cannot and should not be resisted any more. It is unsustainable, first, because the only way the European Union could justify remaining the winner in the distribution of formal power is by behaving like a benevolent hegemon – that is, by providing a public good that would lead the other players to accept its dominance. As developed above, the muted role the European Union plays in substantive international discussions does not justify an overrepresentation.

It is unsustainable, second, because reform of the global economic and financial institutions and the rebalancing of power it implies are not simply required for the sake of fairness. More importantly, they are necessary to ensure a sufficient degree of ownership in the multilateral system. The European Union has every interest to ensure that all countries share ownership in the multilateral system. The more imbalanced this system is, the stronger the temptation will be for those who feel underrepresented to look for alternative solutions. Increasingly, East Asian countries express interest in regional rather than multilateral cooperation. They also count on self-insurance through the accumulation of reserves instead of relying on international financial institutions. This behaviour has the potential to severely undermine the multilateral system – but it is understandable as long as East Asia feels that the system is unfairly dominated by others.

It is unsustainable, finally, because Europe's interests call for a change. Pressure has begun to mount for redistribution. The Europeans are tempted to postpone it, if only because they do not know how to redistribute power among themselves. Even from an entirely selfish viewpoint, this would be a mistake. Europe's share in world GDP is rapidly declining as a consequence of its demography and of the accelerated development of major emerging countries. It is bound to decline further – and rather fast. The more the adjustment is delayed, the lesser the weight of Europe will be in the international institutions.

The European Union needs to trade off formal, but partially ineffective, power for a formally diminished, but more effective, influence in world economic affairs. This does not necessarily imply a complete federalization of external representation, which would not correspond to existing internal arrangements and for that reason would not be effective. The supervised delegation model in use in the trade field offers a middle way. It allows member states to retain control rights through the definition of a mandate and the supervision of its implementation.

The main difficulty the European Union has to solve is the internal redistribution of power that will follow a redefinition of its external representation. This is

The accidental player 35

an admittedly complex issue, which involves at least as much concerns about prestige, as about effective power. However, this is hardly a valid excuse for inaction – unless the European Union wants to demonstrate that it does not deserve the power it has. Fortunately, the multiplicity of institutions and forums offers an opportunity for compromise. For it to be found, action has to start.

Conclusions

I started with the remark that challenges have virtues. The image of the future offered by Arvind Virmani in his thought-provoking paper is for a European an opportunity to revisit the achievements that are often taken for granted. Virmani claims the European Union is not a player in the world economy. I think it should rather be characterized as an accidental player – one which, depending on its internal arrangements or the lack of them, is sometimes at the table and sometimes off the table.

What I wish to stress is that, in the twenty-first century, the Europeans will not any more be able to afford the luxury of this strange position. The choice for them is to be part of the game or to be absent from it. The earlier they choose, the more able they will be to build on the vast formal power they still have in international organizations to exert an effective international influence.

It is therefore long overdue for the European Union to move away from the status of an accidental player.

Notes

1 I am referring here to the finance G20. There is also a trade G20, which was formed on the occasion of the Doha round, and is exclusively composed of emerging and developing countries. They happen to have the same number of members, hence the same name.
2 One hundred and fifty-one, following the membership of Vietnam in January 2007.
3 This has not always been the case, but the current MD, Dominique Strauss-Kahn, was formally designated EU candidate. Unlike his predecessors, he had to campaign for the job and embarked on a world tour to rally emerging and developing countries to his candidacy.
4 Quoted in Truman (2006).
5 Source: Preliminary OECD DAC data for 2007.
6 Sapir (2007) is a significant step in this direction.
7 Jaume Ventura has pointed out to me that European economists have in fact been very active in research on global imbalances – though mostly through US research institutions like the NBER. This is a clear indication that the European Union does not lack the intellectual ability to address global issues.
8 Maskin and Tirole (2001) is a useful reference.

References

Adams, T. (2006) 'The IMF: Back to Basics', in E. Truman (ed.) *Reforming the IMF for the 21st Century*, Washington: Peterson Institute for International Economics.
Ahearne, A., Pisani-Ferry, J., Sapir, A. and Véron, N. (2006) 'Global Governance: An Agenda for Europe', *Bruegel Policy Brief* No. 2006/07.

36   *Jean Pisani-Ferry*

Bini Smaghi, L. (2004) 'A Single EU Seat in the IMF?', *Journal of Common Market Studies*, 42(2).

—— (2005) 'IMF Governance and the Political Economy of a Consolidated European Seat', paper prepared for the IIE conference on IMF reform, September. Online. Available HTTP: http://www.iie.com

—— (2006) 'Powerless Europe: Why Is the Euro Area Still a Political Dwarf?', *International Finance*, 9(2).

Coeuré, B. and Pisani-Ferry, J. (2000) 'Events, Ideas and Actions: An Intellectual and Institutional Retrospective on the Reform of the International Financial Architecture', mimeo.

—— (2007) 'The Governance of the EU's External Economic Relations: How Many Voices?', in A. Sapir (ed.) *Fragmented Power: The EU and the World Economy*, Brussels: Bruegel.

Faini, R. and Grilli, E. (2004) 'Who Runs the IFIs?' CEPR discussion paper (4666), October 2004.

Kagan, R. (2002) 'Power and Weakness', *Policy Review*, No. 113. Online. Available HTTP: http://www.hoover.org/publications/policyreview/3460246.html

Kelkar, V.L., Chaudhry, P.K., Vanduzer-Snow, M. and Bhaskar, V. (2005) 'The International Monetary Fund: Integration and Democratization in the 21st Century', paper presented to the G24 Technical Group Meeting, Manila, the Philippines (17–18 March 2005).

Kenen, P., Shafer, J., Wicks, N. and Wyplosz, C. (2004) *International Economic and Financial Cooperation: New Issues, New Actors, New Responses*, Geneva Report on the World Economy (6), ICMB/CEPR.

Laïdi, Z. (2005) *La norme sans la force: l'énigme de la puissance européenne*, Paris: Presses de Sciences Po.

Lamy, P. (2004) *Trade Policy in the Prodi Commission: An Assessment*, November. Online. Available HTTP: http://trade-info.cec.eu.int/doclib/docs/2004/november/tradoc_120087.pdf

Lane, P. and Milesi-Ferretti, G.M. (2004) 'Financial Globalisation and Exchange Rates', mimeo.

Maskin, E. and Tirole, J. (2001) 'The Politician and the Judge: Accountability in Government', *American Economic Review*, 94(4): 1034–1054.

Nye, J. (2002) *The Paradox of American Power*, Oxford: Oxford University Press.

Pisani-Ferry, J. (2008) 'The End of Europe's Long-Standing Indifference to the Renminbi', in M. Goldstein and N. Lardy (eds) *Debating China's Exchange Rate Policy*, Washington: Peterson Institute for International Economics.

Sapir, A. (ed.) (2007) *Fragmented Power: The EU and the World Economy*, Brussels: Bruegel.

Truman, E. (ed.) (2006) *Reforming the IMF for the 21st Century*, Washington: Peterson Institute for International Economics.

Virmani, A. (2004) 'A Tripolar World: India, China and the US', mimeo, Indian Council for Research on International Economic Relations, May.

3 Complex engagement

The EU and the UN system

Franziska Brantner and Richard Gowan

Introduction

The European Union has developed a strong public commitment to the UN, encapsulated in the European Security Strategy's statement that 'strengthening the United Nations, equipping it to fulfill its responsibilities and to act effectively, is a European priority'.[1] But EU–UN relations are complicated by a history of crises – including the loss of European faith in the UN in the Western Balkans during the 1990s and the European Union's split over the invasion of Iraq in 2003 – and the unresolved puzzle of whether the Union can ever be a coherent actor in an institutional framework based on state sovereignty. Indeed, the structure of the UN contains a number of in-built obstacles to the emergence of a cohesive EU identity. First, it institutionalizes a division between the two European permanent members of the Security Council (SC; Britain and France) and the other EU members. Second, while the European Union is a recognized grouping within the UN system, frequently making common statements and proposing resolutions as a bloc, this comes at the price of constant intra-EU negotiation (involving 1,000 meetings a year in New York alone). As Jørgensen and Laatikainen note, the need to coordinate at the UN highlights the European Union's 'split personality' as 'both actor in its own right and an arena for the expression of member-state interests' (Jørgensen and Laatikainen 2006: 10).[2]

Yet the study of EU–UN linkages is further complicated by the fact that the UN itself is also a combination of 'arena' and 'actor'. More precisely, the UN includes multiple political arenas – including the SC, General Assembly, Human Rights Council (HRC) and Economic and Social Council – but also engages in a huge array of operational activities, including conflict prevention, humanitarian aid and peacekeeping. To complicate matters further, the system also includes funds and agencies, such as the UN Development Programme (UNDP) and International Atomic Energy Agency (IAEA), overseen by stand-alone inter-governmental boards. The European Union's interaction with the UN system cannot therefore, be reduced to its behaviour as an intermittently cohesive bloc within UN political forums, as it also involves significant operational (and financial) cooperation at the field level. An easily visible example of this operational EU–UN relationship in recent years has been the deployment of European Security and Defence Policy (ESDP) missions to support UN peacekeeping in Africa.

38 *Franziska Brantner and Richard Gowan*

While a growing body of academic literature has attempted to define the European Union's degree of 'actorness' (Hill 1996) at the UN, this is challenged by the diffusion of the debates and activities involved. European decision-making on UN issues is very frequently decentralized. European ambassadors to the UN institutions in New York, Geneva and Vienna can in theory refer difficult issues to second pillar committees in Brussels (such as the European Council's Working Party on Human Rights, COHOM, and that on the UN, CONUN) but the pace of UN negotiations often means that they do not do so in practice. The level of 'Brusselization' in European UN policy is thus low. Moreover, the European relationship with the UN system also includes participation in specialized (and often drawn-out) negotiation processes – such as those that led to the approval of the International Criminal Court (ICC) and the Kyoto Protocol – that involve quite different sorts of diplomacy to the regular business carried on in New York and Geneva.

In this context, there is little value in attempting to study the interaction between the European Union and UN as if they were relatively coherent actors, or even relatively cohesive institutions. The degree of common European ambition at the UN varies over time and by issue area, and the coordination that we observe on any one topic or in any one forum may differ markedly from that we perceive elsewhere. We will see, for example, that EU coordination in the SC has lagged behind that in other forums. In our next section, we lay out a number of theoretical frameworks for analysing EU–UN linkages, but we do not wish to argue that any one of these is consistently superior. Instead, it seems probable that different theoretical models explain the European Union's engagement with different elements of the UN. Realism still has an important part to play in explaining the security dimension of EU–UN relations, for example, whereas its approach to human rights is better explained through reference to the European Union's 'natural' attachment to international law. To expand this argument, the remaining sections of the chapter describe the complex legal status of the European Union at the UN, the multi-faceted histories of EU–UN cooperation since the end of the Cold War, current practicalities of EU cooperation in UN forums and resistance to EU positions by other states and blocs. We conclude with a summary of recent European involvement in efforts to reform the UN – this encapsulates many difficulties we identify for European policy in the chapter as a whole.

Yet in spite of the many obstacles to defining an EU identity at the UN, this chapter also shows that there is considerable evidence that one has begun to emerge. At the political level, European cohesion in UN forums such as the General Assembly and the HRC has grown markedly if unevenly. While the highest level of coherence is around rights issues rather than hard security questions such as disarmament, EU members linked security and rights in lobbying for the 'Responsibility to Protect', endorsed at the World Summit marking the sixtieth anniversary of the UN Charter in 2005. This can be related not only to a high level of European support for UN operational activities in countries affected by conflict, but also its commitment to developing international law through the UN, which was demonstrated through its support for the ICC and the Kyoto Protocol. The European preference for basing security in international law has also been seen in its strategy towards Iran's nuclear ambitions, by which the European Union has worked very closely with the IAEA in spite of US doubts.

If this emphasis on linking legality and rights to security appears to represent a common thread in EU behaviour at the UN, it has significant political limitations. Although promoting international law in principle, EU members are often wary of being bound by it in practice through the UN: France and Britain have been accused of taking an 'instrumental' approach to the authority of the SC (Malone 2006), while almost all EU states appear to see themselves as immune to censure by the HRC, thereby alienating other states.

The ostensible European emphasis on legality can thus be interpreted as evidence both of a progressive desire for a rules-based world order and of a conservative goal of preserving power through the structures of the UN at a time of international change. In the closing section of this chapter, we contrast essentially Liberal, norms-based explanations of European behaviour at the UN with more Realist interpretations that highlight the extent to which the European Union's behaviour is motivated by a desire to maintain its own influence – and how, in a period when increasingly assertive global players such as China and India are inclined to exert their own influence, Europe's ability to get the results it wants is in decline. Recent efforts to reform the UN system provide case studies of these dynamics.

Theoretical framework of analysis

Although we wish to highlight the *variability* of EU–UN relations, two unifying questions can be applied across the board. First, what factors affect the degree of EU coordination at the UN: when and why do member states decide to act together, and what role emerges for the European Commission? Second, what factors decide the degree of EU willingness to work through and with the UN system? Why does the European Union choose to prioritize action through UN institutions in some cases, but not in others? It should be noted that a high degree of European unity does not necessarily equate to a desire to prioritize UN action: the European Union is relatively united at the Economic and Social Council, for example, but most European diplomats dismiss it as almost totally irrelevant, at least in private conversation.

A range of theoretical perspectives can be used to explain the degree of EU coherence in UN bodies. Authors inclined towards a realist reading of international relations would argue that EU member states coordinate their policies at the United Nations when it allows them to defend their interests better than going alone (Walt 1987; Allen 1998). EU positions defended at the UN hence largely reflect the compromises found (or not) among its member states based on their exogenously defined preferences. Institutionalists and constructivists alike see the virtue of this case, but argue that the likelihood of such compromises might be higher within the European Union than in other, looser, coalitions of states because of underlying political tendencies within the European Union to search for common positions and institutionalized mechanisms for coordination (Carlsnaes *et al.* 2004; Smith 2006a).

40 *Franziska Brantner and Richard Gowan*

The precise dynamics that lead to greater integration are unsurprisingly heavily developed sources of reflection. Neo-functionalist and institutionalists highlight the *engrenage* effect of EU integration. Neo-functionalists highlight spill-over from one domain of integration into another, requiring further integration in ever more policy fields – so that EU cooperation at the UN may actually be a spill-over from other foreign policy fields. Similarly institutionalists argue that institutionalized coordination constrains and refines member states' preferences. A constant, increasingly institutionalized debate leads to further integration in foreign policy (Smith, M.E. 2003: 246). Constructivist interpretations hold that EU members, and more precisely their delegates in Brussels, New York or Geneva, by coordinating every day on the ground, might be 'socialized' into abandoning unilateral action and extending coordination because they find it 'appropriate' to coordinate their policies at the UN even if it is not necessarily the most rational approach in a given case, or the one likely to maximize benefits (de Schoutheete 1980: 118–120; Nuttall 1992: 312–313; Smith 2004: 58 cited by Smith 2006a). In spite of the differences between these interpretations, they are in many ways complementary, even mutually reinforcing approaches to the sources of EU unity.

The debate over why the European Union may choose to work through the UN in the first place is in many ways more diverse. Robert Kagan argues that multilateral strategies reflect power or, rather, the absence of power, that is, weakness. Because Europe is weak, it pursues multilateral strategies: 'their tactics, like their goal, are the tactics of the weak' (Kagan 2003). Joseph Grieco (1996) also argues that small (weak) states prefer multilateral policies. By contrast, an alternative set of scholars see EU–UN relations in terms of the European Union's normative power (Manners 2002). The European Union's 'DNA' predisposes it to support multilateralism – and that by acting through international organizations such as the UN, it gains the capacity to shape the behaviour of others. It is notable that a parallel school of thought in UN studies highlights the subtle role of UN debates and officials in setting norms (Johnstone 2008).

Both forms of normative power theory imply a critique of US policy. Even if the concept of normative power is not specific to the European Union (Diez 2005), some argue that the European Union's willingness to bind itself to international law is special and specific (Diez 2005: 622). Laatikainen and Smith state:

> The contrast between the US and EU perspectives on multilateralism could not be more stark. While the EU has embraced effective multilateralism as a cornerstone of its foreign policy, the United States has embraced an aggressive policy of pre-emption and a diplomatic tone that is skeptical of and impatient with UN multilateralism.
>
> (Laatikainen and Smith 2006: 7)

However, 'the EU is not yet "good enough at multilateralism" to act as a leader, much less counter US anti-multilateral tendencies' (ibid.: 18).

In spite of these doubts about the European Union's performance, some scholars have gone further in equating the normative bases of the European Union and

UN. European law specialist Bardo Fassbender summarized this position succinctly when discussing EU action at the UN:

> Since the EC/EU and the global multilateral order of the UN are based on the same idea of 'integration through law' and, more fundamentally, the same belief in rational and enlightened human beings able to design and organize their societal life in a reasonable way, a failure of multilateralism on a global level would necessarily have repercussions on the European project. Intellectually and conceptually, the European Union and the United Nations are built on the same foundations. If this ground becomes shaky, both structures are in danger.
>
> (Fassbender 2004: 884)

A final interpretation of EU–UN relations shifts attention from the normative prioritization of international law to an interest in how domestic politics affect European policy towards the UN. As Jørgensen notes in the introduction to this volume, a considerable body of literature reflects on the importance of these factors – such as the composition of governments and public opinion – and there is good reason to think that these factors affect attitudes to the UN. A late 2005 poll found an EU-wide trust rating of 52 per cent for the UN, relative to only 45 per cent for the European Union itself (Gowan 2006). The UN's advantage was higher among traditional leaders in aid and peacekeeping such as the Netherlands (59 to 41 per cent) and the Scandinavian group (72 to 38 per cent). These differentials could shape EU member states' approach to EU–UN cooperation.

Legal and treaty provisions

The legal and treaty provision aspects of the EU–UN relation have two dimensions. The first concerns the *membership* of the European Community (EC) and European Union as an actor on its own at the UN. The second regards the legal basis for the *cooperation* of member states at the UN. Regarding membership, the European Union has not yet a legal (in contrast to political) status at the UN; lacking legal personality it is no subject of international law. Instead, the EC (one pillar of the European Union) was admitted to the UN as observer based on General Assembly Resolution 3208 (XIX) of 11 October 1974. The EC has observer status for the General Assembly and its committees, the Economic and Social Council and its commissions and subsidiary bodies, and for several funds and programmes, but, importantly, not for the SC. The Community can participate in the work of the bodies it has been admitted to, but not in their decision-making. Its status is defined by the UN rules for observers. The participation of the Community is cumulative to that of its members (Dormoy 1997: 45). The EC therefore participates in meetings and conferences in its own right. In contrast, the EC is a full member of one UN specialized agency, the Food and Agriculture Organization (FAO), reflecting the Community's extensive responsibilities in the sectors covered by the FAO. The EC is represented by the Commission.

It is noteworthy that the EC has its own representation at the UN. The Commission, which is responsible for the external representation of the EC, has special responsibilities in areas where there is an exclusive Community competence, such as trade policy or fisheries. Article 302 (Treaty establishing the European Community) allows the Commission 'the maintenance of all appropriate relations with the organs of the United Nations and of its specialized agencies'. On this basis, the Commission has concluded formal agreements with individual UN bodies, for example memorandums of understanding, which have been concluded with the United Nations Development Programme, World Health Organization, Food and Agriculture Organization, United Nations High Commissioner for Refugees and World Food Programme. The European Council secretariat also has an office in New York, even though on a smaller scale, in order to support the presidencies in their coordination tasks and to guarantee the liaison with the Council work in Brussels. This picture will, however, change with the entering into force of the Lisbon Reform Treaty, stipulating a legal personality for the European Union and a common external action service.

Regarding the second dimension, the current legal basis for EU coordination at the UN is the Treaty on European Union (TEU; 1992), with the introduction of the foreign policy (Title V), and the Treaty of Amsterdam (1997), with the strengthening of Common Foreign and Security Policy (CFSP) decision-making procedures and instruments. With regard to the UN, Article 19 of the TEU states:

1   Member States shall coordinate their action in international organizations and at international conferences. They shall uphold the common positions in such forums.

    In international organizations and at international conferences where not all the Member States participate, those which do take part shall uphold the common positions.

2   Without prejudice to paragraph 1 and Article 14(3), Member States represented in international organizations or international conferences where not all the Member States participate shall keep the latter informed of any matter of common interest.

    Member States which are also members of the United Nations Security Council will concert and keep the other Member States fully informed. Member States which are permanent members of the Security Council will, in the execution of their functions, ensure the defence of the positions and the interests of the Union, without prejudice to their responsibilities under the provisions of the United Nations Charter.

The latter part already contains much of the *problématique* of EU cooperation at the UN, as the prerogative of the two permanent members of the SC, France and Britain, not to defend European positions is maintained.

The changing EU–UN relationship: From the Cold War to Iraq

While the Maastricht Treaty gave the European Union an improved legal basis for coordination at the UN, the early 1990s proved a very damaging period for relations between the two organizations. Europe's normative ambitions were already growing at the UN. There were early signs that Europe could lead on non-conventional challenges in the UN system: the EC played an important and effectively coordinated role on climate change and environmental issues as early as the drafting of the UN Framework Convention on Climate Change (1991) and the Rio conference in 1992 (Gupta and Grubb 2000; Gupta 2005). The increasing strength of environmental movements and Green parties in a number of member states can account for one factor contributing to these policies (Oberthür 2007). EU leadership in the environmental field followed earlier progress in the 1980s on establishing common European positions on human rights (Arpio Santacruz 1997).

But this was overshadowed by the UN's unprecedented and scarring involvement of the UN Protection Force (UNPROFOR) in the former Yugoslavia, initially mandated in 1992. While the force was a product of European (especially French and British) policy, and primarily manned by European troops, tensions arose over the inability of the UN to manage the operation or risk the use of force – and (from the UN perspective) a lack of European will to provide sufficient resources or political backing to the operation (Economides and Taylor 1996).

These tensions culminated in the Srebrenica massacre in 1995, and the replacement of UNPROFOR by NATO troops following the Dayton Peace Accords the same year. The humiliation of Dutch forces stationed at Srebrenica, combined with the murder of Belgian troops at the opening of the Rwandan genocide in 1994, left European militaries deeply unwilling to serve under UN command again. Just as the European Union was acquiring a clearer political voice at the UN, the UN had been rendered operationally irrelevant in Europe. This distinction points to a Realist assumption that matters of power and interest are likely to override institutional inclinations in defining the EU approach to the UN in the security field. By the late 1990s, therefore, it was not clear that EU–UN relations would have much significance in the future. Despite this lack of European commitment to the UN, European diplomats did make progress towards unity on many UN issues as the decade progressed.

In UN political forums, the European Union achieved a relatively high degree of coherence: in the General Assembly, for example, the Union's members voted together roughly four-fifths of the time by the late 1990s (see 'Current EU coordination at the UN' below). Those votes on which it continued to split were indicative of the (im)balance of power among EU members: Britain and France often parted company with the rest of the Union on issues relating to nuclear weapons and the legacy of colonialism, whereas there was greater (though as yet incomplete) coherence on issues such as rights. Meanwhile, France and Britain jealously guarded their privileged position on the SC, refusing to hold any formalized consultations on Council affairs with other EU member states throughout the 1990s. The structure of the Council thus arguably led the two powers to take a national view of their interests there.

However, events in the late 1990s pushed the European Union to reconnect with the UN. The initial driver of change was the Kosovo crisis of 1998–1999. As Yugoslav violence mounted in 1998, the United States mooted taking action through NATO without UN approval, but a number of European states (including France, Britain and Germany) initially insisted on working through the UN. Although the Europeans ultimately agreed to action against Yugoslavia without a Council mandate – impossible because of the threat of a Russian veto – they were also influential in insisting that the UN take the lead in post-conflict civil administration in Kosovo, with an EU economic affairs pillar placed under UN authority. Although the UN was forced to take a secondary role in Kosovo, and many observers believed its political legitimacy had been severely damaged as a result, it seemed that European governments were prepared to give it another chance as an operational partner. Particularly important to this process was Germany: the Social Democrat-Green government broke the country's taboo on using force by backing NATO, but nonetheless wished to ensure that the UN framework was not irreparably damaged. Similarly, British Prime Minister Tony Blair was a leading advocate of the use of force, but he balanced this by restating his commitment to the UN (as he would later do, if less successfully, over Iraq). In both the British and German cases, domestic factors – specifically the willingness of centre-left governments to advocate force – were arguably decisive at this moment. UN Secretary General Kofi Annan also assisted the European's cause through a number of statements that implicitly legitimized the intervention.

The period from the Kosovo intervention to the Iraq war saw individual European states back up UN operations elsewhere. In 1999, Portugal made a significant contribution to the UN mission in its former colony of East Timor, emerging bloodily from Indonesian rule; in 2000 and Britain sent a stand-alone force to reinforce the UN mission in Sierra Leone. These cases marked a turning point for UN peacekeeping, which shifted from stagnation into rapid growth, with its primary focus on former European colonies in Africa (including the Ivory Coast, the Democratic Republic of Congo [DRC], Burundi and Sudan).

Although former colonial powers typically refrained from direct contributions to these missions, their political backing was often decisive in the SC decisions. While the Kosovo case can be used to highlight domestic drivers of policy, a Realist IR scholar might explain European support for these interventions in terms of the ex-colonial states' national interests (Ayoob 2005; Ayoob and Zierler 2005). However, their role was to some extent balanced by the emergence of a 'UN lobby' of previously neutral countries in the European Union, with the accession of Austria, Finland and Sweden in 1995. These member states – and the similarly minded Ireland, which had acceded in 1986 – have typically accepted the need to align with the EU majority, but have brought a considerable amount of UN knowledge to the Union.

The European approach to the UN was also shaped by humanitarian and development concerns. At the 2000 Millennium Summit, governments made a series of pledges concerning development that the UN Secretariat codified as the Millennium Development Goals – EU members led the way in committing to these, although their performance in implementing their commitments has been extremely mixed. Meanwhile, a number of European actors – most notably the British government and European Commission – began channelling large quantities of humanitarian aid through UN mechanisms. Climate change also continued to be a topic on which European leadership was essential to the UN. In the run-up to the agreement on the Kyoto Protocol, the European Union proposed a carbon dioxide emissions cut of 15 per cent by 2010 and shouldered the highest emission cut target itself, accepting a target of −8 per cent. The European Union and all its member states then showed leadership by ratifying the Kyoto Protocol in May 2002 and proved 'instrumental in convincing Russia to bring the Protocol into force' (Oberthür 2007: 78). Its equally important contribution to the creation of the ICC is described by Martijn Groenleer and David Rijks in this volume. This combination of progressive successes meant that this period was arguably the point for European normative power at the UN, although it was facilitated by the Clinton administration throughout the late 1990s.

Given the increased European interest in cooperating with the UN across a range of issues, it is perhaps unsurprising that there were growing signs of EU cohesion in UN forums in this period. In January 2001, Britain and France finally began to engage in formalized consultations on SC issues in New York. The number of common EU statements on human rights issues also rose sharply, more than doubling between 1998 and 2000 in this period (Smith 2006a). Prior to the Iraq war debate, the European Union did appear to be moving towards a greater cohesion on UN issues, driven by the variety of issues we have identified. But there were also less positive reasons for cohesion. The Bush administration's rejection of the Clinton legacy of international law, and its broader disdain for working through the UN, meant that the European Union (still at fifteen) found itself increasingly alienated from the United States – arguably causing it to become more unified. Iraq was the exception that proved this rule.

The changing EU–UN relationship: After Iraq

The European Union's progress towards cohesion was sharply interrupted by its very public differences over how to handle the Iraqi crisis. This resulted not only in the failure to win a final resolution for the Iraq intervention, but a sharp drop-off in cooperation on other UN issues in 2003–2004: the number of EU splits at the General Assembly spiked sharply, and common positions on human rights issues fell away. It appeared that the Iraq episode might bring the gradual evolution of EU–UN relations to a grinding halt. But this has not proved correct, as the experience of failure (and an awareness of how much the European Union had at stake in the UN) pushed European governments to invest in rebuilding their own unity and better EU–UN ties.

Indeed, the post-Iraq period has seen an intensification of European cooperation at the UN, and EU–UN operational relations. Early signals of this included the final draft of the *European Security Strategy*, which made a series of references to the UN's importance, and Operation Artemis, the first ESDP mission outside Europe. Artemis was launched in the summer of 2003 to relieve UN forces in the eastern DRC, and while it largely consisted of French troops, it was widely welcomed as a sign that European security cooperation was not dead. It was the first of a series of ESDP missions co-deployed with UN forces, including small-scale

46 *Franziska Brantner and Richard Gowan*

security sector and police reform missions in the DRC; the deployment of a second military mission to back up the UN in the DRC in 2006; and a larger ESDP mission to Chad and the Central African Republic in 2008, designed to work alongside the UN police force. Earlier European support to UN peacekeeping had come from individual ex-colonial powers – and France remains the driver of ESDP in Africa – therefore major efforts have been made to give new missions an EU identity. This has resulted in unexpected deployments, such as that of German troops in the DRC, which are best explained in terms of a desire to prove European integration, but were facilitated and legitimized by UN mandates.

In parallel with this cooperation on security in Africa, there has been a further deepening of European support to UN development and humanitarian efforts. These have included not only the development of joint strategies in cases such as the DRC, but in channelling European aid to Afghanistan and Iraq. Notably, the European Commission has been one of the leaders in supporting the UN: combined Commission funding to UN activities leapt from under € 200 million in 1999 (and just over € 600 in 2003) to € 1,400 million in 2006 (Improving Lives 2007). In the case of Iraq, the Commission has made the third highest set of aid pledges (after the United States and United Kingdom) since 2003 – its contributions have been managed through a joint UN/World Bank mechanism, to which EU members have also contributed.[3] These commitments can be explained in terms of a European desire to reinforce multilateral approaches to aid and reconstruction, in contrast to a US emphasis on bilateral aid to Iraq and Afghanistan.

If operational cooperation with the UN has thus helped the European Union reassert its strategic identity after Iraq, coordination within UN forums has given it the opportunity to demonstrate political coherence within UN forums. The brief spike in splits among EU members in the General Assembly in 2003–2004 was followed by a return to pre-2003 levels of consensus. On human rights, EU consensus in both the General Assembly and the new HRC (discussed below) is virtually complete, at least in terms of votes. One striking feature of this period was that the 2004 enlargement, which brought a large number of pro-US countries into the UN bloc, did not have an appreciable effect on EU voting solidarity – most of the new member states had deliberately shifted towards voting with the European Union before accession. However, as we will note below, the new members have questioned some established EU assumptions on rights, increasing the risk that 'coherence' favours lowest common denominator decisions. While EU members do appear to be increasingly 'socialized' at the UN, following constructivist theory, the process does not necessarily yield positive results.

A further crucial factor in EU–UN relations has been cooperation in addressing the case of Iran. In 2003, EU governments agreed a strategy on Weapons of Mass Destruction alongside the main European Security Strategy – this explicitly states the centrality of the SC and IAEA to non-proliferation. In practice, the EU members have accepted the right of Javier Solana and the 'E3' (France, Britain and Germany) to handle negotiations, and the European strategy has rested on a mixture of incentives and penalties aimed at persuading Iran to cooperate fully with the IAEA (Gowan 2007). Although IAEA–EU cooperation has not always been perfect (especially in 2006 and

2007, during which some observers feared that the IAEA was growing too lenient), the extent to which there has been a joint EU–UN strategy is one of the clearest examples of the two bodies converging to date. This can be explained in Realist terms, as the E3 used EU and UN structures to enhance their influence, but they can also be seen as actively attempting to defend international law in this case.

The European Union also demonstrated resilience and leadership over the ICC (as described by Groenleer and Rijks) and the Kyoto Protocol. Germany has proved a particularly consistent leader on climate issues. Under its presidency in 2007, the European Union committed to reduce carbon emissions by 20 per cent from the 1990 level by 2020. This commitment was again far ahead of other UN member states' promises. The EU leadership among industrialized countries became increasingly tested as the United States attempted to push alternative, non-UN-based approaches in 2007. The success of the Kyoto process despite US opposition is therefore often presented as an example of EU leadership at the United Nations.

The realization of these international commitments inside the European Union has, however, been uneven. Climate policy measures have varied across member states, which can be explained by the inherent logic of the internal burden-sharing agreement among EU members which accorded different emission targets to its member states, but is also due to over-allocation of emission allowances during the first phase of the EU emissions trading scheme. The reluctance of some member states to implement measures with possible short-term negative consequences for some sectors of their industry became evident in the renegotiation of these allocations. The status of the European Union as (an often self-appointed) leader in the UN system has thus often been defined as much by the fact that it is progressive relative to the United States, rather than being absolutely consistent in its policies.

Current EU coordination at the UN

While the European Union's progress towards cohesion at the UN has thus been uneven, it has nonetheless achieved an impressive degree of coherence. The EU presidency now speaks on almost all issues in the UN General Assembly (Luif 2003; Smith 2006a; Young and Rees 2005). EU splits are now only a small percentage of total votes, usually below 15 per cent (Gowan and Brantner 2008: 19). But this analytical focus has obvious weaknesses: it prioritizes the existence of common EU positions over their substance, failing to differentiate between major and minor votes (Kissack 2007).

Nonetheless, the European Union's behaviour has a clear impact in the UN: a further 16 countries from its neighbourhood (ranging from Andorra to Turkey and Ukraine) vote with the European Union so consistently as to be *de facto* members of a single, though still informal, bloc. Yet, the European bloc at its maximum still represents only 23 per cent of the UN membership (Gowan and Brantner 2008: 27).

One might assume that the European Union has a common stance whenever first pillar issues are at stake, while second and third pillar issues should prove to be more difficult to coordinate. Even though such a trend can be observed, cooperation on all pillars is still higher than might be predicted (Laatikainen and Smith

48 *Franziska Brantner and Richard Gowan*

Table 3.1 Distribution of seats on UN forums, by selected political groups, 1 August 2007 (per cent in parentheses)

	General Assembly	Security Council	Human Rights Council	Economic and Social Council
G77	129 (67)	6 (40)	32 (68)	32 (59)
African Union	52 (27)	2 (13)	13 (28)	14 (26)
Organization of the Islamic Conference	58 (30)	2 (13)	16 (34)	15 (28)
European Union	27 (15)	5 (33)	7 (15)	12 (22)

2006). Nonetheless, EU member states are individually active as well – French, British and German diplomats are always engaged and often the first contact points for third countries, if only for the sheer size of their missions to the UN.

When EU member states align according to nationally defined positions, they do not always aim to amplify their influence by acting through the European Union. The Maastricht Treaty's formulation on common EU engagement in the SC (cf. Infra) was deliberately limited, so as not to infringe on the United Kingdom's and France's prerogatives in the SC. Even though member states' ambassadors to the UN meet weekly in New York under the guidance of the presidency in order to discuss upcoming SC agenda items, they are dependent on the willingness of Council members to share information and discuss strategy.

If member state non-cooperation in the security field is often highlighted by the media, donor coordination in UN funds and programmes is another important field where constant and coherent cooperation is still lacking. Member states contribute to the UN budget in three ways, via contributions to the assessed budget, to peacekeeping budgets and finally voluntary donations. The assessed budget contributions are based on an adjusted Gross Domestic Product/habitant factor and finance mainly the UN secretariat. Contributions are unequally shared among EU member states. While the old 15 member states contribute substantially, especially Germany, the United Kingdom, France and Italy, the new 12's contribution, with the exception of Poland, is not significant.

Voluntary contributions are similarly unevenly split among member states and go to funds and programmes, such as the UNDP. In the Fifth Committee of the General Assembly, which decides on assessed contributions, the European Union often speaks with one voice; in the Executive Boards of the funds and programmes (such as the UNDP), which decide on the spending of voluntary contributions, important donors from the European Union coordinate with other donors. The financial involvement of the European Union is often cited as proof of its commitment to the UN (as in Ortega 2005a, 2007), but it should be noted that European efforts to control the disbursement of funds often leads it into conflict with poorer UN members – we will note the impact of their differences over funding on the UN reform process below.

Notably, the Commission is increasingly an important voluntary donor of the UN. EC funding of UN projects has increased by 370 per cent in the period 1999–2004; it is today above 1 billion EUR per year. The Commission is also among

Table 3.2 Assessed UN budget contributions by EU member states, 2005

	EU member state	Percentage of UN budget	Gross contribution in million $
1	Germany	8.662	173,087,081
2	United Kingdom of Great Britain and Northern Ireland	6.127	122,431,834
3	France	6.030	120,493,546
4	Italy	4.885	97,613,760
5	Spain	2.520	50,355,512
6	Netherlands	1.690	33,770,165
7	Belgium	1.069	21,361,128
8	Sweden	0.998	19,942,381
9	Austria	0.859	17,164,835
10	Denmark	0.718	14,347,325
11	Finland	0.533	10,650,591
12	Greece	0.530	10,590,643
13	Portugal	0.470	9,391,703
14	Poland	0.461	9,211,862
15	Ireland	0.350	6,993,821
16	Czech Republic	0.183	3,656,769
17	Hungary	0.126	2,517,776
18	Slovenia	0.082	1,638,552
19	Luxembourg	0.077	1,538,641
20	Romania	0.060	1,198,941
21	Slovakia	0.051	1,019,100
22	Cyprus	0.039	779,312
23	Lithuania	0.024	479,576
24	Bulgaria	0.017	339,700
25	Latvia	0.015	299,735
26	Malta	0.014	279,753
27	Estonia	0.012	239,788

the top three donors in its own right for the World Food Programme and UN Relief and Works Agency for Palestine Refugees in the Near East.

If EU cohesion has not yet been fully achieved in the political and financial fields, it is also sometimes possible to identify cases in which previously achieved coordination appears to be eroding. This is especially true in the human rights field, even though it was one of the earliest areas of progress towards cohesion. An example is the European Union's coordination in the UN Commission on the Status of Women in 2007. The US government under the Bush administration has been very sceptical towards human rights in UN resolutions and conclusions, especially women's reproductive rights and non-discrimination with regard to sexual choice. The European Union has typically attempted to withstand set-backs and defended the status quo. But in 2007, several EU member states, including Poland and Malta, began to defend positions similar to those of the Bush administration in intra-EU discussions – holding up agreement on EU positions on issues of reproductive rights or non-discrimination. Diplomats worried that referring this case to their national governments would create political tensions.

Facing this dilemma, several progressive EU member states envisaged presenting a separate statement inside the General Assembly, together with the Nordic states, in order to show their support for women's rights and to increase pressure on other EU members. This would have meant abandoning EU unity. In the end, this did not occur. Nonetheless, the serious discussion of this option showed the gravity of the problem inside the European Union. Progressive member states start doubting the usefulness of a unified EU position if the only possible EU position is a weak compromise. Would it not be better to have a strong Nordic negotiation position instead and have the few countries inside the EU blocking progress speak up for themselves? Could that also facilitate alliance building across the North–South divide and liberate onerous time for reaching out to Southern partners? While a common position was finally achieved in this case, it has become clear that the European Union's common policy on rights issues may be difficult to sustain if progressive and conservative states continue to clash in future.

European Union's role in the 2005 reform process

In 2003, UN Secretary General Kofi Annan launched a holistic reform effort at the UN; a window of opportunity for the European Union to live up to its promises to strengthen the UN. But Annan's initiative, which culminated in the 2005 UN summit, has been bogged down in North–South stalemate[4] (Laurenti 2005; Luck 2005; Traub 2006). One can blame John Bolton, the polarizing former US Ambassador to the UN, for this situation (Traub 2006). But where is the European Union in all of this? The answer 'in the middle' (Chevallard 2005) is not satisfying. Even if this was the case, we still do not know if that was actually a reform-propitious place.

An analysis of the interplay between EU projections of its power and that of emerging or declining powers within the UN reform process might not provide straightforward answers, but it might allow us to think more critically about the European Union's role in international organizations. The following will draw the larger map, and then locate the European Union on it to analyse how the European Union's power projection has impacted reform efforts.

Security Council reform and the Peacebuilding Commission

Security Council

The reform of the SC is a perennial hobby for some diplomats. Those favouring expansion argue that the SC must reflect the power balances of the twenty-first century; otherwise it will lose its legitimacy to mandate the use of force in those regions of the world which are underrepresented.

As during previous reform rounds, European governments did not speak with one voice (Bourantonis 2005). They were deeply divided. Whereas France and the United Kingdom supported Germany in its bid for a permanent seat in the SC, Italy and Spain and some other smaller member states vehemently opposed such an ascendance of Germany. Nonetheless, observers noted in 2005 that the majority of EU member states had accepted the refined G4 bid, which did not foresee immediate veto rights to the new permanent members and a review clause. Even if internal EU division contributed to reform failure, this division was not the decisive factor blocking reform in 2005. African disunity, Chinese opposition to Japan's bid and the United States' (at least) lack of enthusiasm for reform are at least equally responsible.

France and Britain support a German seat because if the SC was reformed, including a new seat for Germany, the heated discussions currently challenging their own membership would turn into hot air, at least for a decade (Hill 2005). The discussion about a common EU seat – replacing the French and British seats – has mainly been confined to academic circles as France and the United Kingdom have successfully managed to keep this issue off the EU agenda. New York and capitals are the place to discuss the issue and not Brussels.

As Jørgensen states in Chapter 1, Italian and Spanish opposition to a German seat should be interpreted as a relative gains logic 'that is alive and kicking'. An alternative interpretation – Italy and Spain oppose the German seat due to their strong support for a completely integrated European foreign policy – reflected by a common European seat – can be discarded. Neither Italian Prime Minister Berlusconi nor Spanish Prime Minister Zapatero undertook any major initiatives in order to strengthen the CFSP or ESDP.

A permanent seat for Germany would have consequences for the CFSP, probably reinforcing the current trend towards flexible forms of cooperation (Marchesi 2005). At the same time, a common seat of the European Union could potentially have a tremendous impact on the UN system, representing a challenge to the nation-state-based UN system and possibly translating the regional representation logic to other regions, creating potentially negative regional power competition dynamics.

Peacebuilding Commission

On 30 December 2005, the General Assembly and the SC each approved a resolution establishing the UN Peacebuilding Commission (PBC). The idea behind the PBC was to bridge an institutional attention and cooperation gap. The SC deals with conflicts, but rarely with the prevention of conflicts or with their aftermath. The development machinery of the UN helps countries in their economic and social development, but is less effective in situations of failed statehood or not yet established statehood. Who ensures that the delicate transition from conflict to peace and the interplay between security needs and institution building are well managed? The PBC is meant to do just that.

The PBC negotiations were considered mild in comparison to other negotiations. The determination of the PBC's relation to the SC and the General Assembly was the essence of the debate. The battle concerned foremost the PBC's institutional status, but also questions of agenda setting and implementation. Some Non-Aligned Movement (NAM) members, such as Pakistan or Cuba, insisted on the weakest link to the SC; but the majority of the NAM (especially the African group) accepted the argument that the SC had to be closely involved for the PBC to become relevant. Nonetheless, they opposed an increase in SC

52 *Franziska Brantner and Richard Gowan*

powers over new domains and especially automatic P5 permanent membership in the PBC.

The battle was strong inside the European Union. France and Britain wanted the PBC close to the SC, while other members cautioned and preferred a more balanced approach. The P5 claim for permanent membership in the PBC was also outrageous to many inside the European Union. Interestingly, those inside the European Union leaning towards a weaker role of the SC did so, at least partially, because of their sensitivity to the larger membership.[5] The European Union therefore had a carefully drafted compromise position; in that sense, the European Union was in the middle between the SC permanent members that insisted on a 'SC only' body and more radical NAM countries favouring an ECOSOC or GA body. One can argue that the principled US and Russian position on this issue allowed France and the United Kingdom to take a more conciliatory approach.

Internal EU discussions furthermore focused on the representation of the European Union in the PBC. The EU Commission was keen on participating as an important financial donor, whereas the Council wanted to maintain its dominance over second pillar issues. The EU membership evenly split along these two options. The wider UN membership did not quite understand this struggle and only realized that much EU energy was spent on this question. The internal argument over EC/Council representation was especially fierce in view of the EU external action service and its future institutional location.

To summarize, the European Union did not have extreme, but carefully drafted, compromise positions, which were sometimes so weak that the European Union only play a minor role. The conflict lines within the UN over the PBC concentrated on the balance between 'equality and management of power'; so did the conflict lines inside the European Union: between permanent and non-permanent members, between small and large states, between states that have lived through transition recently and those that have not. Overall, the European Union played an important role in promoting the idea of the PBC, but a secondary role in several negotiations over its details. Furthermore, some EU members played individually important roles, such as Denmark, and were highly esteemed for their efforts in the wider UN membership.

Human Rights Council

In March 2006, the General Assembly approved, 170 to 4 votes (United States, Israel, Marshall Islands and Palau against) with 3 abstentions (Belarus, Iran and Venezuela), the resolution creating the HRC. The HRC replaced the Commission on Human Rights, which had come under heavy criticism from the human rights community for being an extremely politicized and rather ineffective body.

The European Union supported from early on the strengthening of the UN human rights machinery. The EU presidencies advocated for a different status of the HRC – a standing body, possibly treaty body – with increased meeting time and new membership rules.[6] The European Union wanted to set criteria for membership (such as 'abiding by the highest human rights standards') and to have the

HRC elected by a 2/3 majority, instead of simple majority.[7] At the same time, the European Union defended the status quo on many other aspects, such as the Commission on Human Rights's mandate to address country-specific situations, or the status of NGOs.[8]

Comparing the European Union with other actors, the European Union was definitely on one extreme. Together with the United States and Canada, Australia and New Zealand (CANZ), they diametrically stood opposed to the few countries blocking any sort of strengthening, such as Iran, Cuba, Belarus or Pakistan. Throughout most of the negotiations, the United States kept silent. Ambassador John Bolton got involved only at a late stage in the negotiations. In fact, the European Union defended a position almost identical to that of the United States, aside from the US strong emphasis on a smaller body that the European Union did not unequivocally share. The fact that the European Union accepted the compromise deal in the end, but not the United States, does not therefore allow the conclusion that the EU position was in the 'middle'.

In general, the wider UN membership was not organized around the developing countries coalitions of the G77 or NAM. Most countries accepted the idea of a new institution and wanted some change, but categorically refused the idea of membership criteria and 2/3 majority voting.[9] In fact, the countries attempting to mediate were foremost Switzerland, Singapore, Liechtenstein and New Zealand.

The question remains why developing, but democratic, countries, such as South Africa, did not support EU positions. Even Liechtenstein argued that 'We do not think that introducing criteria for membership is either feasible or desirable'.[10] Delegates from democratic developing countries opposed 'exclusive clubs' but also substantially argued that excluding those the UN wished to impact was not the most promising strategy. In addition, the European Union (as well as the United States) was criticized for not defining the criteria and who would monitor them and decide on eligibility of candidates. Criteria proposed by some NGOs such as ratification of human rights conventions had to be disregarded as they would have excluded the USA and Australia. The lack of transparency by the European Union and others sustained the fears of many among the developing countries of yet another body dominated by the 'West' setting its standards and applying these in an uneven manner. Furthermore, the proposed criteria as well as the 2/3 majority vote were opposed for exactly the reason the European Union and the United States advocated for them: they increased the control of democratic and human rights defending countries, among which the European Union is in the majority, over the body.

In the end, the EU move to ask for 'no clean slate' per region,[11] an institutional mechanism to ensure more candidates than slots, found broader support among the wider membership. The basic idea was to give all member states a real choice between candidates and trust them not to elect human rights violators. Liechtenstein and others had already earlier in the negotiations argued that 2/3 or simple majority voting would not make any difference if there was no choice. Such an institutional setting would have empowered other democratic countries to make real choices over membership.

54 *Franziska Brantner and Richard Gowan*

Finally, the European Union was challenged based on alleged double standards. The linchpin for many became if the European Union was willing to support resolutions against the United States, and evidence over the past years had shown that this was not the case.[12] This in turn did not increase the credibility of the European Union's claim to strengthen 'universal' human rights, similar to its often manifest unwillingness to discuss internal human rights violations at the UN, for example the situation of minority groups in new EU member states.

To summarize, the European Union's goal was to strengthen the UN human rights machinery and one of the ways it sought doing so was to create stronger control by democratic countries over the UN human rights machinery. Developing countries reacted very sensitively to this and it turns out that, in the end, the European Union lost even more control within the new HRC.[13] By contrast, commitment to an institutional setting that would have empowered other democratic countries to make real choices over membership instead of imposing its (non-specified) criteria might have facilitated a way out of stalemate.

Management of the secretariat, funds and programmes

The quest for improving the management of the UN secretariat and its funds, programmes and agencies is as old as the UN. Heads of states decided in September 2005, after the oil-for-food and secretariat scandals, to commission the Secretary General to write a report on possible management reforms. The United States linked the negotiations over management reforms to the 2006/2007 budget and threatened to withhold payments if reforms were not deep enough. Therefore, the United States introduced a cap on spending – budget approval for a maximum of six months with further approval conditioned on the pace of management reforms. Some inside the European Union attempted to bring the European Union to oppose the spending cap, but France lost and the European Union moved on to support the modified spending cap. In consequence, the European Union was part of the US deal, and its rhetorical moderation did not help to overshadow its alignment with the United States.[14]

Kofi Annan then presented in the spring of 2006 the report 'Investing in the United Nations' that suggested vast management reforms, among which less controversial proposals such as an improvement of the UN's IT system and forever-contenders such as moving budget decisions from the Fifth Committee to a smaller group, and giving more flexibility to the Secretary General to move posts and resources.

The G77 and China strongly opposed these last two proposals. The European Union, however, asked for stronger Secretary General flexibility than even the United States or Japan. Similarly, the European Union was in favour of transferring decision-making away from the Fifth Committee to smaller subgroups. Polarization was at its highest when the G77 and China co-sponsored a resolution in April 2006 that foreclosed further endeavours into changing budgetary decision-making and Secretary General flexibility. The Fifth Committee adopted this resolution by 108 votes with 50 against and two abstentions. Russia supported the G77/China resolution. OECD (Organisation for Economic Co-operation and

The EU and the United Nations 55

Development) countries and potential EU candidates stood alone in their opposition; Norway abstained.

Only after intense negotiations were some management reforms adopted in June and the budget cap lifted on the last possible day. These reforms mainly concerned non-conflictual areas. Observers argued that, without the polarization over budgetary processes, further more confined reforms regarding accountability and oversight could have been adopted. Interestingly, over the tricky 'flexibility of the Secretary General' issue, the European Union was isolated. Japan (the United States had aligned with Japan's position before) had found a deal with the G77, while the European Union was still insisting on much larger leeway for the Secretary General. In the end, the European Union had to give in and accept the compromise found between Japan and the G77.

Regarding the European Union's position on reform of the budgetary decision-making structure, European member states, when acting together, need only one representative. With increasing EU funding to the UN and EU cooperation in the Fifth Committee, it becomes less and less relevant for EU member states to have necessarily all its members around the table (some might even be happy not to have to send a delegate and to leave the job to the presidency).

The EU (and US) refusal to share power has increasingly negative consequences in times of an emerging new conscience among several powers in the South. China, India, Brazil and South Africa know that their power is increasing. They also have the perception that the United States and the European Union today depend much more on the UN. Surely, they need the UN as a forum to present their new strength, but they do not receive important financial support from the UN and the one issue of major importance to them – trade – is negotiated at the WTO. Their perception is that the United States and the European Union need the UN in order to legitimize their security policies be it in Afghanistan, Iraq or Congo, or to legitimize their democracy and human rights policies, and the European Union its environmental policies.[15] This perception – be it right or wrong – also contributed to the Southern countries not accepting the financial whip.

To summarize, in the management case, the European Union conducted and explicitly supported polarizing policies. To a large extent these were polarizing because of their content: aiming at increasing control over budgetary processes. The European Union, as much as the United States, did not come up with institutional mechanisms to ensure adequate accountability standards.

The US-proposed spending cap was clearly a strategic decision that inflamed the wider membership and soured the atmosphere sustainably. The European Union might not have proposed it itself, but the fact of supporting it, no longer allowed the European Union to play a broker role.

Conclusion

Much of the EU–UN literature recommends the European Union to speak increasingly with one voice, to coordinate its policies better and to punch according to its weight (Ortega 2005b; Laatikainen and Smith 2006). Martin Ortega

56 *Franziska Brantner and Richard Gowan*

concludes an EU Institute for International Security paper collection with the following: 'The Europeans have the ideas, the means; what is lacking is self-confidence, leadership and determination' (Ortega 2005b: 100). To a large extent, the critique of the European Union in the UN falls in the rubric of the 'expectations–capabilities gap' (Hill 1993) – if only the European Union had the capabilities for doing what is right and good.

But this amounts to taking the European Union's mantra of 'effective multilateralism' at face value. Is the question really if the European Union uses its weight and power *enough*, the challenge that member states and EU institutions coordinate and cooperate *better and more*? This does neither illuminate the impact of EU policies and strategies nor does it ask what the European Union should punch harder for (and how) or, for that matter, what the substance of 'one voice' should be in order to strengthen the UN.

While calling for a stronger and united European Union, the same authors sometimes have statements in their work that seem to prove the opposite or at least raise questions. Laatikainen and Smith write that 'a common EU stance can even spark the automatic opposition of developing countries, because they perceive the EU as domineering and neo-colonial' (Laatikainen and Smith 2006: 18). But this is not followed up – what sparks 'automatic opposition', what policies are perceived as 'neo-colonial'? Similarly, Biscop and Drieskens mention that the European Union did not wish to highlight the similarities between EU approaches to current global challenges and recommendations of the High Level Panel on Threats, Challenges and Change, which was tasked to develop UN reform recommendations in 2004. The European Union did not want to seem to be a leader because it fears perceptions of 'European/western dominance in discussions of UN reform ... since such perceptions might provoke outsiders to resist European positions and ideas' (Biscop and Drieskens 2006).

The omission of the above questions is partially the consequence of non-clarity by these authors about the central concern of their research. Is the central question how the European Union can be a catalyst for improved and enhanced international cooperation or rather how the European Union can exert influence beyond its borders? Even if the two are obviously linked, equating the two amounts to equating EU interests to 'interests of the globe'. This tendency is latent in much of the EU–UN work – the European Union knows what is in the interest of the rest of the world.

At least two remedies to this bias can be imagined; neither assumes that the European Union is inherently a force for good. The first one looks inward and attempts to understand who precisely within the European Union is pursuing what kind of 'effective multilateralism' strategy, in whose interest they act, and by which objectives they are motivated. A second approach developed in this work looks first outward at the larger picture, in this case coalition constellations facilitating cooperation, as a starting point of its analysis. It then focuses on how the European Union fits into the larger picture, in this case what forms of EU power projection enable conditions favourable to reform. Research in this area is promising and a more refined understanding of the European Union's role in the UN will shed light on general assumptions about EU foreign policy.

The sheer complexity of EU engagement with the UN ultimately makes it impossible to say whether or not the European Union is effective within it. Its impact varies over issues and time, and there is no one political or theoretical definition of success that can be applied to topics as diverse as peace operations and climate change. If, however, we consider the European Union's pursuit of international law and norm-building through the UN as essential to its 'multilateral DNA', we come to a mixed conclusion. The European Union clearly has been central to constructing and defending international law through the UN, but it has failed to develop a long-term understanding by the United States and much of the South on the necessity of this project. Without such an understanding, its multiple forms of engagement with the UN system – although impressive in their scale – are liable to remain fragmented and *ad hoc*.

Notes

1 European Council (2003) *A Secure Europe in a Better World. European Security Strategy*, Brussels, 12 December. Communication from the Commission to the Council and the European Parliament.
2 Hill and Wallace similarly argue that

> the member states of the European Union have established a collective 'presence' in the international arena, without achieving the ability to act collectively except through cumbersome consultative procedures and partially effective diplomatic, economic and military instruments. ... Its presence in the world is therefore real but incoherent, leaving third countries ... to cope with relations with the European Community (through the Commission) alongside bilateral relations with the member states.
>
> (Hill and Wallace 1996: 13)

3 Details of this mechanism, the International Reconstruction Fund Facility for Iraq, are at http://www.irffi.org
4 At the UN, North–South refers to Western powers against the Group of 77 (G77, 130 members) and the Non-Aligned Movement (NAM, 118 members).
5 Interviews with UN delegates conducted in New York by Franziska Brantner, June and July 2006.
6 EU priorities for the 60th session, http://www.europa-eu-un.org/articles/en/article_4599_en.htm
7 EU speaking points for the Informal Consultations of the United Nations Plenary on the Human Rights Council, New York, 11 January 2006.
8 In professional EU 'speak': 'The establishment of such a body [the Human Rights Council] must take into account the valuable aspects of the *acquis* in the field of human rights' (emphasis in original) – EU general statement on UN reform on 6 April 2005.
9 Interviews with UN delegates conducted in New York by Franziska Brantner, June and July 2006.
10 Statement by Christian Wenaweser, Liechtenstein's ambassador to the UN, 24 October 2005.
11 Due to the principle of equitable geographic representation, each region of the UN has assigned number of seats in the HRC, which are, however, voted on individually by the entirety of the membership – this was one of the compromises of the Eliasson document.
12 For example, votes on resolutions regarding Guantanamo Bay, draft resolution E/CN.4/2005/L.94/Rev.1, question of detainees in the area of the United States of America naval base in Guantánamo.

58 *Franziska Brantner and Richard Gowan*

13 The European Union has proportionally less votes in the HRC than it did in the CHR, as the new forum is based on equal geographic representation. The number of members on the Council from the Organization of the Islamic Conference (OIC) – currently 18 out of 47 Council members – is seen as playing a major role in the current tension within and around the Council. The terms of OIC members Algeria, Bahrain, Indonesia, Morocco and Tunisia will expire in 2007. If they are replaced with non-OIC members of the African and Asian groups, it is thought that HRC dynamics could shift. However, it is also possible to be re-elected for a second term.

14 For this argument, see also Laatikainen (2006a: 15).

15 Without having been asked, many delegates from developing countries interviewed mentioned this perspective.

References

Allen, D. (1998) 'Who speaks for Europe? The search for an effective and coherent external policy', in J. Peterson and H. Sjursen (eds) *A Common Foreign Policy for Europe?*, London: Routledge, pp. 41–58.

Arpio Santacruz, M. (1997) 'L'Union européenne et l'action des Nations Unies dans le domaine des droits de l'homme', in D. Dormoy (ed.) *L'Union Européenne et les organisations internationales*, Bruxelles: Editions Bruylant.

Ayoob, M. (2005) 'What trans-Atlantic crisis?', *International Herald Tribune*, 24 February.

Ayoob, M. and Zierler, M. (2005) 'The Unipolar Concert: The North–South divide trumps transatlantic differences', *World Policy Journal*, XXII (1), Spring.

Biscop, S. and Drieskens, E. (2006) 'The European security strategy: Confirming the choice for collective and comprehensive security', in J. Wouters, H. Hoffmeister and T. Ruys (eds) *The United Nations and the European Union: An Ever Stronger Partnership*, The Hague: TMC Asser Press, pp. 267–279.

Bourantonis, D. (2005) *The History and Politics of UN Security Council Reform*, London and New York: Routledge.

Carlsnaes, W., Sjursen, H. and White, B. (eds) (2004) *Contemporary European Foreign Policy*, London: Sage.

Chevallard, G. (2005) 'UN reform: A test of European leadership', *The International Spectator*, No. 4.

Diez, T. (2005) 'Constructing the Self and changing Others: Reconsidering "Normative Power Europe"', *Millennium: Journal of International Studies*, 33(3): 613–636.

Dormoy, D. (1997) 'Le statut de l'Union Européenne dans les organisations internationales', in D. Dormoy (ed.) *L'Union Européenne et les organisations internationales*, Bruxelles: Editions Bruylant.

Economides, S. and Taylor, P. (1996) 'Former Yugoslavia', in: J. Mayall (ed.): *The New Interventionism 1991–1994. United Nations Experience in Cambodia, Former Yugoslavia and Somalia*, Cambridge: Cambridge University Press, pp. 59–93.

Fassbender, B. (2004) 'The better peoples of the United Nations? Europe's practice and the United Nations', *European Journal of International Law*, 15(5): 857–884.

Ginsberg, R. (1989) *Foreign Policy Actions of the European Community. The Politics of Scale*, Boulder: Lynne Rienner.

Gowan, R. (2006) 'The European security strategy's global objective: Effective multilateralism', in S. Biscop and J.J. Anderssen (eds) *The EU and the European Security Strategy: Forging a Global Europe*, London: Routledge.

—— (2007) 'The global objective: Effective multilateralism', in S. Biscop and J.J. Andersson (eds) *The EU and the European Security Strategy: Forging a Global Europe*, London: Routledge.

The EU and the United Nations 59

Gowan, R. and Brantner, F. (2008) *A Global Force for Human Rights? An Audit of European Power at the UN.* London: European Council on Foreign Relations.

Grieco, J.M. (1996) 'State interest and institutional rule trajectories: A neorealist interpretation of the Maastricht Treaty and European Economic and Monetary Union', *Security Studies*, (Spring) 5(3): 261–305.

Gupta, J. (2005) 'L'Union Européenne, leader de la politique international du changement climatique?', in D. Helly and F. Petiteville (eds) *L'Union Européenne, acteur international*, Paris: L'Harmattan, pp. 253–266.

Gupta, J. and Grubb, M. (eds) (2000) *Climate Change and European Leadership: A Sustainable Role for Europe?* Dordrecht: Kluwer Academic Publishers.

Helly, D. and Petiteville, F. (eds) (2005) *L'Union Européenne, acteur international*, Paris: L'Harmattan.

Hill, C. (1993) 'The capability–expectations gap, or conceptualizing Europe's international role', *Journal of Common Market Studies*, 31(3): 305–328.

—— (ed.) (1996) *The Actors in Europe's Foreign Policy*, London: Routledge.

—— (2005) 'The European dimension of the debate on UN Security Council membership', *The International Spectator*, 4: 31–39.

Hill, C. and Wallace, W. (1996) 'Introduction, actors and actions', in C. Hill (ed.) *The Actors in Europe's Foreign Policy*, London: Routledge.

Improving Lives (2007) Results from the partnership of the United Nations and the European Commission in 2006, United Nations System in Brussels.

Johnstone, I. (2008) 'Normative evolution at the UN: The impact on operational activities', in S. Forman and B.D. Jones (eds) *Cooperating for Peace and Security*, Cambridge: Cambridge University Press.

Jørgensen, K.E. and Laatikainen, K.V. (2006) 'The EU @ the UN: Multilateralism in a new key?', paper prepared for presentation at the ISA Annual Convention, San Diego, California, USA, 22–25 March.

Kagan, R. (2003) *Paradise and Power: America Versus Europe in the Twenty-first Century*, London: Atlantic.

Kissack, R. (2007) 'European Union Member States coordination in the United Nations system: Towards a methodology for analysis', European Foreign Policy Unit Working Paper 20071/1.

Laatikainen, K.V. and Smith, K.E. (eds) (2006) *The European Union at the United Nations: Intersecting Multilateralisms*, Basingstoke: Palgrave Macmillan.

Laurenti, J. (2005) 'Summit asymmetry: The United States and UN reform', *The International Spectator*, No. 4 (October/December), pp. 7–18.

Luck, E.C. (2005) 'How not to reform the United Nations', *Global Governance*, 11: 407–414.

Luif, P. (2003) *EU Cohesion in the UN General Assembly*, EU-ISS Occasional Paper No. 49.

Malone, D. (2006) *The International Struggle Over Iraq: Politics in the Security Council 1980–2005*, Oxford: Oxford University Press.

Manners, I. (2002) 'Normative power Europe: A contradiction in terms?', *Journal of Common Market Studies*, 37(3): 235–258.

Marchesi, D. (2005) *The United Nations Security Council Reform and the European Union – Assessing the Impact on CFSP*, thesis presented for the Degree of Master of European Studies, Academic Year 2004–2005, College of Europe.

Oberthür, S. (2007) 'The European Union in international climate policy: The prospect for leadership', *Intereconomics*, March/April.

Ortega, M. (2005a) *The EU and UN: Implementing Effective Multilateralism*, EU Institute for Security Studies paper, March.

60 *Franziska Brantner and Richard Gowan*

—— (ed.) (2005b) *The European Union and the United Nations: Partners in Effective Multilateralism*, Chaillot Paper 78, European Institute for Security Studies.

—— (2007) *Building the Future: The EU's Contribution to Global Governance*, Paris: Institute for Security Studies.

Smith, K.E. (2001) *European Union Foreign Policy in a Changing World*, Cambridge: Polity Press.

—— (2003) *European Union Foreign Policy in a Changing World*, Cambridge: Polity Press.

—— (2006a) 'Speaking with one voice? European Union coordination on human rights issues at the United Nations', *Journal of Common Market Studies*, 44(1): 97–121.

—— (2006b) 'The European Union', human rights and the United Nations', in K.V. Laatikainen and K.E. Smith (eds) *The European Union at the United Nations: Intersecting Multilateralisms*, Basingstoke: Palgrave Macmillan.

Smith, M.E. (2003) *Europe's Foreign and Security Policy – The Institutionalization of Cooperation*, Cambridge: Cambridge University Press.

Traub, J. (2006) *The Best Intentions. Kofi Annan and the UN in the Era of American World Power*, New York: Farrar, Strauss, Giroux.

Walt, S.M. (1987) *The Origins of Alliances*, Ithaca, NY: Cornell University Press.

Wouters, J., Hoffmeister, F. and Ruys, T. (eds) (2006) *The United Nations and the European Union: An Ever Stronger Partnership*, The Hague: TMC Asser Press.

Young, H. and Rees, N. (2005) 'EU voting in the UN General Assembly, 1990–2002: The EU's Europeanising tendencies', *Irish Studies in International Affairs*, 16: 193–207.

4 A single EU seat in the International Monetary Fund?[1]

Lorenzo Bini Smaghi

Introduction

The creation of the euro and the discussion that took place in the run-up to the new Treaty of Lisbon have revitalized the debate on the role of the European Union in international financial matters, in particular in the context of the International Monetary Fund (IMF).[2] Some have even suggested that EU member states should merge their quotas in the IMF in order to be represented as a single member. Such a merger would imply that the Fund would be transferred to Europe.[3]

These proposals have partly grown out of the frustration experienced by European countries with IMF decision-making. Despite the fact that EU countries hold over 30 per cent of the votes, nearly double that of the United States, the European Union's influence on IMF matters is rather limited. An interest in rationalizing EU representation in international fora has also been voiced strongly outside Europe. Several emerging market economies, Japan and the United States have occasionally expressed the view that Europeans are overrepresented (see, e.g., Van Houtven 2002).

The issue of EU representation in the Fund was examined on several occasions by Ecofin, the EU Council of Finance Ministers, and the Eurogroup.[4] The main conclusion was that cooperation should be further intensified, but the current institutional arrangements should continue to apply for the time being.

This chapter examines the rationale for consolidating the position of EU member states in the IMF. It considers in particular whether the creation of EMU has provided additional grounds for moving in that direction.[5] The starting point of the analysis is the principle of subsidiarity, according to which EU member states' policy competencies should be allocated to the European level only if they cannot be performed efficiently at the national level.[6]

The chapter is organized into three main sections. The first examines the current situation in the IMF, where the 27 EU countries are represented in ten different constituencies. A substantial amount of coordination already takes place. Moreover, on issues related to the single monetary and exchange rate policy, as well as on a number of other euro area-specific issues, the euro area speaks with one voice. The second and third sections apply the principle of subsidiarity to IMF issues. Two aspects are of relevance in the analysis: the heterogeneity of

62 *Lorenzo Bini Smaghi*

preferences across countries on IMF issues and the economies of scale and/or externalities that can be achieved by unifying representation. If economies of scale and/or externalities dominate, there might be a case for unifying representation at the IMF. If, instead, heterogeneity of preferences dominates, IMF-related policies are better dealt with at the national level (see Alesina *et al.* 2001). The second section examines the degree of heterogeneity among EU member states' positions on IMF issues. The third section examines the economies of scale that can be achieved through stronger EU representation on the IMF Board.

The current situation

The system of constituencies

Table 4.1 shows how the 27 EU countries are represented on the IMF Executive Board:

- Germany, France and the United Kingdom each have a single chair;
- Italy, The Netherlands and Belgium lead their respective constituencies, where other countries participate. Greece, Portugal and Malta are members of the constituency chaired by Italy, together with Albania, San Marino and East Timor.[7] Austria, Luxembourg and Slovenia are members of the constituency chaired by Belgium, together with other EU countries, that is, the Czech Republic, Hungary and the Slovak Republic, as well as other countries from outside the European Union, that is, Belarus, Kazakhstan and Turkey.[8] The Netherlands chairs a constituency, which includes one euro area country (Cyprus), two EU countries (Bulgaria and Romania) and several non-EU countries, including Israel and the Ukraine;
- Sweden, Finland and Denmark are part of the Nordic–Baltic constituency, together with the Baltic countries, Norway and Iceland. The chair rotates between the five Nordic countries every two years;
- Ireland is a member of the constituency chaired by Canada, which also includes other countries mainly of the Caribbean region;[9]
- Spain participates in a constituency together with Mexico, Venezuela, Costa Rica, El Salvador, Guatemala, Honduras and Nicaragua, with the chair rotating every two years between the first three countries;
- Poland is part of the constituency led by Switzerland.

Except for the countries holding a single chair, the current situation is the result of decisions made by each IMF member. Each constituency has its own decision-making system, as allowed by the IMF statutes. The IMF statutes require the five major countries to have single chairs.

Changes in constituency composition have occurred over time. For instance, Spain participated in the constituency chaired by Italy until 1978, holding the position of Alternate Executive Director, but then decided to join the constituency of Mexico and Venezuela, holding the position of Executive Director every four years.

Table 4.1 EU constituencies in the IMF

EU countries	Other countries	Constituency chair	Votes (%)
Germany (5.87)		Germany	5.87
France (4.84)		France	4.84
United Kingdom (4.84)		United Kingdom	4.84
Italy (3.19), Greece (0.38), Portugal (0.4), Malta (0.06)	Albania (0.03), San Marino (0.02), Timor-Leste (0.01)	Italy	4.09
Netherlands (2.33), Bulgaria (0.3), Cyprus (0.07), Romania (0.47)	Armenia (0.05), Bosnia-Herzegovina (0.09), Croatia (0.18), Georgia (0.08), Israel (0.43), Macedonia, FYR (0.04), Moldova (0.07), Ukraine (0.63)	Netherlands	4.74
Austria (0.85), Belgium (2.08), Czech Republic (0.38), Luxembourg (0.14), Hungary (0.48), Slovenia (0.12), Slovak Republic (0.17)	Belarus (0.19), Kazakhstan (0.18), Turkey (0.55)	Belgium	5.14
Denmark (0.75), Finland (0.58), Sweden (1.09), Estonia (0.04), Latvia (0.07), Lithuania (0.08)	Iceland (0.06), Norway (0.76)	Rotating every two years between Denmark, Finland, Sweden and Norway	3.43
Spain (1.38)	Costa Rica (0.09), El Salvador (0.09), Guatemala (0.11), Honduras (0.07), Mexico (1.43), Nicaragua (0.07), Venezuela (1.21)	Rotating between Spain, Mexico and Venezuela	4.45
Ireland (0.39)	Antigua and Barbuda (0.02), Barbados (0.04), Belize (0.02), Canada (2.88), Dominican Republic (0.11), Grenada (0.02), Jamaica (0.13), St. Kitts and Nevis (0.02), St. Lucia (0.02), St. Vincent/ Grenadines (0.01)	Canada	3.27
Poland (0.63)	Azerbaijan (0.08), Kyrgyz Republic (0.05), Switzerland (1.57), Tajikistan (0.05), Turkmenistan (0.05), Uzbekistan (0.14)	Switzerland	2.57

Source: IMF and author's calculations.

64 *Lorenzo Bini Smaghi*

Further single country constituencies are held by the United States (16.73 per cent of the votes), Japan (6.0), China (3.65), Russia (2.69) and Saudi Arabia (3.16). Overall, 185 countries are grouped together in 24 constituencies, some of which are composed of a relatively large number of countries.[10] Each constituency can express only one view in the Board. Being a member of a constituency forces members to agree on a common position, or to abstain from voting.

The voting share of each country is determined mainly by the respective quota share, which is calculated on the basis of a set of formulae combining the ability to contribute, that is, national product, and the need for Fund resources, calculated on the basis of countries' vulnerability to external shocks linked, in particular, to openness to international trade (see IMF 2001). The IMF has agreed on a quota and voice reform with the aim of better aligning members' voting shares with their economic weight in the global economy and enhancing the participation and voice for low-income countries. This reform package was approved at the spring meetings in 2008. It includes inter alia a new quota formula, quota increases for several countries and a tripling of the basic votes. However, its implementation will have to await the consent of the US Congress to the necessary changes of the IMF Articles of Agreement.

Cooperation among constituencies

As in most public companies, individual shareholders have very little influence on decisions. Cooperation arrangements between shareholders are thus the key to influence. In the IMF, such arrangements are based on two main criteria: country size and debtor/creditor position.

Country size is the main factor behind the Group of Seven (G-7),[11] which holds around 45 per cent of the votes on the Board (Table 4.2). The finance ministers and central bank governors of the G-7 meet the day before the spring and annual meetings of the IMF and World Bank to discuss the main issues on the agenda and try to reach common positions. Proposals for reforming the international financial institutions are generally initiated at G-7 meetings (see Group of Seven 1999). The G-7 deputies, representing their respective finance ministers, meet frequently and hold teleconferences to review and discuss major systemic and country-specific issues, developing a consensus on the major topics discussed at the Board. The executive directors of the G-7 countries ensure that the positions they take at the IMF Board are consistent with the prevailing G-7 consensus.

The Group of Ten (G-10) was created on the basis of both size and creditor position. It groups together the major potential creditor countries, adding The Netherlands, Belgium, Sweden and Switzerland to the G-7. The overall voting share of the G-10 constituencies amounts to 62 per cent of the votes. Although the Fund is known to be a cooperative institution which tries to reach decisions by consensus and in the interest of all its shareholders, the fact that creditors hold a majority of the votes is crucial for the financial viability of the institution.

Developing countries' constituencies, which are also the main debtors, also cooperate actively on some key strategic issues. The Group of 11 (G-11) is made

Table 4.2 Groupings' voting shares in the IMF (per cent)

Groups	Members	Votes of members	Votes of constituencies
G-7	Canada (2.88), France (4.84), Germany (5.87), Italy (3.19), Japan (6), United Kingdom (4.84), United States (16.73)	44.35	45.52
G-10	United States (16.73), Japan (6), Germany (5.87), France (4.84), United Kingdom (4.84), Italy (3.19), Canada (2.88), Netherlands (2.33), Belgium (2.08), Switzerland (1.57), Sweden (1.09)	51.42	62.12
G-11	Argentina (0.95), Brazil (1.61), China (6.14), Egypt (2.55), Rwanda (0.41), India (1.46), Indonesia (5.34), Iran (1.32), Saudi Arabia (1.03), Kenya (1.27), Belgium (7.29)	29.37	29.37
G-20	United States (16.73), Japan (6), Germany (5.87), France (4.84), United Kingdom (4.84), China (3.65), Italy (3.19), Saudi Arabia (3.16), Canada (2.88), Russia (2.69), India (1.88), Australia (1.47), Mexico (1.43), Brazil (1.38), Korea (1.33), Argentina (0.96), Indonesia (0.95), South Africa (0.85), Turkey (0.55)	64.65	80.84
Euro Area	Germany (5.87), France (4.84), Italy (3.19), Netherlands (2.33), Belgium (2.08), Spain (1.38), Austria (0.85), Finland (0.58), Portugal (0.4), Ireland (0.39), Greece (0.38), Luxembourg (0.14), Slovenia (0.12), Cyprus (0.07), Malta (0.06)	22.68	36.21
EU-27	Germany (5.87), France (4.84), United Kingdom (4.84), Italy (3.19), Netherlands (2.33), Belgium (2.08), Spain (1.38), Sweden (1.09), Austria (0.85), Denmark (0.75), Poland (0.63), Finland (0.58), Hungary (0.48), Romania (0.47), Portugal (0.4), Ireland (0.39), Greece (0.38), Czech Republic (0.38), Bulgaria (0.3), Slovak Republic (0.17), Luxembourg (0.14), Slovenia (0.12), Lithuania (0.08), Cyprus (0.07), Latvia (0.07), Malta (0.06), Estonia (0.04)	31.98	43.84

Source: IMF and author's calculations.

Note: *The G-11 is composed of 11 IMF constituencies.

66   *Lorenzo Bini Smaghi*

up of the chairs of most developing countries, amounting to almost 30 per cent of the votes.

Cooperation between EU countries

Cooperation between EU countries in the IMF is still evolving. It is not based on the criterion of country size, since most EU countries have a relatively small share, but rather mirrors the progress in European integration. This is, in particular, reflected in the commitment made at the Vienna European Council to strengthening the European Union's role in international fora.[12]

When issues related to the euro are discussed in the Fund, euro area countries are supposed to speak with one voice. The President of EURIMF[13] makes a statement on behalf of all euro area countries for the Article IV consultation of the euro area. The section of the statement dealing with the single monetary policy and exchange rate policy of the euro is prepared and agreed with the European Central Bank (ECB). A representative of the ECB attends the Board meetings as an observer when issues of pertinence to the euro are discussed, and actively participates in the coordination within EURIMF.

This arrangement is partly reflected in other international fora, such as the G-7, where the President of the Eurogroup and the President of the ECB represent the euro area during the surveillance part of the meeting.[14]

Another example of the euro area speaking with one voice is the IMF multilateral consultation on global imbalances.[15] The euro area was represented in the series of meetings by three members, representing the Eurogroup, the Commission and the ECB, respectively. The intensive cooperation between these three institutions before and in the meetings allowed the euro area to effectively speak with one voice. At an Executive Board meeting on these multilateral consultations, a euro area statement was delivered by the EURIMF President.

At the spring and annual meetings of the IMF, the finance minister holding the Presidency of the EU Council of Ministers gives a speech on behalf of the European Union. The speech covers the main economic developments in Europe and other parts of the world, and strategic issues for the IMF. The speech is prepared by the Economic and Financial Committee (EFC).[16] It is discussed and approved at the informal meetings of the Ecofin, which are also attended by central bank governors, taking place generally in April and September, prior to the spring and annual meetings of the IMF. Meetings of the International Monetary and Financial Committee (IMFC) are also attended by the ECB President as an observer and by the President of the Eurogroup. It has now become a standard practice that the former is invited to speak at the IMFC on euro area developments after his US colleague.

The work of the EFC on IMF and related issues is prepared by a working group on IMF and related issues, set up in early 2001. The working group was transformed into a permanent sub-committee (SCIMF) in 2003. It is composed of representatives of finance ministries and central banks of the EU member states, plus the Commission and the ECB. A representative of the EU Presidency on the IMF Board generally attends SCIMF meetings to ensure consistency with the coordination taking place among European representatives in Washington. SCIMF conducts work on a series of issues discussed at the IMF Board, and prepares common understandings endorsed by the EFC and Ecofin. Common understandings have been produced on issues such as private-sector involvement in crisis prevention and resolution, access limits to Fund resources, streamlining of IMF conditionality, cooperation between the IMF and the World Bank, the role of the Fund in the poorest countries, IMF surveillance and highly indebted poor countries. Common views have also been produced on issues related to development finance, related in particular to the Monterrey and Johannesburg Conferences on sustainable development that took place in 2002. Recently, the SCIMF and the EFC have also frequently discussed how to position the European Union in the quota reform debate at the IMF. Moreover, regular discussions also took place on the other elements of the Fund's strategic review, such as the modernization of the Fund's surveillance framework and the reform of the IMF's income model as well as measures to limit expenditures. Common views or understandings prepared in Brussels are used by EU countries' representatives in the Fund as a basis for their cooperation and their statements at the IMF Executive Board discussions. Moreover, at times, they are transmitted to the Fund staff with a view to contributing to the shaping of the debate in the Fund and in other fora such as the G-7.

There is an active interaction between the SCIMF in Brussels and the EURIMF to build upon and complement each other's work. The Presidency of EURIMF has also established direct links with the Fund management and staff, with a view to contributing to the Fund agenda and to pushing forward EU views. In order to improve the visibility and the continuity of relations of the European Union in the Fund, the Ecofin has decided to set up a more permanent EURIMF presidency, elected for two years, who represents EU countries in the Fund. In 2007, the German Executive Director was selected to hold this two-year position for the first time.

It has also recently been recognized that there might be a case for closer euro area coordination on IMF-related matters beyond the core set of issues that are directly and exclusively related to euro area common policies, such as the euro area Article IV or exchange rate issues. Countries realized that it might also be sensible for the euro area to coordinate their positions on a wider range of issues, such as the IMF's biannual World Economic Outlook, Article IV consultations with systemically important third countries, and possibly also some other policy issues. Going forward, it will depend on the political willingness of the euro area countries whether and how to intensify their coordination. They will have to decide on a case-by-case basis whether they opt for the strongest form of coordination, that is, a common statement like they do for the Article IV consultation with the euro area, or whether they prefer to stick to some looser form of coordination, in which case they could continue to deliver their own statements, possibly in addition to a EURIMF Presidency statement. This process is likely to develop only gradually since euro area-specific coordination among Executive Directors is not yet well developed, and the SCIMF and EURIMF deliberations always involve all EU countries. The Eurogroup Working Group (i.e. EFC

68 *Lorenzo Bini Smaghi*

members meeting in euro area composition) could certainly play a more important role in strengthening euro area coordination on international issues.

To sum up, the current situation can be characterized as one of increasing cooperation on an *ad hoc* basis. There is no *ex ante* commitment to achieve and defend common positions. Cooperation remains focused on broad issues considered strategic to the Fund. In specific country cases, in particular on emerging market programmes, coordination is still limited. This is a key difference from the G-7, which aims at building consensus not only on general policy issues but also in specific cases where major Fund programmes are at stake. Such cooperation provides the G-7 with a key role as interlocutor of the Fund staff and management.

Do EU countries have common views on IMF issues?

A similarity in objectives and views on the key policy issues is a crucial prerequisite to ensuring that cooperation would lead to a stronger EU role in the Fund rather than to watered-down positions and thus reduced influence.

The role of the Fund in the International Financial System

The main reason for divergences of views between EU countries in the IMF derives chiefly from the different importance given to international financial issues in the respective countries. Typically, large countries (where size does not depend only on the weight of the economy but also on the international exposure of the private sector) tend to see IMF matters as closely related to their domestic political agenda. They are thus keen to play an active role in the IMF and are keener to influence the decision-making. For smaller countries, participation in the IMF tends to be rather distant from domestic political issues. This leads to a hands-off approach to the day-to-day business of the Fund, delegating decisions to the management or the Executive Director.

The different political interest in international financial issues makes it difficult to achieve in the European Union the same type of commitments as in the G-7. Several EU finance ministers do not attend the spring or annual meetings of the IMF and World Bank. In several EU countries, the competence for these matters is delegated to the central bank.

In certain EU countries, not being a key player in the international community is sometimes considered as an advantage. It has been claimed by some that a strong European voice could be damaging, not only for the country itself but also for the IMF as an institution. A single EU chair in the IMF could imply a polarization in the Board with the United States, with a shared veto power on the most important decisions, and creating tensions with less developed countries, which would in turn try to coordinate more intensively.[17] According to this view, this could undermine the cooperative nature of the Fund, and thus impair its effectiveness.

Coeuré and Pisani-Ferry (2000) also attribute the lesser interest of Europe in IMF issues to European academic circles. Comparing the annual meetings of the American Economic Association with those of the European Economic

Association, it can easily be seen that US academics are much more involved in discussing IMF and related issues.

Aside from the differences, EU countries tend to have a common view on the role to be played by the Bretton Woods institutions, deriving from their democratic legitimacy and universal representation, in addressing issues of interest for the international community. The United States, Japan and some emerging market economies have at times promoted other fora for discussing major issues affecting the International Financial System (IFS). The reason, in their view, is that not all players are adequately represented in the International Financial Institutions (IFIs) and the existing groupings such as the G-10. In this context, the Group of 22 was launched in 1998 to assess the effects of the Asian crisis and propose remedies. The G-22 evolved into a G-33 in 1999 and finally into the G-20 later that year (Table 4.2).

Multilateral surveillance

European countries share a common interest in multilateral surveillance, as they are affected by developments in other areas of the world, be it the United States, Japan or emerging market countries. This is especially the case for the euro area, which is increasingly seen as an economic and political entity with a strong impact on the rest of the world. The IMF *World Economic Outlook*, for instance, treats the euro area as a whole.

EU countries, in particular those of the euro area, share common views on the world economy. As mentioned above, the recent multilateral consultation on global imbalances was an example of the euro area speaking with one voice. The EFC regularly prepares common understandings on global developments, including the US and Japanese economies, which are used to prepare G-7 meetings, and also by EURIMF to coordinate their positions in the Board. The EURIMF always meets to discuss the IMF's *World Economic Outlook* and the *Global Financial Stability Report*.

Overall, multilateral surveillance is an area where EU countries tend to coordinate and aim at conveying common messages. As explained above, it remains to be seen whether the member countries, especially those of the euro area, are ready to move ahead and even present their position in single statements at the Board. This will be even more pertinent in the future since multilateral surveillance is becoming more important in the light of the integration of financial markets and the emergence of new players in the world economy.

Crisis prevention and resolution

Europe has in the past contributed to the resolution of international financial crises as the United States, although not in the same proportion across countries. For instance, the four largest EU countries contributed financially as much as, if not more than, the United States to support Korea and Brazil ($6 and $7 billion respectively, against $5 billion by the United States; see Table 4.3).

70 *Lorenzo Bini Smaghi*

Table 4.3 Financial support of major sponsors ($US bn)

	Indonesia 1997	*Korea 1997*	*Thailand 1997*	*Brazil 1998*
IMF	10.1	21.1	4.0	18.1
WB and MDBs	8.0	0.6	0.1	9.0
Bilateral, of which:	19.8	21.1	10.5	14.5
USA	3.0	5.0	5.0	5.0
Japan	5.0	10.0	0.2	1.3
EU:		6.0	5.0	7.0
UK		1.3		1.3
Germany		1.3		1.3
France		1.3		1.3
Italy		1.3		0.8
Total	37.9	58.4	17.2	41.0

Source: Bini Smaghi (2000).

In the aftermath of the Asian crisis, criticisms have been made of the role played by the Fund as lender-of-last-resort to bail countries out. EU countries have been at the forefront of such criticism, pointing to the need to involve the private sector to finance part of external imbalances. The issue of private sector involvement (PSI) has been brought onto the agenda of the Fund and the G-7 mainly by EU countries. Two documents have been produced on this issue by the EFC, feeding the debate within the Fund.

Without going into details, PSI represents a clear example of how EU countries can express common positions on key strategic issues for the Fund. However, differently from the G-7, EU countries have expressed little interest in trying to coordinate views on specific country programmes and financing. As a result, views have at times differed on how the private sector has been involved in specific country cases such as Argentina.

There may be several reasons for such differences of views. The first is the degree of involvement in the Fund decision-making process, as indicated above. Larger countries, involved in the G-7, tend to have a more discretionary, case-by-case, implementation of agreed principles. Smaller countries tend instead to follow a rule-based approach. A second factor is the political relevance of programme countries for the different constituencies. Geopolitical considerations do matter in Fund decisions. The question is whether EU countries have sufficient common geopolitical interests to coordinate in the Fund or whether, in specific cases, they may find it more efficient to act alone. In specific cases, some EU countries may have special interests and thus be induced to hold different positions from those of other Europeans. As cooperation in the field of foreign policy intensifies in the European Union, it will be easier to develop common views on specific country programmes. The experience of the Monterrey and Johannesburg summits has shown that common positions taken by EU foreign affairs ministers in international policy fora strengthen cooperation between finance ministers on international financial matters. Common EU geopolitical interests are bound to create the conditions for common positions in the IFIs.

The role of the Fund in poor countries

Europe is the biggest provider of development aid in the world. At the level of the European Union, the European Development Fund and the EU budget allocate on average over € 4 billion every year to the ACP countries.[18] Further assistance is provided in the form of emergency, humanitarian aid and macro-financial assistance managed by the European Commission. The European Investment Bank can also provide up to € 300 million preferential loans per year to projects in the ACP countries. EU financial support is based on a common political strategy, linked to the programmes developed by the IMF and the World Bank, in particular the poverty reduction strategy papers. Again, some EU countries may have a specific interest in some IMF-assisted countries or regions. It remains to be seen whether these specific interests can be promoted more efficiently by acting alone than by fostering a common position by the European Union.

The European Union in IMF decision-making

The advantages of coordination in the IMF

This section looks at the second part of the subsidiarity test, examining whether EU countries are effective in pursuing their objectives in the IMF within the existing cooperation mechanism, and whether there is scope for further synergies.

The IMF is an institution which tends to decide mainly by consensus. In general, countries or constituencies can achieve very little by themselves and have very little decision-making power. This is the reason why coalitions and cooperation agreements tend to develop, grouping together countries with similar objectives. This applies also to the largest shareholder, the United States, which benefits from a veto power on key issues where a qualified majority is required (85 per cent), but cannot alone impose decisions on the rest of the institution. One important way for the largest shareholders to influence decisions is through a constant dialogue with the management and the staff, to push ideas and provide political input.

Coordination with other constituencies on key issues is essential to influence Fund decisions. All large countries participate in some form of agreement. Countries that are outside established coordination agreements tend to have little impact.

As far as EU countries are concerned, the key issue is whether they could be more effective by further strengthening intra-EU coordination. A related question is whether strengthened EU coordination would be compatible or inconsistent with other cooperation agreements such as the G-7.

The limits of ad hoc coordination among EU countries

Even if EU countries agreed on all issues related to IMF activities, the current institutional set-up, whereby the 27 EU countries are spread in ten constituencies, undermines effectiveness. There are various reasons for this.

72   Lorenzo Bini Smaghi

First, in the present IMF constituency system, some EU countries, like Ireland and Spain, are in a minority position in their own constituencies, and thus have a difficult task in pushing forward a European position when the latter differs substantially from those of the other members of the constituency. One example is the discussion that took place at the Board in early 2003 on the proposal for a sovereign debt restructuring mechanism. While EU countries gave strong support to the proposal, as expressed in several common understandings and EU speeches, the constituency in which Spain belongs opposed it, as the negative views of the other members, in particular Venezuela and Mexico, prevailed.

Difficulties in cooperation between European countries arise also from the participation of countries that receive substantial financial support in European constituencies, notably those chaired by Belgium and The Netherlands. The position of the borrowing members of the constituency cannot be ignored when financial issues such as access quotas, repayment conditions, interest rates, penalties, and so on are discussed. The same applies for issues such as the role of the Fund in protecting the integrity of the IFS against money laundering, or the financing of terrorism, or on questions related to crisis resolution or the Fund's transparency policy. Another example was the decision taken by the Board in July 2003 on the publication of surveillance reports that are the core of IMF activity for crisis prevention. While most EU members supported the idea that the reports should be presumably published, the constituencies chaired by Belgium and Spain were not able to support this position.

Mixed constituencies, which include both creditor and debtor countries, are considered to play a special role in the IMF as they contribute to reinforcing the cooperative nature of the Fund (Mahieu *et al.* 2003). The participation of non-EU countries in EU constituencies, or vice versa, may also be a way to enlarge the basis for consensus around EU positions. However, these advantages are rather limited and are counterbalanced by the fact that EU positions tend to be less cohesive. The supposed special role of 'mediation' that mixed constituencies might have in a cooperative institution like the Fund is not borne out by evidence. It is generally the management which plays such a role when shareholders have split views. Alternatively, it is the constituencies with different opinions who try to find a compromise. For instance, on the issue of transparency, the solution came from a negotiation between the G-11 and the G-7. Furthermore, the leverage that can be obtained from mixed constituencies depends on the relative position of EU countries within these constituencies. The votes that can be mobilized by constituencies where EU countries participate sum up to 43.84 per cent of the total, nearly 12 percentage points more than the sum of EU countries' votes alone (Table 4.2). However, excluding the constituencies that are led by non-EU countries or where the latter have fewer than one-third of the votes (those of Ireland, Spain and Poland), the sum of EU constituencies' votes falls to 32.95, only around 1 percentage point higher than the sum of EU countries' votes. Finally, in the constituency led by The Netherlands, the latter can hardly ignore the non-EU countries' positions, even though EU countries sum up to two-thirds of the votes.

Overall, the leverage that can be gained by incorporating non-EU countries in EU constituencies seems rather limited. What matters in an institution like the

IMF, which tends to decide mainly on the basis of consensus, is the strength and cohesion of coalition agreements, rather than the overall size of a constituency voting power. That is the reason why the United States and the G-11 tend to have more impact on IMF decisions than the European Union. The United States is also able to express consistent positions and to influence decisions before they are presented to the Board. This is the reason for the influence of the G-7, which holds a constant dialogue with the Fund staff and management.

Another reason for the weakness of EU coordination in the existing institutional context is the segmentation of EU representation on the Board, which creates strong incentives for differentiation, even when there is fundamentally a common underlying view. If only the Presidency of the EURIMF intervenes on key issues, as is currently the case when euro-related issues are discussed, there is little scope for the other European representatives to participate in the meetings, unless they differentiate their position slightly from that expressed by the Presidency. This creates a negative incentive, at the political and bureaucratic level, to achieve common EU positions on the Board. Incidentally, the repetition of similar positions by different European representatives at Board meetings tends to irritate other members of the Board.

The current system of representation encourages countries to look for extra-EU cooperation arrangements. In particular, the difficulties experienced in coordinating EU positions induce the four large EU countries to maintain their links with other G-7 countries.

The opposite argument has also been made, that is, that the participation in the G-7 by the four large EU countries is an obstacle to EU coordination. However, EU cooperation cannot be an alternative to G-7 cooperation since EU countries alone do not have a majority in the Fund. Cooperation with the other major shareholders, in particular the United States and Japan, will always be needed. EU cooperation is, rather, a way to increase the weight of EU countries within the G-7 coordination process, and to increase the weight of the G-7 itself. EU cooperation must thus be consistent with G-7 cooperation. It requires willingness to compromise with non-EU countries, something that not all EU countries are always able to achieve.

In the past, another problem with EU representation in the IMF derived from the lack of continuity, especially in dialogue with the Fund management. With the EU Presidency changing every six months, it was difficult to sustain a consistent dialogue between the IMF staff and management and EU representatives. This situation has now been improved with the creation of the two-year EURIMF Presidency.

The fact that IMF issues are rarely discussed among EU finance ministers and central bank governors further limits the ability to shape consistent EU policies. It is a surprising fact that G-7 finance ministers and central bank governors meet more often (at least three times a year) than their European counterparts do to discuss international issues.

To sum up, EU coordination has intensified but there are limits to further cooperation as long as representation remains segmented. Indeed, the institutional framework influences the contents of coordination.

74   *Lorenzo Bini Smaghi*

A single EU constituency

Constituencies in the IFIs are established through a system of self-determination. If EU countries decided to join the same constituency, it would be difficult to prevent them from doing so. The statutes of the Fund indicate, however, that the five largest shareholders should be represented individually. A change in the statutes would thus be required. This would presumably also entail a recalculation of the quota and voting share of the new constituency and a reallocation of quotas and votes to other members.[19] It would be unlikely that the single EU constituency maintain the same voting power as the sum of the current country votes, which is nearly twice as large as that of the United States and is already considered excessive by other members.

The variables currently used for the calculation of country quotas could be used for the European Union as a whole. For instance, the indicators of openness as well as of variability, which are used to model countries' vulnerability to external shocks, could exclude intra-EU trade. This would make sense since, with the creation of the euro, intra-area payments cannot be considered a factor of vulnerability. According to these calculations, an EU constituency with 27 members could have 29 per cent of the votes compared with a voting share of 32 per cent at the moment and a calculated quota share of around 38 per cent (Table 4.4).

The difference would mainly be allocated to the United States, Japan and some emerging market economies that are underrepresented in the present distribution of quotas, in the sense that their quotas do not reflect their current economic weight in the world economy.[20]

The reduction in the voting share of EU countries would be compensated for by the fact that the EU constituency would, as a whole, not only be the largest, but would also have a veto power, similar to the United States. The decision-making system of the EU constituency would have to be defined.

The creation of a single EU constituency would have implications for other groups, bearing in mind that a certain number of non-EU countries that currently participate in constituencies with EU member states would be compelled to join other groups. It would also imply changes on the Executive Board, depending on the solution adopted to reallocate the number of appointed Executive Directors given up by EU members.

In the European Union, the creation of a single chair would raise three main issues: legal/institutional, organizational and political. From a legal/institutional point of view, the creation of an EU constituency can be achieved in two different ways: through an intergovernmental agreement between the member states, or through a change in the EU Treaty.

In the first option, the participation in the Fund would remain a national competence. Representation would be defined through an intergovernmental agreement, similar to those governing other constituencies. This would not be a novelty for 24 of the 27 EU countries which are already members of multi-country constituencies. For the three countries which have a single constituency, such a decision might have to be submitted to their respective Parliaments.[21] This solution would preserve the existing mechanisms of national accountability, through which finance ministers report to Parliament on the positions taken on the IMF Board.

Table 4.4 EU-27 countries' quota and voting shares in the IMF

| | Excluding intra-EU-27 trade | | | | |
	Calculated quota (1)	*Actual quota (2)*	*Voting share (3)*	*Calculated quota share (4)*	*Voting share (5)*
Germany	6.85	5.98	5.87	5.49	5.47
France	4.13	4.94	4.84	2.87	2.86
United Kingdom	5.24	4.94	4.84	5.99	5.97
Italy	3.32	3.24	3.19	2.42	2.41
Netherlands	2.90	2.37	2.33	2.73	2.72
Belgium	2.27	2.12	2.08	1.21	1.20
Spain	2.24	1.40	1.38	1.40	1.39
Sweden	1.17	1.10	1.09	1.06	1.06
Austria	1.13	0.86	0.85	0.62	0.62
Denmark	1.04	0.76	0.75	0.71	0.71
Poland	0.78	0.63	0.63	0.51	0.51
Finland	0.53	0.58	0.58	0.59	0.59
Hungary	0.49	0.48	0.48	0.28	0.28
Romania	0.25	0.47	0.47	0.20	0.20
Portugal	0.48	0.40	0.40	0.24	0.24
Ireland	1.66	0.39	0.39	0.95	0.95
Greece	0.48	0.38	0.38	0.36	0.36
Czech Republic	0.59	0.38	0.38	0.28	0.28
Bulgaria	0.13	0.29	0.30	0.11	0.12
Slovak Republic	0.25	0.16	0.17	0.11	0.12
Luxembourg	1.37	0.13	0.14	0.64	0.64
Slovenia	0.15	0.11	0.12	0.09	0.09
Lithuania	0.10	0.07	0.08	0.09	0.09
Cyprus	0.06	0.06	0.07	0.04	0.05
Latvia	0.06	0.06	0.07	0.05	0.05
Malta	0.05	0.05	0.06	0.05	0.05
Estonia	0.07	0.03	0.04	0.06	0.06
Euro Area (15 countries)	27.62	23.00	22.68	19.70	19.65
Total EU-27	37.77	32.36	31.98	29.16	29.09
United States	16.28	17.08	16.73	18.74	18.66
Japan	7.01	6.12	6.00	8.07	8.03
Other	38.94	44.45	45.29	44.03	44.22

Source: IMF, except for trade data for EU-27 without intra-area trade (Eurostat).

Notes: Columns 1 to 3 show the current picture at the IMF. Columns 4 and 5 simulate the effects of excluding intra-EU trade for the calculated quota shares and consequently the voting shares.

The creation of an EU constituency based on individual membership would not alter the position of the United States as the largest individual member of the IMF. Indeed, each EU member state would continue to hold its quota share. On the Board, however, the Executive Director representing the EU constituency would cast a total amount of votes equal to the sum of the votes of the individual EU member states participating in the EU constituency. Therefore, while the EU constituency would

76 *Lorenzo Bini Smaghi*

dispose of the largest voting power on the Board, the United States, as an individual member of the Fund, would continue to be the member with the largest quota in the Fund.[22] Therefore, the creation of an EU constituency would have no implications for the location of the Fund that, according to Article XII, section 1, of the IMF statute, will 'be located in the territory having the largest quota'.

In the second option, the competence over IMF issues would be transferred to the European Union.[23] This would require a change in the EU Treaty (making the option look less likely, in current circumstances). The role of the various EU institutions, in particular the Council, the Commission and the Parliament, would have to be clarified. On the basis of existing procedures, the Commission would have the right of proposal, while the Council would take decisions. A voting system in the Council would have to be defined, for instance, with qualified majority voting. The European Parliament would have to be consulted on key strategic issues and be involved in ensuring accountability. The Commission (together with the ECB) would have a role as executive branch, and thus in representing the EU positions.

From an organizational point of view, the procedure for the nomination of members of the office of the Executive Director would have to be decided. In addition to the Executive Director and its alternate, advisers and assistants would have to be nominated. If the ECB is to give up its observer status, a position in the EU office would have to be reserved for the ECB. In addition, a mechanism for ensuring adequate support and guidance on the positions to be taken at the IMF Board on behalf of EU countries would have to be organized in Europe. The EFC (and SCIMF) would be in charge of this task, referring to Ecofin on the most important issues. To address the most urgent topics, the EFC would resort to tele-conference systems and *ad hoc* meetings, as is currently the case in the G-7.

From a political point of view, the creation of an EU constituency in the IMF would entail a much greater involvement of Ecofin in IMF issues. The representation of the European Union in the IMF and other fora would require greater continuity. The Commissioner for Economic and Monetary Affairs could play such a role, similar to the position of the High Representative for Foreign and Security Policy who, under the new Treaty of Lisbon, will become a Vice-President of the European Commission.

The creation of a single EU constituency would entail changes also in EU external representation in other institutions, fora and groupings, such as the World Bank, the G-7 or the G-20. In the G-7, there would be little scope for having the four largest countries continue to attend, together with the governor of the respective central bank.

Conclusions

The issue of a single EU seat in the IMF is not on the agenda for the immediate future, although many observers, academics and even finance ministers would agree that, sooner or later, this might happen (possibly in a euro area format, as a first step). What could be the reasons for Europe making such a step forward? What could be the political and institutional implications on member states' sovereignty?

EU countries have become aware that the role they are able to play in international issues is relatively limited compared with their overall size and financial contribution. This has led EU countries to broaden the range of issues on which they cooperate to cover international aid and financial assistance, the fight against money laundering and the financing of terrorism and the promotion of financial stability. All these areas are closely interlinked with the work of the IMF.

There is scope for further improving cooperation. However, there are natural limits to what can be achieved within the existing cooperation framework. A single EU constituency would enable EU member states to have a strong impact on IMF policies, potentially as strong as that of the United States. However, this may not be an objective for all EU countries. Some countries might prefer to keep the current system of representation, which gives some visibility to national representatives.

If EU countries wish to improve their collective influence in international issues and the IMF, some institutional changes in the way European interests are represented and promulgated may be necessary. Institutional changes require two main forces: vision and political leadership. This chapter is a contribution to the former, in the expectation that the latter will soon emerge.

Notes

1 The views expressed in this chapter reflect only those of the author. I would like to thank Vincenzo Zezza, Silvia Zucchini, Stefan Huemer and Regine Wölfinger for their valuable comments and assistance, and Daniel Daco for providing some of the data used in the tables.
2 The new Treaty of Lisbon opens up new prospects for coordination and representation of euro area countries in the international financial institutions. In particular, the Treaty of Lisbon explicitly refers to the need 'to secure the euro's place in the international monetary system' and 'to ensure unified representation within the international financial institutions and conferences' (Article 115 C).
3 The IMF statutes indicate that the institution is located in the country with the largest quota share. The relocation of the IMF would occur only if the EU member states cease to be individual members of the Fund and the European Union replaces them as an IMF member. In contrast, if the EU member states maintain their individual membership in the Fund but join a single EU constituency, the United States would remain the member with the largest quota share. Therefore, in the latter case the IMF would continue to be located in the United States.
4 The Eurogroup is an informal body which brings together the euro area Finance Ministers, the Commissioner for Economic and Monetary Affairs, and the President of the ECB.
5 The question whether there is a case for a single euro area chair at the IMF has been examined in Bini Smaghi (2006).
6 In areas which do not fall within its exclusive competence, the Community shall take action, in accordance with the principle of subsidiarity, only if and in so far as the objectives of the proposed action cannot be sufficiently achieved by the member states and can therefore, by reason of the scale or effects of the proposed action, be better achieved by the Community (Article 5 of the Treaty establishing the European Community).
7 Greece holds the position of Alternate Executive Director.
8 Austria holds the position of Alternate Executive Director.
9 Ireland holds the position of Alternate Executive Director.

78   *Lorenzo Bini Smaghi*

10 The two African constituencies group together 19 and 24 countries each, representing 2.67 and 1.4 per cent of the votes, respectively.

11 The Group of Seven comprises Canada, France, Germany, Italy, Japan, the United Kingdom and the United States.

12 'It is imperative that the Community should play its full role in international monetary and economic policy cooperation within fora like the G-7 and the IMF', European Council Conclusions, Vienna, December 1998.

13 The EURIMF was established in Washington in 1997 as a coordination device at EU level in parallel to the coordination activities in Brussels. It brings together the representatives of the EU member states and the ECB observer in the Executive Board. A representative of the Commission also participates in the meetings to discuss relevant agenda items ahead of IMF Board meetings, that is, especially Article IV consultations with EU member states.

14 This is the understanding which has led to the agreement in the G-7 for the organization of meetings of G-7 finance ministers and central bank governors, according to which discussions on multilateral surveillance are attended, on the euro area side, by the finance ministers of Germany, France and Italy and the Presidency of the Eurogroup and the President of the ECB, but not by the governors of the three respective national central banks (the latter are only invited to attend the discussion on issues not directly related to the euro area). For the G-7/G-8 summit, and the preparatory meetings by finance ministers, the Presidency of the European Union attends some parts of the meetings.

15 In spring 2006, the IMF launched this new procedure of multilateral consultation, which aims at addressing major issues of systemic importance. The first multilateral consultation was launched in June 2006 to deal with global imbalances, for which the IMF invited five parties, that is, the United States, Japan, China, Saudi Arabia and the euro area. The consultations involved bilateral meetings with individual parties as well as multilateral meetings with all parties concerned.

16 The EFC is composed of high-level officials of finance ministries and central banks. The representatives of the finance ministers of France, Germany, Italy and the United Kingdom are also the respective G-7 deputies.

17 In particular the US and the EU chair together would also have veto power on decisions requiring a 70 per cent qualified majority.

18 The ACP states are African, Caribbean and Pacific countries that are signatories of the *Lomé Convention*, i.e. a cooperation programme originally between 15 countries of the European Union and 46 countries of Africa, the Caribbean and the Pacific (ACP).

19 The financial implications of a single EU chair at the Fund have been explored by Mahieu *et al.* (2003).

20 This can be measured by the difference between calculated quotas and actual quotas. This difference is particularly relevant for emerging market economies in Asia, and also for Turkey.

21 In other international institutions, such as the regional development banks (Asian Development Bank, Inter American Development Bank, African Development Bank), France, Germany and the United Kingdom are members of multi-country constituencies.

22 The US quota would continue to be well above the quota pertaining to any EU country. As was pointed out in footnote 3, a change in the location of the Fund could be envisaged only if the European Union itself were to become an IMF member, instead of its individual member countries. However, this is only a theoretical hypothesis given that EU membership would require a change in the Articles of Agreement, and that the United States would probably veto a change that could move the institution outside its territory.

23 As far as this is not already the case: for instance, euro area monetary policy and exchange rate policy, as well as their external representation (including at the IMF), are Community competencies.

References

Alesina, A., Angeloni, I. and Schuknecht, L. (2001) 'What Does the European Union do?', *NBER Working Paper*, No. 8647.

Bini Smaghi, L. (2000) *Chi ci salva dalla prossima crisi fi nanziaria?*, Bologna: Il Molina.

Bini Smaghi, L. (2006) 'Powerless Europe: Why Is the Euro Area Still a Political Dwarf?', *International Finance*, 9(2): 1–19.

Coeuré, B. and Pisani-Ferry, J. (2000) 'Events, Ideas and Actions: An Intellectual and Institutional Retrospective on the Reform of the International Financial Architecture', Mimeo.

Group of Seven (1999) 'Report of the G-7 Finance Ministers to the Köln Economic Summit'. Online. Available HTTP: http://www.G7.utoronto.ca

International Monetary Fund (IMF) (2001) *Alternative Quota Formulas: Considerations*, Washington, DC: IMF.

Kiekens, W. (2003) 'What Kind of External Representation for the Euro?' Mimeo. Online. Available HTTP: http://www2.oenb.at/tagung/eu_konvent/paper/statement_kiekens.pdf

Mahieu, G., Ooms, D. and Rottier, S. (2003) 'The Governance of the International Monetary Fund with a Single EU Chair', *Financial Stability Review*, Brussels: National Bank of Belgium, June.

Van Houtven, L. (2002) *Governance of the IMF*, Washington, DC: IMF.

5 The World Trade Organization and the European Union

Jens Ladefoged Mortensen

What the European Union[1] does in the World Trade Organization[2] (WTO) is a matter for not only the Europeans but also the rest of the world. The relationship is arguably one of the cornerstones in contemporary global governance. Europe is an undisputed giant in the global economy. It is the biggest trader in the world, responsible for roughly a fifth of global trade in goods and services. The stakes are high for the European Union in global trade but outsiders have little confidence in what the European Union does in the WTO, whereas the European Union sees itself as its most loyal supporter. The European Commission speaks for 'Europe' in the WTO. This institutional set-up is unique. The European Union is one of the original WTO members in its own right. For all purposes, the Commission acts like all other foreign policy actors in the WTO. Yet, domestic and transnational politics pull the Commission in different directions. The Commission itself is often fragmented. This duality is often framed as a multilevel game (Putnam 1988; see also Conybeare 1992; Paarlberg 1997; Meunier and Nicolaïdes 2005). The two-level game model continues to produce insightful analyses of EU behaviour in WTO negotiations but is of little use when it comes to EU behaviour in the dispute settlement system, the *raison d'être* of the WTO institution.

Currently, the European Union is faced with many difficult choices in the WTO. The Doha process is close to a complete collapse. Prospects of continued growth rates in the global economy look gloomy. Bilateral trade agreements flourish. Key economies are heading towards recession. China is increasingly perceived as a commercial rival, even within the Commission, despite strong interdependencies. The weak dollar and yen put EU exports under pressure. The parallels to the early 1980s are all too clear. The structural determinants of the European Union's trade policy have come back into play. Yet, I argue, it is important to put the current crisis into perspective. Not even a breakdown of the Doha Round, I argue, can overshadow the historical significance of the transformation of Europe from a defensive player to proactive leader. Consequently, the WTO stands on a firmer political foundation today than the General Agreement of Trade and Tariffs (GATT) did in the 1980s.

The chapter is organized into three sections. The first section looks at the transformation of the European Union in the multilateral trade system from a slow, reactive GATT player (1960s to early 1980s) to an aspiring WTO leader (1994 to

The WTO and the EU   81

2003) in the Doha Round. It concludes by discussing the current crisis. The second section examines the sources of these transformations. It starts off by contrasting structural systemic explanations to domestic explanations. It proceeds to argue that the two-level image captures much of the interplay between internal and external dynamics within the convoluted set-up of the European Union. However, the model ignores the multilateral orientation of EU trade diplomacy. The European Union is arguably more neoliberal today but remains loyal to the idea of multilateralism. The two-level game also tends to downplay the systemic change that follows from the legalization of trade politics and globalization of production and trade, and consequently the growing relevance of issue-specific networks, transnational actors (firms and NGOs) and experts in EU trade politics.

Who are the EU trade diplomats?

It is helpful to start off by asking a seemingly simple question: Who are the EU trade diplomats? I suggest that these can be understood in terms of overlapping concentric circles, as depicted in Figure 5.1.

The legal basis for the Common Commercial Policy is Article 133 of the European Community Treaty that provides for the delegation of powers from the national to the supranational level on all matters concerning international trade. Consequently, the Commission negotiates in Geneva in consultation with the Article 133 Committee (which meets on a weekly basis). All agreements must be ratified by the Council of Ministers by a qualified majority. At the centre is the DG External Trade unit in the Commission. According to latest budget figures, the DG Trade consists of roughly 550 people, currently headed by Commissioner Peter Mandelson. It is telling that the former Trade Commissioner, Pascal Lamy, is the current Director General (DG) of the WTO. The first Director General of the WTO, Peter Sutherland, was a former Commissioner for Competition 1985–1989. The 'EU representation to International Organizations in Geneva' is also part of the core trade diplomacy even if it also manages relations with other Geneva-based IOs. It consists of roughly 18 people, being one of the largest in Geneva.[3] To this, one must add each national representation of the member states in Geneva. The relevant European Parliament Committees (like those on International Trade or Development, respectively) are also considered part of the permanent machinery of the EU trade diplomacy. The current status of the EP is limited to that of an advisor.

One of the peculiar features of the EU–WTO relationship is that the European Community is a member of the WTO itself alongside the EU member states.[4] It is common practice to let the EU delegate speak on behalf of all member states in the WTO – even if individual member states are present. A few comments on the voting issue are in order as it is in stark contrast to those relating to EU business in the IMF and World Bank (see Chapter 4). Since both the European Union and its member states are formally represented in the WTO process, critics have – particularly in the United States – argued that EU interests have double weight in the WTO. Yet, Article IX of the WTO Agreement determines that the number of votes cannot exceed the number of the individual European Community (EC) member states (Matsushita

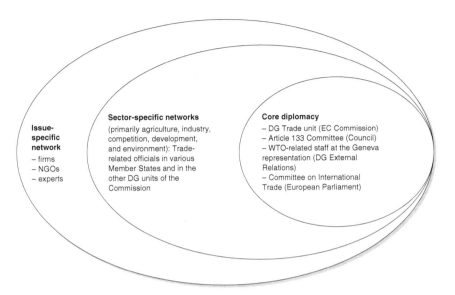

Figure 5.1 Levels of EU trade diplomacy.

et al. 2006: 11). In any event, the WTO Councils and bodies operate on a consensus voting norm. WTO issues are almost never put to a formal vote. Consensus is determined in the corridors and not by counting votes at meetings. Nonetheless, the special status of the European Union in the WTO is indicative of how prominently the European Union is positioned throughout the WTO process.

The next circle of the EU diplomacy is slightly more fluid, open ended and policy sector specific in its composition. Yet, EU trade diplomacy cannot be understood without references to the different segments of the Commission. Also, as the WTO involves the member states directly, these interests are represented either directly via the Council in the core diplomacy or through sector-specific networks involving the relevant parts of the national governments. The outer layer of the EU trade diplomacy is an extremely fluid trade policy network that includes sections of the civil society, the trade policy expert community and other private actors. This layer is the issue-specific aspect of the EU–WTO process. These networks are increasingly integrated into the policy process, however, as reflected by WTO dispute settlement, anti-dumping proceedings or the trade barriers regulation.

Putnam's two-level game model stresses the fact that trade diplomats play different games simultaneously in the various capitals, in Brussels, in Geneva and in Washington. An explanation of what the European Union does in the WTO must take the dynamics at different levels into consideration. Putman-inspired analysis explains trade diplomacy as outcomes of 'synergistic policy linkage' and 'reverberation' between the external and internal negotiations (Paarlberg 1997; Patterson 1997). The relationship resembles a principal–agent relationship. Member states may well have accepted the political benefits of having the Commission to speak on behalf of the European Union in the WTO, but they remain 'at pains to ensure that such de facto authority ... does not lead to an increase in the acquired powers of the Commission' (Woolcock 2005: 379). When negotiating, DG External Trade meets frequently with the Article 133 committee (comprised of senior national officials). Member states have also limited the scope of the exclusive competence by excluding audio-visual services, health services and education (Article 133, para. 5–6). Although the transfer of powers following Article 133 is uniquely strong, the room of manoeuvre for an independent-minded Commission in the WTO confronts several control mechanisms. Yet, the power of the EU trade bureaucracy in day-to-day WTO matters is considerable. Issue-specific WTO governance requires extensive legal and diplomatic expertise. This puts the Commission in the driving seat in most day-to-day activities in the WTO.

A defensive GATT player becomes the proactive WTO leader

Ever since 1957, European trade diplomacy has undergone many transformations. It is beyond the scope of this chapter to provide details on all relevant subject matters. Two such transformations are of particular relevance here: the shift from defensive neo-mercantilism in the GATT to the rise of European proactive leadership in the WTO.

1957–1985: Defending Europe at all costs

The first phase started in 1957. As internal tariff walls were gradually dismantled within Europe, starting with the Treaty of Rome in 1957, a common set of tariffs towards the rest of the world replaced these. All duties on internal trade were demolished in 1968. Authority to manage the common tariff wall was delegated to the EC according to Article 133 (formerly Article 113). The provisions will be examined later. Viewed from the outside, the Rome Treaty itself was a product of the GATT regime. The GATT promoted trade liberalization on the basis of non-discrimination, transparency and reciprocity. GATT also defined a number of important exceptions to these principles, continued use of tariffs, import quotas, anti-dumping duties, subsidies, among others. One of these exceptions (GATT Article XXVI) concerned free trade areas and customs unions. The GATT enabled the EC to be formed in the first place. Nor must it be forgotten that it was the United States who demanded an exception to agricultural trade in 1955. The GATT regime thus legitimatized a lot of government intervention in the market but aimed for a negotiated disarmament of these policies.

Bretherton and Vogler (1999: 55) point out that the EC commercial policy was from its outset 'something of a *tabula rasa*; its developments and the understandings and practices adopted by the Community as it emerged as a trade actor were very much the outcome of a mutual process of structuration'. Indeed, 'structuration' is a good description of how the EC and the GATT came to shape each other. Both were multilateral regimes shaped by broader US foreign policy concerns of the 1950s. Both replaced previous structures of imperial and bilateral trade preferences.

84 *Jens Ladefoged Mortensen*

External circumstances permitted internal factors to shape EC behaviour in the early GATT years, allowing domestic priorities to dominate the trade diplomacy. A defensive version of European neo-mercantilism was more or less tolerated by the Americans although concrete trade conflicts were fought out bilaterally and occasionally inside the GATT. None of these cause fundamental problems – except in agricultural trade. As the US farmers felt the effects of the CAP on falling world market prices, they intensified their attack on the CAP in Washington and Geneva. The Kennedy Round (1964–1969) was a consolidation of the EC as a defensive GATT player. Both the European member states and industry representatives spent their energies fending off US demands for market liberalization. The GATT was at standstill for the rest of the 1960s. The Tokyo Round (1973–1979) kick-started the GATT but failed to produce new GATT rules on new forms of protectionism, namely with respect to non-tariff barriers. Grieco (1990) concluded – as a structural realist – that relative gains always triumphed over absolute gains (for an alternative analysis, see Winham 1986). A liberal interpretation points to internal demands for better GATT enforcement and broader issue-coverage to include new issues. Hampson (1999: 183) found that the EC played the 'role of spoiler' in the GATT. Ostry concluded that the Europeans 'skilfully blocked any meaningful reform on dispute settlement thereby ensuring that its preference to handle disputes bilaterally through non-transparent negotiations could continue' (Ostry 1997: 86).

Perhaps the EC used the GATT for defensive purposes. Yet, it never challenged the GATT regime directly. It never played the part of an aggressive neo-mercantilist power. Its strategy was reactive. It was about bending the letter of the law without undermining the GATT regime altogether. It was about shielding domestic economic priorities from outside pressures, not securing specific advantages for European exporters.

1986–1993: GATT diplomacy under transformation

By the early 1980s, exporters on both sides of the Atlantic demanded renegotiations of the Tokyo Round. Globalist interpretations go further. Neoliberal ideas and transnational interests had decisively transformed the EC game (Balanyá *et al.* 2003; Van Appeldorn 2006). The ideational balance shifted towards neoliberalism within the European policy elites. The Single Market process did by no means transform the EC trade diplomacy overnight. From 1986 to the early 1990s, it still looked as if the European defence of the CAP would spell doom for the GATT. Structuralist interpretations – like Bergsten (1992: 59) – equated the Single Market with an external 'Fortress Europe':

> The Europeans are so preoccupied with their internal and regional development, the deepening and broadening of their community, that they aren't paying attention to the rest of the world. … Indeed, if the multilateral trade negotiations … do break up, it will be over European intransigence to liberalize on agriculture and a few other things.

The WTO and the EU   85

Initially, the Uruguay Round exceeded all expectations. It started in 1986 (in Punta del Esta, Uruguay) with high ambitions. Fourteen negotiation groups were formed to conclude agreements on issues like agriculture, intellectual property rights, and services as well as institutional reforms.[5] In 1988, at the Montreal Midterm Ministerial, some negotiations had already been concluded and progress was reported on most issues. A realistic deadline for the entire Round was set for the Brussels Ministerial in December 1990. It was a spectacular failure. Yet, it was a critical juncture for the EC as well as the GATT. The story about the Blair House (1991–1992) agreement shows how the domestic game that so often had paralysed the EC trade diplomacy for years was being transformed.

Most accounts of the Brussels failure point to the flawed institutional set-up of the EU trade diplomacy. The EC agricultural ministers were put in charge of the GATT negotiations. As Moyer put it, 'The organization with the strongest interests in maintaining the CAP is placed in the driver's seat of the actual conduct of the negotiations' (Moyer 1993: 103). An insider account also points to the domestic stalemate: 'The agricultural ministers were not listening. They had their constitutional and sacred duty to defend the common agricultural policy, reinforced by a personal ambition to represent the interests of their own member states with appropriate firmness and vigour in Brussels' (Paemen and Bensch 1995: 177–178). It was German resistance to a CAP report that proved decisive in tilting the internal balance. The EC found itself 'between a rock of the US and the hard place of French intransigence' (Hampson 1999: 233). Eventually, the EC produced a compromise acceptable to the United States, overriding agricultural resistance.[6]

A conjunction of internal and external developments explains why the Blair House agreement was possible. Outside pressures (i.e. a looming trade war after defeat in the oilseed case, expiration of 'fast-track authority' of the US Trade Representative, the NAFTA debate) played into the free-traders within the Commission (who also linked the outside trade pressures to the budgetary problems of the EC itself). In the two-level game, Blair House was a product of synergistic reverberation between different games. The trade diplomats within the Commission had used the two-level game strategically.

Yet, agriculture was an exception. Other key issues displayed little disagreement across the Atlantic. EC diplomats played a leading role in all other areas of the Round. After some hesitation, the EC joined forces with the Americans on the GATS and TRIPS issues, and endorsed US leadership on the inclusion of services (Drake and Nicolaïdis 1993: 68; Dunkley 2000: 176) and on intellectual property rights (Drahos 2002). Some point to the impact of transnational business interests, suggesting that the TRIPS was a 'brainchild of an industry coalition' spanning across North America, Europe and Japan (Balanyá et al. 2003: 129; Sell 2003: 104–105). Both issues grew into North–South confrontations.

Initially, the UR was 'business as usual' but something had changed. The external pressures coincided with a domestic policy shift in key governments and within the Commission. Moreover, transnational business interests came into play as evident by the alignment of EU and US business strategies on TRIPS and GATS. Agriculture may have provided much of the drama but breakthroughs on

86 *Jens Ladefoged Mortensen*

the GATS, TRIPS and dispute settlement reforms proved more significant. Both agreements are today safeguarding European competitiveness in designer goods, pharmaceuticals and the global service industries.

1994–2003: EU leadership in the WTO

This marked the beginning of attempted EU leadership in the WTO. It was the European Union who put forward a new agenda, the so-called 'trade and ... agenda'. The European Union pushed for inclusion of labour standards, for better environmental exceptions, procurement liberalization and global competition rules (Woolcock 2005: 394). Falke (2005) links this to a shift towards 'positive regulation' of trade and the 'post-modern trade agenda' (see also Dymond and Hart 2000). However, the rest of the WTO was hostile, especially to issues like social rights and the environment. The developing world had little confidence in the European Union. To them, this looked more like neo-colonialism and green protectionism than free and fair world trade.[7]

Inside the European Union, the member states and the Commission clashed on the issue of 'shared' and 'exclusive' competences.[8] However, the practical effects of this were minimal. It was the European Union who pushed for a new comprehensive Round, or 'a global negotiation without limits' (Paemen 2000: 53). At the Singapore Ministerial (1997), the European Union specified that 'deep integration' included WTO rules on investment, competition, public procurement and trade facilitation (Singapore issues). It was hinted that CAP reforms were acceptable in return for this. Yet, not even the breakdown of the Seattle Ministerial Meeting would dampen the European optimism. As the European Union saw it, this only confirmed the urgency of addressing the 'systemic flaws' in the WTO.[9]

In hindsight, the European Union misread 'the Battle in Seattle' completely. It failed to accept the new topography of global trade politics. The Doha Round was launched in October 2001 under exceptional circumstances after the 9/11 attacks. It was intended to be a showcase of global pro-trade/pro-development solidarity. The European Union and the United States had even reached a pre-Cancun compromise on agricultural trade, a sort of Blair House agreement of the Doha Round. The seasoned EU and US trade negotiators were certain that the Cancun Ministerial in September 2003 would prove successful. The full weight of the European Union was mobilized in support of the Singapore issues. Yet, times had changed. Cancun marked the end of bilateral co-hegemony in multilateral trade. Falke (2005: 340) concludes that Cancun was 'the failure of the EU's attempt to shift to a post modern trade strategy'. Others found no evidence on 'post-modernity' of the European Union. It was by many interpreted as a cynical neo-colonialist power exercise (Jawara and Kwa 2003). The retreat from the Singapore issues was a tactical defence of the CAP. In any event, the European Union had to accept the fact that the Singapore issues were off the agenda. The EU trade diplomacy was dismal but still in support of the WTO.[10]

Since then, the Doha Round has broken down several times. In July 2006, the European Union was quick to blame Washington, stating that the United States was 'unwilling to accept, or indeed to acknowledge, the flexibility being shown by others in the room and, as a result, felt unable to show any flexibility on the issue of farm subsidies' (press conference, 24-7-2006). This infuriated the United States who felt that the European Union (and others) was inflexible when it came to market access offers (USTR 2006). The blame game continues even today. However, it was also apparent that old divisions in the European Union were intact.[11]

The post-trade agenda resembled an embryonic Global Single Market. Perhaps this is why the EU diplomats ignored the structural transformations in global trade. The European Union offered an agenda projecting EU experiences onto the global level. It failed to see that most other WTO members wanted to return to the basics of trade diplomacy, to renegotiate tariffs, subsidies and market access. Perhaps the developing world mistrusted the EU motives. Perhaps four decades of defending the CAP at all costs had stained the credibility of EU trade diplomacy in the end. Instead, the new agenda has found its way into the bilateral trade diplomacy of the European Union.

EU impact on the WTO reforms: Membership and dispute settlement

The institutional design of the WTO itself has been much influenced by the European Union. This section will briefly look at two aspects of this, namely WTO membership, especially the entry of China but also possible entry of Russia and the Ukraine, as well as the legalization of the WTO dispute settlement.

WTO accession and the European Union

Concerning WTO membership, although accession to the WTO requires two-third majority in the WTO Council, consensus is the norm. The People's Republic of China became the 143rd WTO member on 11 December 2001. Former DG Mike Moore called it 'an historic moment for the WTO, for China and for international economic cooperation'. Few disagree today. Chinese accession has changed everything in the WTO. The road to Chinese WTO membership was particularly long. A GATT Working Party was established in March 1987. A breakthrough was achieved in 1995–1997 as China accepted full convertibility for current account transactions, that is, IMF membership, full implementation of TRIPS obligations and a phase-out of trading monopolies. The European Union itself stressed its role as a broker, suggesting that the critical momentum in 1996 was created by EU proposals that granted China transition periods for certain WTO obligations. The EU–China agreement (May 2001) paved – together with the China–US agreement (February 2001) – the way forward for formal accession. The industry had major concerns about enforcement of intellectual property rights and market access. European insurance industries were particularly pleased with the result whereas the telecommunications and audiovisual sectors felt left out of the agreement. The EU negotiators had the strategic advantage of being the last hurdle for Chinese WTO membership since the United States already had

88 Jens Ladefoged Mortensen

completed its negotiations six months earlier. Yet, as a commentator noted, the European Union failed to exploit its hold-out position to pressure China into further concessions (Laprès 2000).

Today, the accession of Russia and the Ukraine are the last two pieces missing in the global coverage of WTO law. Mandelson has declared that '2008 should be the year that sees both Russia and the Ukraine accede to the WTO and begin to look towards deeper economic integration agreements with the EU' (speech, 12 December 2007). If the United States was the key to China's accession, the European Union now has the strongest strategic interests in a successful outcome. Russian accession is stalled due to worries about market transparency and systemic lack of intellectual property rights protection. The United States shares similar concerns. The situation is not that different from China's accession. The Ukraine is a different story. Economically, the Ukraine has a highly productive agricultural sector. Mandelson ensured that EU farmers should not fear this competition: 'there is plenty of demand to go round at the moment' (*Financial Times* 17-1-2008). The rise of food prices has for the time silenced the powerful EU agricultural lobby. Politically, however, the Ukraine will enter the WTO before Russia. Although the EU supports rapid Ukrainian WTO accession, it is also dreading the broader consequences of having delayed Russian accession.

European Union and the design of the WTO dispute settlement system

China's accession to the WTO was one of the defining moments in modern trade diplomacy. Another defining moment was the decision to strengthen the GATT dispute settlement as a part of the Uruguay Round, paving the road for the legalization of trade politics.[12] Since the early 1970s, the Americans had pushed for more effective GATT enforcement. Business was dissatisfied with the ineffective, consensus-driven GATT regime. It was, during the 1970s, used as a scapegoat for declining US market shares in Europe and Japan. A more legalistic system was deemed necessary. Aggressive trade litigation had dominated US trade politics for years. Initially, the EC was sceptical. By the late 1980s, the European negotiators seemed to accept a legalist design of the GATT. Again, a mix between external events and internal shift in policy orientation provides one explanation. Externally, the 1988 enactment of the US Trade and Omnibus Act (known as Section 301) threatened the GATT institution. The EC was forced to accept the US demands. Internally, the Single Market process also supported an ideational shift towards accepting legalization as a legitimate mode of GATT governance. Perhaps the Cassis de Dijon case provided a learning experience. Just as the EC diplomats supported US demands on TRIPS and GATS issues, they also accepted the legalist turn in the institutional reform. Yet, it should have stopped there. The United States had achieved what it wanted. It was the European Union who – together with the Canadians – persuaded other GATT members that a legal unification of GATT enforcement required a new organization.[13] And it was the United States who was put on the defensive and argued against the reform, stating that it would distract attention away from 'more important topics' (GATT 1990a). Even towards the end, the Europeans fended off US threats and maintained that the

The WTO and the EU   89

Table 5.1 Overview of major changes in EC–GATT/EU–WTO relations

Trade policy ideas and interests strategy in GATT/WTO	Inward-looking neo-mercantilism	Outward-looking pro-liberal
Defensive, reactive	EC 1960s–1985	EC 1986–1992
Proactive, aggressive		EU 1993–2003

organization was 'an essential and indispensable' component (GATT 1993: 10). After decades of being reactive in the GATT, the European Union can praise itself of being one of the founding fathers of the WTO. In the end, the new head of the GATT – former Competition Commissioner Peter Sutherland – had to reassure the Americans that 'the intention is not to set up a new international super-bureaucracy' (GATT 1993). Since the creation of the WTO, talks on continuing the legal reform of WTO dispute settlement has continued but with no significant result. Instead, the legal integration into the WTO is pushed forward by the Appellate Body on a case-by-case basis.

Explaining the European Union in the WTO

The transformation of Europe from a defensive neo-mercantilist GATT player to the proactive, post-modern trade liberalizer in the WTO cuts across several dimensions. Table 5.1 indicates what is here considered to be the key dimensions of these changes: trade policy content (including dominant interests and ideas) and diplomatic strategy (including choice of instruments).

The period of defensive neo-mercantilism was driven by inward-looking domestic interests as well as economic nationalist ideas. Again, the EC never challenges the GATT institution directly. The EC and the GATT were 'structurating' each other. The shift to proactive diplomacy coincided with an internal shift towards outward-looking export interests and new ideas within the relevant policy elites who had embraced the neoliberal ideals of the early 1980s, calling for unconditional market liberalization, stronger enforcement and fewer exceptions in the GATT. The other distinction concerns the choice of strategy. Early on, a passive strategy prevailed, allowing for external events and pressures to shape the behaviour of the EC in the GATT. EC-style neo-mercantilism was shaped by the defensive policy orientation of the elites and an internal policy process driven by domestic interests. The period after 2003 is left open for interpretation.

What has shaped these transformations? As mentioned, the two-level game is a useful starting point for unlocking the interplay between the inside and the outside but the structural conditions underpinning these games cannot so easily be eliminated.

Structural explanations: Towards a new realism in EU trade diplomacy?

The degree of openness in world trade has always been the trade mark of International Political Economy studies. Hegemonic Stability Theory (Gilpin 1987; Kennedy 1987; Bergsten 1992) explained the erosion of the GATT by the

90 Jens Ladefoged Mortensen

Table 5.2 Combined top traders in world merchandise trade (2006)

Rank	Market share (imports + exports)	Billion €	% World
1	EU-25	2,516.6	17.1
2	USA	2,296.5	15.6
3	China	1,312.1	8.9
4	Japan	921.5	6.3
5	Canada	609.6	4.2
	World	14,678	100.0

Source: Eurostat 2007.

decline of US hegemony. European integration itself was treated as a symptom of declining US hegemony. Today, there are strong parallels between the early 1980s and the late 2000s. Compared with the 1980s, China has replaced Japan as the principal challenger of the existing order. Trade statistics reveal a significant redistribution of market shares between the Quad (United States, European Union, Canada and Japan) and the emerging markets (primarily China, India, Russia and Brazil). Yet, the European Union has maintained its share of world trade in goods, whereas Japan and the United States have lost market shares. China has doubled its share during the past decade.

The European Union is the biggest trader in the world. It has benefited enormously from global market integration. When excluding intra-EU trade (extra-EU), almost a fifth of world exports in goods originated from Europe. When including intra-EU trade, Germany ranks as the biggest exporter in the world economy. A closer look at the United States and China – key markets or economic rivals of the European Union in the globalization game – is worthwhile. The US trade deficit (–€ 555.3 billion) was about five times higher than that of the European Union (–€ 113.6 billion) in 2004 (DG Trade 2006a: 1). China had grown rapidly into the second largest trading partner of the European Union, amounting to 9.4 per cent of total EU exports and imports combined.

Europe is a leader in some of the most lucrative sections of the global economy. It displays good export performance in up-market, high-quality products. Yet, the EU trade performance is at 'an unstable equilibrium … because the European industry is losing ground in high technology products' (Commission 2005: 5). Up-market products account for about half of EU exports. The European economies are at their most competitive in expensive products, when competing on non-price factors like innovative features, quality, reputation and post-sale services. However, these positive economic fundamentals are contradicted by the creeping competitiveness discourse within the European Union. Europe does not seem poised to lose the globalization game. Perhaps certain sectors are not benefiting as much from globalization as others. Some have pleaded for a new era of 'Pan-European realism', arguing that the old mode of Euro-centric economic thinking must be replaced with a pro-liberal competitiveness strategy.[14] These are structural arguments. Global competition pressures the European Union into a new direction.

The WTO and the EU   91

Table 5.3 Key quotes from Commission strategy paper, 2006

WTO	'There will be no European retreat from multilateralism. We stand by our commitment to multilateralism and are prepared to pay, reasonably, to keep the system thriving.'
Bilateral trade	'... a new generation of bilateral free trade agreements with key partners to build on WTO rules by tackling issues which are not ready for multilateral discussion and by preparing the ground for the next level of multilateral liberalisation.'
China	The 'greatest challenge for EU trade policy in the years to come'.
IPRs	Must be included in future bilateral agreements.
Market access	Focus on non-tariff barriers and direct contracts with EU industries.
Procurement issues	Better access for EU companies to public procurement markets.
Defence instruments	'The EU economic interests are global and highly complex. We need to be sure that our trade defence instruments and our use of them take account of these new realities.'

Source: Commission 2006: 10–12.

A recent Commission strategy paper also promises to be active in 'opening markets abroad' while rejecting 'protectionism at home'.

Structural explanations have thus come into play again. The European Union has not turned towards 1970s-style protectionism. Bilateralism today is not about quotas. It is about market access. The calls for reforms of trade defence instruments are made in light of global supply chains and investment. Globalization has made these counterproductive. By 2006, the Commission is reformulating its strategic priorities in trade governance. The Commission stresses that multilateralism remains a first choice. While reaffirming that new EU bilateralism will not contradict the WTO, it suggests that future trade agreements (competitiveness-driven free trade agreements) are to be 'ambitious in coverage and to include ... far-reaching liberalization of services and investment' (Commission 2006: 11).

Structural theories offer two predictions to how Europe reacts to global pressure. It can become an economic predator or an inward-protectionist. The analysis here suggests that it is unlikely that the European Union will reverse back to 1980s-style reactivism in the WTO. Internal constraints (the Single Market, Lisbon) are in place and the external context (economic globalization, WTO dispute settlement) will almost certainly punish such behaviour. The mindset of the EU trade diplomacy itself is also very different today. Yet, hegemonic realists maintain that structures shape behaviour. Back in the early 1990s, Conybeare coined the term 'economic predator' as a universal description of how struggling trade powers act in times of crisis:

> history and social science would suggest that the EC might become an economic predator, bargaining bilaterally with other predators, promoting oligopolistic restrains on world markets, linking its economic power to non-economic issues, and baffling outsiders as to how it makes decisions.
>
> (Conybeare 1992: 160)

92 *Jens Ladefoged Mortensen*

It remains an unlikely scenario but, given the current crisis mood, it is no longer an unthinkable scenario. Realism in the European Union's WTO diplomacy will be more assertive and predatory than passive and inward looking. Structural transformations in the world economy may ignite a global recession which in turn may tilt the balance towards predatory neo-protectionism within the European Union. Not by choice or conviction but out of necessity. Yet, the potential new realist assertiveness in the WTO will be of neoliberal orientation. The old defensive neo-protectionist school of thought dominating within elites throughout the 1970s is unlikely to return in the late 2000s.

'Domestic' explanations: How the two-level game matters in EU–WTO relations

Analytically, the two-level game is the bridge builder between structural and domestic levels. It allows us to think of trade diplomacy in terms of strategic competition but it prioritizes domestic factors. Yet, its emphasis on interlocked, nested games comes closer to reality than most other negotiation theories. As suggested in the preceding analysis, the two levels were strategically exploited by the Commission at most of the critical junctures in past trade diplomacy. For instance, the combined pressure from the inside (budget, exporters) and outside (US threat of unilateralism) enabled the MacSherry reform and the Blair House agreement.

The two-level game stresses internal divisions between globalization winners and losers. Domestic socio-economic interests shape the trade preference which then ultimately drives the WTO diplomacy. Yet, what really matters is actual influence on the trade policy. It does not argue that institutions determine what the European Union does in the WTO – it is not a constructivist argument – yet it emphasizes how institutional factors frame the strategic behaviour of actors. The Commission is the Chief Negotiator in Europe, the actor who strategically controls the interface between different games. DG External Trade occupies the commanding heights of most matters in actual WTO diplomacy. Yet, as the Blair House story illustrated, the European Union has problems whenever 'negotiations are formulated through a multi-tiered, compartmentalized, consensus-driven decision-making process that favours agricultural interests' (Moyer 1993: 95). Yet, the fragmentation issue is a sector-specific problem. It is not an institutional one.

The assumption that only one actor controls the interface between the different games is a basic weakness of the two-level game approach. Just as suggested by the three concentric circles model of the EU trade diplomacy outlined earlier, the two-level game must be modified in order to fit the reality of the EU process. The EP must be included. Unlike the United States, the EP has had little say in what the European Union does in the WTO. Only their assent is required. The Commission developed a practice of consulting the relevant Committees. However, this will most likely change. The draft Constitution proposed to grant the EP more influence by transforming the decision process from assent to co-decision. The EP can therefore be expected to be more involved in the future. In addition, the NGO community must be included. A 'Civil Society Dialogue' mechanism was instituted in 1998. It serves as a platform for meetings between NGO representatives and top-level EU diplomats. Although 32 meetings took place in 2007, not much seems to have been achieved (Dür and de Bièvre 2007). However, it is difficult to assess precisely what has been achieved but – like the EP involvement – it is part of a broader strategy of legitimizing EU trade policy. Regardless of its achievements, both measures do not challenge the core argument of the two-level game – that is, essentially what the European Union does in WTO negotiations remains controlled by the relevant sections of the Commission and Council jointly.

Beyond the two-level game: The business of WTO dispute settlement

However, firms trade, trade diplomats do not. Firms are indirectly actors in their own right throughout the WTO process. Much of what happens in the WTO today is about dispute settlement. Day-to-day WTO governance is much more open to the transnational game of globalization than the restricted intergovernmental level suggests. This is why even Mandelson (2006a) acknowledged that 'globalization collapses distinctions between what we do at home and what we do abroad'. The two-level game neglects the dual track influence of transnational actors. Firms can act like 'European interests' at the Commission level or as 'national interest' at the national level according to their strategic interest. NGOs have – in principle – the same option. Yet, the high costs of the dual track lobbying implies that only a handful of mega-corporations have the resources to fully exploit both options (as argued by Balanyá *et al.* 2003: 8).

Thus, the conventional two-level game is problematic with respect to day-to-day WTO governance in dispute settlement. The outer layers of the EU trade diplomacy are increasingly important. Any analysis of EU diplomacy in the WTO is incomplete without an analysis of how the European Union acts in the WTO dispute settlement system (Shaffer 2006). As the biggest trader in the world economy, the European Union also is defending its commercial interests in the WTO court rooms. The European Union has been involved in 76 cases as complainant and in 59 cases as a respondent (as of 18 January 2008; see Commission 2008). Only the United States has been more active (88 and 99 cases, respectively). Thirty-one disputes are currently pending. The European Union has been a frequent target of legal complaints. Sixteen active cases have been launched against the European Union, whereas 15 disputes have been launched by the European Union. The transatlantic trade frictions dominated the WTO system in the past. Almost half of all WTO cases involve the two superpowers in one way or another. Even so, the European Union has currently eight cases against the United States and the United States has three ongoing cases pending against the European Union.[15] The number of transatlantic trade wars has declined dramatically in recent years but some remain exceptionally dangerous for the WTO.

The prominence of agricultural conflicts sits in stark contrast with its economic significance: a mere 4.3 per cent of EU agricultural imports originate in the

94　*Jens Ladefoged Mortensen*

United States, while 4.8 per cent of EU agricultural exports go to the United States (DG Trade 2006a: 8). Considering the occasional anti-EU rhetoric in Washington, it is easy to forget that the European Union is the most important trade partner of the United States, the largest exporter to the US market (19.5 per cent of total US imports) and second largest importer of US products (21.3 per cent of total US exports). Transatlantic trade amounts to 20.3 per cent of total US trade, slightly more than that between the United States and Canada, and twice as much as that between the United States and China (DG Trade 2006a: 3). Far more important to the European Union is the trade relationship in commercial services. Some 34.8 per cent of combined EU exports and imports in services in 2004 are with the United States while trade in commercial services with China is of marginal importance (2.6 per cent). Switzerland (12.6 per cent) and Japan (4.7 per cent) are more important trade partners to the European Union.

Only the Commission or individual member states may initiate a dispute in Geneva. Firms have no legal standing in WTO law. In practice, the Commission initiates in consultation with the Article 133 committee legal proceedings in the WTO. This political control on EU trade lawyers goes against the transnational argument. However, EU firms have direct access to the Market Access Unit in the Commission under the Trade Barrier Regulation (TBR, following Council regulation 3286/94). The use of the TBR is part of the new Global European strategy, as mentioned above. It permits the Commission to act on private complaints, thus bypassing political controls of national governments (Sherman and Eliasson 2006: 475). It does not require the Commission to convert every TBR complaint into a WTO complaint. The Council must approve the initiation of WTO cases by QMV and the Commission is obliged to have exhorted all other alternatives. Even so, the Commission can approach foreign governments directly without involvement of the member states, the domestic game, if a TBR complaint has been filed by an EU firm or industry.

The TBR option exists only for market access issues. It cannot be used with respect to regulatory barriers (like food standards). The TBR empowers the Commission in the conduct of day-to-day WTO business. It grants private actors access to the WTO process but not to the legal WTO proceedings. Like anti-dumping investigations, it engages EU industry directly.[16] WTO business is directly tied into the domestic 'competitiveness game'. This link is not necessarily pro-liberal. The southern block of 'protectionists' are also in a position to capture the EU trade policy as when it can authorize controversial anti-dumping duties by a simple majority.[17]

What are the consequences of future EU activities in the WTO? The legalization of the WTO seems self-enforcing. EU trade politics might be transformed into US-style 'private litigation'. The Commission will invest more in legal resources and adopt an even more activist legal strategy in the WTO. It will work much closer with not only business but also trade experts. Indirectly, I have argued, the legalization of the WTO has empowered private actors within the European Union as well as in the WTO. They now enjoy multiple access points. In other words, the issue-specific trade networks are likely to become more prominent in EU–WTO relations. As Shaffer writes,

The WTO and the EU 95

[t]he judicalization of international trade relations has spurred the formation of public–private coordination strategies in the EU whose dynamic has
become more outward looking and proactive.

(Shaffer 2006: 847)

The growth of the issue-specific networks may counterbalance the systemic
pressures of economic rivalry discussed earlier. Resourceful firms, industry
groups and super NGOs can bypass political controls and time-honoured practices in the future WTO diplomacy of the European Union. Both pro-liberal and
protectionist business will have a much larger say in future day-to-day WTO governance. Transnational firms and other resourceful actors will be privileged by
the WTO process. As trade disputes are extremely knowledge-intensive activities, the Commission will be in need of resourceful partners in the WTO process.

Conclusions

The chapter argues that the EU trade diplomacy is undergoing a number of transformations. It is no longer the spoiler of international trade liberalization. What
determines how the European Union acts in the WTO? Part of the answer is due to
the growing emphasis on exports within the European Union. Moreover, globalization has made the EU trade policy more visible to the public. The answer also
depends upon the specific WTO activity in question. When Europe negotiates in
Geneva, the Commission has the exclusive competence to negotiate. Like other
governments, the European Union is divided on controversial issues. Unlike other
governments, the EU trade diplomats are watched closely by its member states.
Yet, the convoluted, multilayered decision-making process has passed the test of
time. Five decades of trade diplomacy suggests that the European Union is capable
of defending and promoting itself. Neither the Commission nor the individual EU
governments control the WTO process to the same extent as earlier. Paths created
by 50 years of practice are being altered. The last remains of its 'deep integration'
approach – perhaps best understood as a projection of the EU model to the global
level – have been washed away by the Doha breakdown. All but one of the
Singapore issues has disappeared from the agenda. The WTO is in crisis. Emerging
trade powers like China, India and Brazil have asserted themselves in the WTO. It
is beyond the scope here to look deeper into how WTO politics are being transformed. Like other WTO members, the European Union turned towards bilateral
liberalization. This is, however, not the same as saying that the European Union has
abandoned the WTO. Rather, external circumstances have forced the European
Union into adapting its WTO strategy for a new competitive global environment.

Notes

1 It is the EC who formally acts in the WTO. Reflecting common usage, 'EU' is used –
except 'EC' when used in a historical context (1957–1992). The 'EU trade policy' is a
shorthand used here for 'The common commercial policy of the European Communities'
as defined by Treaty of the EU Article 133 (formerly Article 113).

96   *Jens Ladefoged Mortensen*

2 The WTO 'replaced' the General Agreement of Trade and Tariffs (GATT) on 1 January 1995. The GATT agreement from 1947 exists today as GATT 1994 (Annex 1 of the Marrakesh Agreement establishing the WTO). GATT 1994 regulates trade in goods. Fourteen issue-specific WTO agreements (agriculture, technical barriers, subsidies or anti-dumping) exist. The General Agreement on Trade in Services (GATS) and Agreement on Trade-Related Intellectual Rights (TRIPS) are the two other principal WTO agreements. The GATT was never formally an organization. It had a small secretariat that operated on a provisional basis. The WTO is recognized as an international organization with legal personality and capacity (Trebilcock and Howse 2005: 20–26). With a permanent staff of 625 (WTO 2007: 100), the WTO remains much smaller than the OECD (about 2,500), the World Bank (about 10,000) or the IMF (2,678 in 2007).

3 Top 5 in an unofficial headcount of professional staff in Geneva. Jawara and Kwa (2003: 20–21) found that Japan (with staff of 23) exceeds the EU representation (18), Korea (16), United States (14), Thailand (13) and Brazil (12). A direct comparison is difficult as some like the US mission are exclusively devoted to the WTO, whereas others like the EU representation are not (covering all other Geneva-based IOs).

4 The non-membership of the EC was one out of many peculiar features of the GATT (Jackson 1989: 47). The European Union is one of the original WTO members. GATT 1994 article XXXIII permits WTO membership of 'separate custom territories possessing full autonomy of the conduct of its external commercial relations'. Chinese Taipei and Hong Kong China are members alongside PR China. Only the European Union enjoys this privilege in the WTO. Other organizations – like, for example, the African Union, Organization of the Americas, or secretariats of the ADEAN or the Caribbean Communities – are granted observer status in most WTO bodies. Outside observers are not permitted in some WTO bodies like, for example, the Dispute Settlement Body.

5 For good insider accounts, see Croome (1995) and Paemen and Bensch (1995).

6 A deal struck within the Commission was rejected by Delors. Agricultural Commissioner MacSherry resigned but Delors was forced to reinstate him. Intense diplomacy in Washington, Geneva and Brussels made a breakthrough at Blair House in Washington possible (Paemen and Bensch 1995: 205–218).

7 See Bhagwati (2004: 135–161) for Southern pro-trade criticism of the Northern 'trade and environment' and 'fair trade' agenda.

8 The ECJ was asked to decide whether the Commission had exceeded its mandate by concluding the Uruguay Agreement. Its Opinion I/94 confirmed the UR agreements but ruled that the certain aspects of the GATS and TRIPS exceeded the mandate (see MacLeod *et al.* 1996: 268–274). The Amsterdam treaty solved the issue (Dashwood 1998).

9 Lamy demanded that 'liberalization must be accompanied by a much-needed updating of the WTO rule-book' but also that 'the longer time goes on without a response to the systemic issues behind the headlines of Seattle relating to globalization and development – the greater the risk of the WTO itself becoming marginalized, and of a dangerous vacuum in international economic policy' (Lamy 2000).

10 Commissioner Lamy's (2003) infamous outburst on this occasion illustrates this well:

> [T]he WTO remains a medieval organization. … There is no way to structure and steer discussions amongst 146 members in a manner conducive to consensus. The decision-making needs to be revamped. The EU remains committed to a strong rules-based multilateral trading system and will continue to work in this direction within the WTO.

11 The *Financial Times* reported that 'officials within the 13 or 14 agrarian EU member states periodically orchestrated by France to prevent bigger cuts in European farm tariffs have also been privately half-hoping that the talks would fail' (24-7-2006).

12 Legalization is here used as shorthand for institutionalization characterized by binding legal obligations, more precise rules and high degree of delegation (Abbott *et al.* 2000: 17). The Dispute Settlement Understanding (Annex 2 of the WTO Agreement) comes

The WTO and the EU 97

close to this ideal with its quasi-automatic procedures, such as (1) a right to a panel investigation upon second request, (2) right to appeal to the Appellate Body, and (3) automatic adoption of rulings unless consensus goes against it.

13 The Canadians first proposed a 'WTO'. Shortly afterwards, the EC proposed a 'Multilateral Trade Organization' (GATT 1990a). The name was later changed back into the WTO due to American resistance.

14 As Gordon Brown (2005) put it:

> The challenge for Europe now is that of global competition. … [I]t is because global competitive pressures bearing down upon Europe are so intense … that Europe must reform and reform quickly. And the question for us is how Europe can move from the older inward-looking model to a flexible, reforming, open and globally-oriented Europe – able to master the economic challenge from Asia, America and beyond.

15 Four clusters of transatlantic disputes have emerged: (1) anti-dumping 'Byrd amendment' (DS 217), 'Zeroing' (DS 294), steel bars (DS 319) and 'Zeroing Methodology' (DS 350); (2) TRIPS ('Irish Music' [DS 160], Havana Club [DS 176]); (3) strategic trade policies in global aircraft industry (EU cases: DS 317, DS 353; US cases: DS 316, DS 347); (4) food wars (US: Hormones [DS 26] and GMO [DS 291]; EU complaint about continued retaliations [DS 320]. The US complaint in the Banana case remains unsolved after more than a decade [DS 27].

16 The authorization of anti-dumping duties is not subject to qualified majority voting but by simple majority vote in the Council. This was a concession to France in return for ratification of the Uruguay Agreements (Woolcock 2005: 242).

17 The southern block (led by Italy) won a Council vote of 13–12 in favour of a two-year 16.5 per cent AD duty on imported leather shoes from China and Vietnam (BBC 6-10-2006).

References

Abbott, K.W., Keohane, R.O., Moravcsik, A., Slaughter, A.-M. and Snidal, D. (2000) 'The Concept of Legalization', *International Organization*, 54: 17–35.

Balanyá, B., Doherty, A., Hocdeman, O., Ma'anit, A. and Wesselius, E. (2003) *Europe Inc. Regional and Global Restructuring and the Rise of Corporate Power*, London: Pluto Press/Corporate Europe Observatory.

Bergsten, C.F. (1992) 'The World Economy after the Cold War', *California Management Review*, 34(2): 51–65.

Bhagwati, J. (2004) *In Defense of Globalization*, Oxford: Oxford University Press, Ch. 11, pp. 135–161.

Bretherton, C. and Vogler, J. (1999) 'The EU as an Economic Power and Trade Actor', in *The European Union as a Global Actor*, London: Routledge, pp. 46–79.

Brown, G. (2005) *Global Britain, Global Europe: A Presidency Founded on Pro European Realism*, HM Treasury, Speech at Mansion House, London, 22 June 2005. Online. Available HTTP: http://www.hm-treasury.gov.uk/newsroom_and_speeches/press/2005/press_57_05.cfm

Commission (2005) *Trade and Competitiveness – Issues Paper*, Bruxelles: DG Competition, dated 01-09-2005.

Commission (2006) *GLOBAL EUROPE: Competing in the World – A Contribution to the EU's Growth and Jobs Strategy*. Online. Available HTTP: http://trade.ec.europa.eu/doclib/docs/2006/october/tradoc_130376.pdf

Commission (2008) *General Overview of Active WTO Dispute Settlement Cases Involving the EC as Complainant or Defendant and of Active Cases under the Trade Barriers*

98 Jens Ladefoged Mortensen

Regulation 18 January 2008. Online. Available HTTP: http://trade.ec.europa.eu/doclib/docs/2007/may/tradoc_134652.pdf

Conybeare, J.A.C. (1992) '1992, The Community and the World – Free Trade or Fortress Europe?', in D.L. Smith and J.L. Ray (eds) *The 1992 Project and the Future of Integration in Europe*, New York: M.E. Sharpe.

Croome, J. (1995) *Reshaping the World Trading System. A History of the Uruguay Round*, Geneva: WTO.

Dashwood, A. (1998) 'External Relations Provisions of the Amsterdam Treaty', *Common Market Law Review*, 35(5), October.

Drahos, P. (2002) 'Negotiating Intellectual Property Rights: Between Coercion and Dialogue', in P. Drahos and R. Mayne (eds) *Global Intellectual Rights – Knowledge, Access and Development*, Houndsmill: Palgrave.

Drake, W.J. and Nicolaïdis, K. (1992) 'Ideas, Interests, and Institutionalization: "Trade in Services" and the Uruguay Round', *International Organization*, 46(1): 37–100.

Dür, A. and de Bièvre, D. (2007) 'Inclusion without Influence? NGOs in European Trade Policy', *Journal of Public Policy*, 27(1): 79–101.

Dymond, W. and Hart, M. (2000) 'Post Modern Trade Policy – Reflections on the Challenges to Multilateral Trade Negotiations after Seattle', *Journal of World Trade*, 34(3): 21–38.

Esserman, S. and Howse, R. (2003) 'The WTO on Trial', *Foreign Affairs*, 82(1): 130–140.

Eurostat (2007) *Top Trading Partners*. Online. Available HTTP: http://trade.ec.europa.eu/doclib/docs/2006/september/tradoc_122531.xls

Falke, A. (2005) 'EU–USA Trade Relations in the Doha Development Round: Market Access Versus a Post-modern Trade Policy Agenda', *European Foreign Affairs Review*, 10: 339–357.

GATT (1990a) *Communication from the EC*, MTN.GNG/NG/14/W/42, dated 1-7-1990.

GATT (1990b) *Communication from the United States*, MTN.GNG/NG/14/W/44.

GATT (1993) *Twenty-Ninth Meeting: 31 August 1993*, Trade Negotiation Council, MTN.TNC/33.

Gilpin, R. (1987) *The Political Economy of International Relations*, Princeton: Princeton University Press.

Grieco, J. (1990) *Cooperation among Nations. Europe, America and Non-Tariff Barriers to Trade*, Ithaca: Cornell University Press.

Hampson, F.O. (1999) *Multilateral Negotiations: Lessons from Arms Control, Trade, and the Environment*, Baltimore and London: Johns Hopkins University Press.

Hilf, M. (1995) 'The ECJ's Opinion 1/94 on the WTO – No Surprise, but Wise?', *European Journal of International Law*, 6(2): 245–259.

Jackson, J.H. (1989) *The World Trading System: Law and Policy of International Economic Relations*, Cambridge, MA: MIT Press.

Jawara, F. and Kwa, A. (2003) *Behind the Scenes at the WTO: The Real World of International Trade Negotiations*, London: Zed Books.

Kennedy, P. (1987) *The Rise and Fall of the Great Powers: Economic Change and Military Conflict from 1500 to 2000*, London: Fontana Press.

Lamy, P. (2000) 'Trade is Changing – So Must Europe', *Financial Times*, 5 December.

Lamy, P. (2003) 'Press Conference Closing the World Trade Organization 5th Ministerial Conference', *5th WTO Ministerial Conference*, Cancun, 14 September.

Laprès, A. (2000). *The E.U.–China WTO Deal Compared*. Online. Available HTTP: http://www.chinabusinessreview.com/public/0007/lapres.html

The WTO and the EU   99

MacLeod, I.I., Hendry, S. and Hyatt, S. (1996) *The External Relations of the European Communities*, Oxford: Clarendon Press.

Mandelson, P. (2006a) *Global Europe: Competing in the World*, Speaking points, Press room, European Commission, 4 October. Online. Available HTTP: http://ec.europa.eu/commission_barroso/mandelson/speeches_articles/artpm030_en.htm

Mandelson, P. (2006b) *Bilateral Agreements in EU Trade Policy*, speech by Peter Mandelson at the London School of Economics, London, 9 October.

Mandelson, P. (2007) *Europe and the World in 2008*, speech, University of Ljubljana, Slovenia, 12 December. Online. Available HTTP: http://ec.europa.eu/commission_barroso/mandelson/speeches_articles/sppm187_en.htm

Matsushita, M., Schonenbaum, T. and Mavroidis, P. (2006) *The World Trade Organisation: Law, Practice and Policy*, 2nd edition, Oxford: Oxford University Press.

Meunier, S. and Nicolaïdis, K. (2005) 'The European Union as a Trade Power', in C. Hill and M. Smith (eds) *International Relations and the European Union*, Oxford: Oxford University Press.

Mortensen, J.L. (1998) 'The Institutional Challenges and Paradoxes of EU Governance in External Trade: Coping with the Post-hegemonic Trading System and the Global Economy', in A. Carfuny and P. Peters (eds) *The Union and the World*, The Hague: Kluwer.

Moyer, H.W. (1993) 'The European Community and the GATT Uruguay Round: Preserving the Common Agricultural Policy at all Costs', in W. Avery (ed.) *World Agriculture and the GATT*, Boulder: Lynne Rienner.

Ostry, S. (1997) *The Post-Cold War Trading System: Who's on First?*, Chicago: University of Chicago Press.

Paarlberg, R. (1997) 'Agricultural Policy Reform and the Uruguay Round: Synergistic Linkages in a Two Level Game?', *International Organization*, 51(3): 413–444.

Paemen, H. (2000) 'The EU Approach to the New Round', in J. Schott (ed.) *The WTO after Seattle*, Washington: Institute of International Economics.

Paemen, H. and Bensch, A. (1995) *From the GATT to the WTO: The European Community in the Uruguay Round*, Leuven: Leuven University Press.

Patterson, A.L. (1997) 'Agricultural Policy Reform in the European Community: A Three-level Game Analysis', *International Organization*, 51(1): Winter.

Putnam, R. (1988) 'Diplomacy and Domestic Politics: The Logic of Two-level Games', *International Organization*, 42(3): 427–460.

Richard, S. and Aliasson, J. (2006) 'Trade Disputes and Non-state Actors: New Institutional Arrangements and the Privatisation of Commercial Diplomacy', *World Economy*, 29(April): 473–489.

Sell, S.K. (2003) *Private Power, Public Law – The Globalization of Intellectual Property Rights*, Cambridge: Cambridge University Press.

Shaffer, G. (2003) *Defending Interests: Public–Private Partnerships in WTO Litigation*, Washington, DC: Brookings Institution Press.

Shaffer, G. (2006) 'What's New in EU Trade Dispute Settlement? Judicialization, Public–Private Networks and the WTO Legal Order', *Journal of European Public Policy*, 13(6): 832–850.

Sherman, R. and Eliasson, J. (2006) 'Trade Disputes and Non-state Actors: New Institutional Arrangements and the Privatisation of Commercial Diplomacy', *The World Economy*, 29(4): 473–489.

Smith, M. (2001) 'The European Union's Commercial Policy: Between Coherence and Fragmentation', *Journal of European Public Policy*, 8(5): 787–802.

100 *Jens Ladefoged Mortensen*

Trebilcock, J. and Howse, R. (2005) *The Regulation of International Trade*, 3rd edition, New York: Routledge.

USTR (2006) Statement by Office of the US Trade Representative, 25 July 2006. Online. Available HTTP: http://www.ustr.gov/Document_Library/Press_Releases/2006/July/Statement_by_Office_of_the_US_Trade_Representative.html

Van Appeldorn, B. (2006) 'The Transnational Political Economy of European Integration: The Future of Socio-economic Governance in the Enlarged Union', in R. Stubbs and G.R.D. Underhill (eds) *Political Economy and the Changing Global Order*, Oxford: Oxford University Press.

Weaver, R. and Abellard, D. (1993) *The Functioning of the GATT System*, Deventer: Kluwer Law and Taxation Publishers.

Whalley, J. and Hamilton, C. (1996) *The Trading System after the Uruguay Round*, Washington, DC: Institute for International Economics.

Wiemann, J. (1996) 'Green Protectionism: A Threat to Third World Exports?', in M.P. Van Dijk and S. Sideri (eds) *Multilateralism versus Regionalism: Trade Issues after the Uruguay Round*, London: Frank Cass.

Winham, G.R. (1986) *International Trade and the Tokyo Round Negotiation*, Princeton: Princeton University Press.

Woolcock, S. (2005) 'European Union Trade Policy: Domestic Institutions and Systemic Factors', in D. Kelly and W. Grant (eds) *The Politics of International Trade in the Twenty-First Century: Actors, Issues and Regional Dynamics*, Palgrave: Houndmills.

Woolcock, S. and Hodges, M. (1996) 'EU Policy in the Uruguay Round: The Story Behind the Headlines', in H. Wallace and W. Wallace (eds) *Policy-making in the European Union*, 3rd edition, Oxford: Oxford University Press, pp. 301–324.

World Trade Organization (2005) *International Trade Statistics 2005*, Geneva: WTO.

World Trade Organization (2007) *Annual Report 2007*, Geneva: WTO. Online. Available HTTP: http://www.wto.org/english/res_e/booksp_e/anrep_e/anrep07_e.pdf

6 The European Union and NATO

'Shrewd interorganizationalism' in the making?

Johannes Varwick and Joachim Koops

After precisely half a century of structured separation and complex coexistence, the European Union and the North Atlantic Treaty Organization (NATO) announced in their December 2002 Declaration on European Security and Defence Policy (ESDP) the establishment of a strategic and mutually reinforcing partnership in crisis management. Barely three months after, the conclusion of the so-called Berlin Plus agreement consolidated this partnership even further by providing for the European Union's access to NATO's military assets and planning capabilities. It was on the basis of this arrangement that the European Union was able to launch its first ever military mission, *Concordia*, in Macedonia in March 2003. This did not only take one of the closest and most densely negotiated interorganizational relationships to the practical realm, but also signalled a military revolution in the European Union's evolution as an international actor.

It is therefore unsurprising that the European Union's European Security Strategy (ESS) also refers to NATO's importance in its outline of 'an international order based on effective multilateralism' (Council of the European Union 2003: 9). In view of reinforcing the European Union's 'progress towards a coherent foreign policy and effective crisis management', the ESS stresses that 'the EU–NATO permanent arrangements, in particular Berlin Plus, enhance the operational capability of the EU and provide the framework for the strategic partnership between the two organizations in crisis management. This reflects our common determination to tackle the challenges of the new century' (ibid.: 11–12).

In this light, the EU–NATO relationship indeed provides an important and rather intriguing empirical case study for assessing the European Union's practice of its interorganizational foreign policy concept of effective multilateralism in the realm of military crisis management. In this chapter, we shall thus analyse the evolution, implementation and function of the European Union's cooperation with NATO and assess the impact both organizations have had on each other within and as a result of their relationship. This should provide us with a useful basis for evaluating one interorganizational aspect of the European Union's approach to its strategy of effective multilateralism in the field.

The chapter, in line with the general analytical approach of this volume, is structured as follows. In the first section, we provide an outline of the three main phases in the evolution of the EU–NATO relationship and highlight key developments

102 *Johannes Varwick and Joachim Koops*

and turning points therein. Next, we analyse the main internal and external factors of change behind this evolution and assess their relative importance. In the final section, we provide an overall evaluation of the EU–NATO relationship in the wider context of the European Union's strategy of effective multilateralism. By applying our previous findings to a comparative analysis of the European Union's and NATO's impact on each other's policies, developments and institutional designs, we seek to assess what the empirical example of the EU–NATO nexus can indeed tell us about the European Union's actual implementation and pursuit of its foreign policy concept of effective multilateralism in practice. We conclude by arguing that the European Union's relationship with NATO is less characterized by the interorganizational altruism often associated with the European Union's 'foreign policy philosophy' (Barroso 2004) of effective multilateralism. Instead, the European Union seems to have developed a distinctly instrumental approach to its cooperation schemes with NATO.

By progressively applying its experiences and lessons learned with NATO to the launch and conduct of more and more autonomous missions, the European Union seems to be intent on strengthening and advancing its own profile as a visible international actor in the realm of crisis management. Instead of an effective multilateralism in the field, therefore, we seem to be rather witnessing the emergence of an EU-led 'shrewd interorganizationalism' in the making.

The evolution of the 'EU–NATO relationship': From structured separation to ambiguous interaction

In this section, we provide a brief overview and analysis of the main developments and key changes in the evolution of the EU–NATO relationship, including the shifting balance of power between both organizations. We identify three major phases in the emergence of EU–NATO relations.

The first phase, roughly covering the first post-Cold War decade, highlights the European Union's and NATO's search for adapted roles and a new interorganizational equilibrium in response to the new demands and opportunities of the fundamentally altered international environment. Whilst NATO succeeded in establishing its primacy as an effective military actor during this period in the Balkans, the European Union's increasing ambitions in the security and defence field – most forcibly foreshadowed by the Franco-British St Malo declaration in 1998 – reinforced the pressing question of what kind of new post-Cold War balance and bargain should be struck between the two rapidly evolving organizations.

The second phase, ranging from the establishment of the ESDP in 1999, via initial contacts between EU and NATO officials, to the final 'Berlin Plus' agreement in March 2003, comprises the actual onset and formalization of a direct EU–NATO relationship at the political and operational level.

The third and indeed current stage in the evolution of EU–NATO relations is as much defined by increasing interactions as by deliberately ambiguous relations between both organizations. Despite the European Union's operational dependence on NATO for the European Union's first ever military mission, *Concordia*,

The EU and NATO   103

from March to December 2003 in Macedonia and the indispensable need for cooperating with NATO in the context of the more ambitious mission *Althea* in Bosnia since December 2004, the European Union has nonetheless been keen to stress its political and operational autonomy by conducting independent military missions without recourse to NATO's capabilities and assets. As we shall argue below, a key underlying feature of this period is thus the slow but clear shift in the overall power balance between both organizations: away from NATO and decidedly towards a more assertive European Union. Questions surrounding the implications of this power shift for the functions, practice and meaning of 'EU–NATO effective multilateralism' will be central to the chapter's remaining analysis.

Towards a new post-Cold War EU–NATO balance: 1990–1998

The lifting of the Iron Curtain in 1989 not only removed the geopolitical separation between Western and Eastern Europe, but also blurred the clear organizational division of labour, roles and functions that have characterized the distinct relations between NATO and the European Community throughout the Cold War. Whilst NATO, with the dissolution of the 'Soviet enemy' in 1991, was forced to rethink its *raison d'être* and to justify its continued existence, the negotiations on the transformation of the European Community into the European Union in 1991 were also accompanied by some new-found ambitions in the security policy realm (Deighton 2002: 724). The creation of the European Union's Common Foreign and Security Policy (CFSP) signalled the first tentative indications of the European Union's readiness to venture into what had hitherto been NATO's exclusive domain. Indeed, sensing a new activism, reorientation, overlap of ambitions and the general search for a new post-Cold War balance amongst the major European and international organizations, such as the Organization for Security and Co-operation in Europe, Council of Europe or the UN, NATO Secretary General Manfred Wörner already called in 1991 for a cooperative scheme of 'interlocking institutions' (Biermann 2008: 152).

Ironically, however, their inadequate responses to the exogenous shock and challenge of the Balkan Wars from 1991 to 1995 served to reinforce NATO and US primacy. The Dayton Peace agreement of 1995 not only underlined that solely a US-led NATO was capable of an intervention decisive enough to bring the warring parties to the negotiation table, but also woefully exposed the European Union's marginal role and its 'capability–expectation gap' in the wider security realm (Hill 1993). The Balkan experience, initial American reluctance to get involved in an essentially European conflict it had little strategic interest in and Europe's eventual and woeful dependence on US military power reinforced the sense of urgency amongst European leaders for the need of developing their own European military capacities.

A key bone of contention for the relationship between the European Union and NATO has been in which precise organizational context Europe's new-found militarization project should take place. Whilst US administrations have welcomed and constantly called for European moves towards greater 'burden sharing', they also remained adamant that these initiatives should not be undertaken outside the NATO framework (Varwick 2008: 120). In this vein, the Clinton administration supported the idea of a European Security and Defence Identity (ESDI) within NATO, which had already been hinted at in NATO's Strategic Concept of November 1991. In the wake of the Europeans' efforts to reactivate the dormant Western European Union (WEU), a compromise and new, albeit temporary, institutional post-Cold War balance was struck at NATO's ministerial meeting in Berlin in June 1996. The WEU, as the European Union's extended defence arm, was offered access to NATO's military assets and planning capabilities for the launch of missions 'where NATO as a whole is not engaged'. Thus, conditional on US approval in the North Atlantic Council, NATO's highest political decision-making body, the European Union could, via the WEU, draw on combat forces that were 'separable, but not separate' from NATO. This 'Berlin agreement' thereby reinforced NATO's political pre-eminence, whilst enhancing the European Union's military capabilities and operational options, indirectly, through the WEU.

However, barely two years after, this compromise seemed to be already overtaken by events, in the form of the Franco-British declaration at St Malo in December 1998 (UK FCO 1998). Signifying a historical shift in the British position, Tony Blair and Jacques Chirac agreed on the need for the European Union's *direct* development of autonomous military capacities (Howorth 2007). This declaration – which, rather tellingly, the Americans had not been previously consulted on – did not only herald the onset of the European Union's more assertive ESDP, but also raised the issue of the balance and relations between the European Union and NATO afresh, and indeed, more acutely than ever before.

Compromising the 'Grand Bargain': Towards the 'Berlin Plus' arrangement 1999–2003

Whilst the St Malo declaration signified the beginning of the European Union's development of autonomous military capacities, the decision reached at the EU Council Summits at Cologne in June 1999, to transfer the majority of the WEU's structures and tasks to the European Union, implied the end of the EU–WEU–NATO triangle and marked, by default, the commencement of a direct EU–NATO relationship. The central question at this stage was how exactly this new EU–NATO relationship should be organized, formalized and internally balanced.

Madeleine Albright's famed 'three Ds' conditions revealed the Clinton administration's suspicions about ESDP as an institutional rival that was potentially capable of undermining NATO. Thus, in her article she demanded that the development of ESDP should neither lead to the decoupling of North American and European security, nor to the duplication of NATO assets, nor to the discrimination against non-EU NATO members (Albright 1998). Arguably, the very fact that the US administration felt to have a right and duty to attach conditions to the European Union's unfolding military project is telling evidence of the perceived EU–NATO hierarchy and assumed transatlantic power balances at this critical juncture.

The EU and NATO   105

NATO's reaction to ESDP was more ambiguous. At its 50th anniversary summit in Washington in April 1999, it welcomed the European Union's initiative with some reservations. Whilst the Summit Communiqué stressed that the European Union's ESDP should develop only in close coordination with NATO, based on the WEU–NATO agreements reached at Berlin in 1996, NATO's new Strategic Concept – adopted on the same day as the final communiqué – still referred to the ESDI within NATO instead of acknowledging the realities of an autonomous ESDP outside of NATO (Yost 2007: 75).

However, spurred by a repeated demonstration of the military inadequateness of the European troops participating in the US-led NATO air-strikes in Kosovo from March to June 1999, EU governments stepped up the deepening of the ESDP's institutional and operational structures. Whilst the first Helsinki Headline Goal, agreed upon at the December EU Council summit, called for the creation of a European Rapid Reaction Force of up to 60,000 troops to be deployed within 60 days and to be sustained for at least one year – incidentally, the same number of troops required by NATO's Implementation Force (IFOR) in Bosnia in 1995 – the Treaty of Nice formalized the creation of the Political Security Committee (PSC), European Union Military Committee (EUMC) and European Union Military Staff (EUMS). These developments signified indeed a military revolution in the European Union's evolution as an international actor and spelt the end of the European Union's long-established self-image as a purely 'civilian power' (Gnesotto 2004).

For EU–NATO relations, this shift meant a further EU move into NATO's operational domain. Yet, despite ESDP's institutional advances, by 2002, the European Union still lacked the operational capabilities for conducting its own crisis management mission. As long as the build-up of the European Union's own capacities was still incomplete, functional cooperation with NATO – and the European Union's use of NATO assets in particular – was still essential. Despite earlier reservations, particularly by the French, about the detrimental effect a formally institutionalized EU–NATO relationship – including the danger of an over-reliance on NATO replication – could have on the independent development of ESDP, the formalization process of EU–NATO relations gained a clear momentum by the summer of 2000 (Reichard 2006: 124–125). Parallel to the increasing number of informal meetings between key individuals of both organizations since 1997 and between the European Union's interim PSC and NATO's North Atlantic Council (NAC) at ambassadorial level since autumn 2000,[1] negotiations on permanent and formalized cooperation arrangements between the European Union and NATO lasted from 1999 to 2003. After having overcome several obstacles and objections, particularly from non-EU NATO members, most notably Turkey, a political and diplomatic break-through in the evolution of EU–NATO relations was achieved at the EU Council summit in Copenhagen in December 2002. After half a century of structured separation between both organizations, the 'EU–NATO Declaration on ESDP' announced the establishment of an effective 'strategic partnership' (NATO 2002) in the field of crisis management. This 'mutually reinforcing' EU–NATO 'relationship' was to be founded on the principles of

106 *Johannes Varwick and Joachim Koops*

'effective mutual consultation, dialogue, cooperation and transparency' as well as on 'equality and due regard for the decision-making autonomy and interests of the EU and NATO' (ibid.). Thus, whilst the declaration stressed that the 'European Union and NATO were organizations of a different nature', it nevertheless called for overall close cooperation and coordination 'with a spirit of openness' between the European Union and NATO 'in order to provide one of the indispensable foundations for a stable Euro-Atlantic security environment' (ibid.).

Three months after this declaration, the practical details of this arrangement were eventually concluded on 17 March 2003 in the form of over a dozen classified agreements and under the overall label of 'Berlin Plus' – indicating its more technical nature as well as its actual proximity to the WEU–NATO Berlin Accords of 1996. Indeed, despite the December 2002 declaration's promisingly ambitious tone and wider political scope, in practice the Berlin Plus arrangement turned out to be a highly technical and rather limited mechanism on the secure exchange of information and, above all, for EU access to NATO's military assets and planning capabilities in the case of an EU-led crisis management mission.[2] As pointed out by a NATO official, 'Berlin Plus itself is a technical manual, not a political tool' (cited in Crisis Group 2005: 29). Hence, for those who expected a comprehensive 'grand bargain' on a more precisely defined EU–NATO role in collaboratively shaping the post-Cold War security environment as well as on the persistent transatlantic question of burden sharing, divisions of labour and EU autonomy, Berlin Plus represented a comprehensive disappointment (for a more in-depth critique, see Cornish 2006: 12). As soon as Berlin Plus was formally concluded, there was a tacit understanding that these questions and the precise nature and operability of the EU–NATO relationship had to be decided on an *ad hoc*, bottom-up basis in the field.

Increasing interactions, ambiguous relations: The question of EU autonomy revisited

Two weeks after the formal conclusion of the EU–NATO Berlin Plus agreement, the European Union's operation *Concordia* in Macedonia not only represented the European Union's first ever military mission, but also marked the first instance of actually putting Berlin Plus into practice in the field. The aim of this rather modest mission, which lasted from March to December 2003 and involved 357 troops, was to continue the stabilization efforts of the preceding NATO mission *Operation Allied Harmony* in Macedonia. In line with the EU–NATO procedures, the EU relied on NATO's operational headquarters in Mons, Belgium, and 'borrowed' NATO's Deputy Supreme Allied Commander Europe (D-SACEUR) as *Concordia*'s Operational Commander. The Force Commander on the ground was a French EU general. The mission was regarded as a success for both the European Union's military debut and, more importantly, for the actual implementation of 'Berlin Plus'. Thus, *Concordia* not only signalled the advancement of the EU–NATO relationship into the practical realm, but also served as an important preparation for the second, more ambitious and more complex military

The EU and NATO   107

operation under the EU–NATO Berlin Plus mechanisms: the European Union's mission EUFOR *Althea* in Bosnia. Launched in December 2004 in direct succession to NATO's Stabilization Force, this remains the European Union's largest and longest military operation to date. Bearing in mind the European Union's ineptitude and disastrous handling of the Bosnian war during the 1990s, the cooperation with NATO, and indeed NATO's continued presence in Sarajevo, was vital (Grevi *et al.* 2005: 7). Following the Berlin Plus procedures, the European Union has once again relied for its Operation Commander on NATO's D-SACEUR, whilst providing its own force commander. The European Union's Political and Security Committee exercises the overall strategic direction of the mission and the EU Military Committee monitors its implementation.[3] NATO's D-SACEUR mainly reports to the EU's Military Committees. Indeed, overall, *Concordia* and *Althea* have demonstrated a successful and promising implementation of the Berlin Plus arrangements in the field (Kupferschmidt 2006). Furthermore, as a result of both Berlin Plus military missions, a dense network of frequent and effective interactions between EU and NATO military staffs and strategic planners has been progressively forged. This has contributed to stronger bonds and mutual organizational understandings between the European Union and NATO in the realm of crisis management (interview with NATO official, Crisis Management Unit, November 2007).

Yet, beyond these two carefully controlled missions, the EU–NATO relationship as a whole remains more ambiguous, mostly due to two major reasons. First, on the wider political level, interorganizational cooperation and formal exchanges between the European Union and NATO have become rather limited. This is mostly due to the blocking manoeuvres by France and, since the European Union's 2004 enlargement, increasingly by Turkey. Whilst France has persistently viewed closer EU–NATO relations as a constant limitation on the European Union's autonomy, Turkey's refusal of any official EU–NATO exchanges in the presence of the non-NATO EU member Cyprus has been explained by Turkey's frustrations over the unsettled Cyprus conflict, over its stalling EU accession process and over its lack of decision-making influence in ESDP (Hofmann and Reynolds 2007: 2–4). As a result, the political EU–NATO dialogue has almost come to a halt in recent years. Second, the European Union's continued eagerness to demonstrate its military autonomy from NATO has not only reinforced the underlying tendencies of interorganizational rivalry, but has also in several instances directly undermined the spirit of the Berlin Plus arrangement itself. This was most acutely highlighted by the lack of agreement between the European Union and NATO on who should respond to the African Union's request for a strategic airlift for its military mission in Sudan in 2005. Whilst the United Kingdom, Italy and The Netherlands preferred a NATO mission, France, Germany and Greece supported the idea of an EU mission (Touzkovskaia 2006: 252). In the end, after severe interorganizational procrastination that did as much damage to the credibility of each organization's rapid reaction mechanism as to the relevance of Berlin Plus itself, both organizations launched separate missions.

108   *Johannes Varwick and Joachim Koops*

In addition to this head-on collision, further instances of the underlying process of the European Union's *autonomization* in the field of crisis management – that is, the build-up and promotion of ESDP capacities and activities independent and distinct from NATO and outside the Berlin Plus framework – have heightened the tensions within the EU–NATO relationship. They ranged from the fractious proposal for an autonomous EU operational planning cell made by France, Germany, Belgium and Luxembourg at their Tervuren Summit in April 2003 and the launch of three autonomous military crisis management missions in support of the United Nations (*Artemis* and *EUFOR RD Congo* in the Democratic Republic of Congo in 2003 and 2006, respectively, as well as the currently planned *EUFOR Chad/RCA* in Eastern Chad and North Eastern Central African Republic) to the creation of so-called EU Battlegroups. The Tervuren proposal provoked fierce reactions from the United States, which perceived it as a direct threat to NATO and as a further hostile act from 'old Europe' in the wake of the transatlantic controversies over the invasion of Iraq. In the end, a compromise was reached by the establishment of a EU cell within NATO's Supreme Headquarters Allied Command for the operational planning of Berlin Plus missions and a small civil–military cell (Civ-Mil cell) at the EUMS for the planning of EU autonomous, but primarily small-scale, civilian–military crisis management missions (Howorth 2007: 111–112). It was thus specifically designed to avoid rivalry with NATO in the realm of 'pure' military missions. However, in December 2004, the Civ-Mil cell was tasked to set up an EU 'Operations Centre', which had been fully activated in June 2007 and is now also envisaged to be used for autonomous 'predominantly military operations' (European Council Secretariat 2007a: 2). Thus, the previous compromise's limitation on civilian–military operations has been quietly dropped and reveals the strong *autonomization* tendencies of the ESDP. These have been reinforced by the European Union's autonomous military missions. In the case of *Artemis*, the lack of prior consultation with NATO or the United States in the run-up to the operation raised some diplomatic eye brows and hedged further mistrust (Kupferschmidt 2006: 26). *EUFOR RD Congo* provides another illuminating case. Whilst an initially reluctant Germany was persuaded both by French policy-makers, and in particular by the EU High Representative Solana, to take on the overall command of the mission (interview with German EU Council Secretariat Official, Brussels, 6 July 2007), Germany at first suggested a mission under the 'Berlin Plus' arrangement in cooperation with NATO. In the end, the French insistence on an independent EU mission run from the German Operation Headquarters in Potsdam prevailed (Shimkus 2007: para. 24), highlighting the urge for EU autonomy. Finally, the practical experiences drawn from the ESDP's first autonomous military mission *Artemis* had a direct 'spill over' effect on the emergence of the British–French–German initiative for the so-called EU Battlegroups. Operational since January 2007, the 1,500 troop-strong rapid reaction forces are either formed by a single nation or composed multinationally of up to four member states, and are specifically but not exclusively designed for UN support missions on the African continent (European Council Secretariat 2007b). Concerns have been voiced over the potential rivalry between the Battlegroups and NATO's

Response Force (NRF), which essentially draw on the same national sets of resources (Lindstrom 2007: 48–49). However, with NATO's announcement in September 2007 that national contributions to the NRF were severely falling short, the European Union's Battlegroup concept seemed to have become the member states' preferred option (Dempsey 2007). The Battlegroups not only seem to function as a 'catalyst' for the European Union's promotion of multinational interoperability and military transformations, but also for further advances in the progressive integration and *Europeanization* of national defence policies within the context of the European Union's ESDP (Shimkus 2007: para. 11; Boyer and Quille 2007). Taken together, these developments not only highlight the European Union's increasing strife for UN-centred, NATO-independent missions, but also show that the European Union's move towards *autonomization* is deeply embedded in an underlying process of *Europeanization*. This does not only mean that national military policies and cultures are increasingly influenced by the ESDP-level or by the preferences of other member states, but also that, in the context of the EU–NATO relationship, such a process is intimately related to a 'de-NATOization' of national policies: the partial shift of national preferences from NATO to the European Union's ESDP. Thus, parallel to the European Union's successful interaction with NATO in the context of their two Berlin Plus missions in the Balkans, the European Union's instances of choosing autonomy over EU–NATO cooperation, or at least consultation, render the EU–NATO relationship as a whole and as acutely ambiguous. Indeed, in combination with the current short falls of the EU–NATO consultation mechanism at the political level, these tendencies have led some commentators to speculate whether *Althea* has indeed been the last operation under Berlin Plus (Yost 2007: 89).

In the short and medium term, however, this seems unlikely. Despite the cumbersome and technical nature of Berlin Plus, the European Union is still not in a position to run a long-term and complex military mission, such as *Althea*, on its own without recourse to NATO's capabilities. A common feature of the European Union's three autonomous missions in Congo and Chad is that they remain rather faint in terms of military impact and strong in terms of Europeanized symbolism. Ironically, at the current stage of EU–NATO relations, the European Union seems to apply the lessons learned from its cooperation with NATO – such as the design of the ESDP's military institutions or the operational procedures in the field – to missions that aid and contribute to the European Union's proliferation and visibility as an international actor in the realm of military crisis management on the one hand, and the European Union's slow but increasing 'emancipation' from NATO on the other. This autonomy reflex at the interorganizational and increasingly *Europeanized* national level raises some doubts about the European Union's long-term interest in the EU–NATO collaboration system, at least at the political level. At the operational level in the field, however, cooperation and coordination attempts remain strong and effective. This will have to be kept in mind when assessing the EU–NATO nexus within the wider context of the European Union's pursuit of its foreign policy strategy of effective multilateralism in the final section. At first, however, we shall take a

110   *Johannes Varwick and Joachim Koops*

closer look at the external and internal factors and causes of the major changes identified in this section.

Potential explanations and drivers of change: External and internal factors

In this section, we summarize and analyse the key factors and processes driving the changes in the EU–NATO relationship. In line with the analytical approach of this volume, we distinguish between external and internal factors of change and assess their relative importance. By external factors, we refer to major structural changes, power shifts, and exogenous shocks in the international system. Furthermore, the external factor of 'other organizations and governments' – predominantly, the United Nations and the United States – will be looked at. Internal factors, on the other hand, include the impact of shifts at the national, organizational, interorganizational and individual level. These range from policies pursued by key member states, direct interorganizational interaction and the role of individuals in executive positions either at the organizational or national level. The influence of political and military cultures will also be touched upon in this category. Finally, we will be looking at the underlying process of Europeanization as an important internal, but also increasingly externalized, underlying process of change.

The end of the Cold War: The underlying structural factor

The end of the Cold War represents in many ways the crucially permissible 'master variable' and was a decisive, structural factor of change in the early stages of the evolving EU–NATO relationship. It was the end of the East–West conflict that both permitted and forced a re-evaluation of the European Union's and NATO's roles in the newly uncertain, fundamentally re-forming international system. With the demise of the Soviet Union, the Euro-Atlantic Security architecture that had persisted – French ambitions notwithstanding – without any major challenges throughout the Cold War lost its key disciplining threat and, in the case of NATO, its actual *raison d'être* overnight. Whilst NATO was forced to fundamentally adapt and transform in order to justify its post-Soviet existence, the European Union faced, for the first time in the history of the integration project, an external environment which gave it the legitimacy to create a *Common Foreign and Security Policy*. This was a major development that had been unattainable throughout the Cold War, when Western European leaders had little incentive to organize their own defence within a separate organizational set-up, beyond – let alone outside – the US security guarantee embodied by NATO. This, however, changed dramatically in the post-Cold War context, where European leaders could no longer count on, or were no longer content with, a dominant US military engagement in Europe. The creation of a European Security Defence Policy in the context of the European Union – and thus the subsequent need for some sort of EU–NATO arrangement – was facilitated by a combination of further external factors intimately connected to

The EU and NATO   111

the main underlying structural change of the international system: exogenous shocks as well as the external role of the United States and United Nations.

Exogenous shocks: The Balkans, '9/11', Iraq and Sudan

Exogenous shocks, such as the Bosnian War from 1991 to 1995, the Kosovo War in 1999, the terrorist attacks on New York and Washington in 2001 as well as the Iraq War of 2003, were important factors with differing consequences for the European Union, NATO and their common relationship. As we have seen, the Europeans and European Union's own inability to intervene militarily in the Bosnian and Kosovo conflicts, coupled with a US reluctance to get involved in this essentially European affair, served as an important impetus for the European Union's subsequent militarization. For NATO, both conflicts presented external opportunities for re-establishing its post-Cold War relevance in the field of crisis management. Furthermore, the emergence of NATO's consolidated role and military primacy in the context of the Bosnian conflict and the formative and positive experience gained by European armed forces participating in NATO's IFOR convinced European leaders in the mid-1990s to pursue an ESDI within NATO (Wallace 2005: 439; Medcalf 2006: 84). Kosovo, however, represented both the zenith and key turning point for NATO's primacy as a crisis manager. Although externally perceived, despite numerous complications, as another demonstration of NATO's military effectiveness, the mission itself was hampered by intra-Alliance disputes on the selection of targets, the use of ground forces and the avoidance of civilian casualties, which particularly in US circles led to severe frustrations over the multilateral drawbacks of such a 'war by committee' (Clark 2002). Once again, the fact that the United States had to provide the vast majority of air strikes, due to a lack of European resources, but was still restrained in its decision-making autonomy, meant that Kosovo marked the beginning of the end of NATO's usefulness in the eyes of US military strategists. As a Pentagon official vividly explained, 'if anyone thinks that the US is ever going to use the North Atlantic Council to run another military campaign, they must be smoking pot' (cited in Biscop 2006: 8). At the same time, the Kosovo episode convinced in particular French leaders to press ahead with an autonomization of ESDP outside NATO and safely beyond US dominance (Howorth 2007: 157).

For NATO, the consequences of Kosovo were the beginning of waning support from both the Europeans and the United States, which brought the organization under fierce existentialist pressures once more. The US post-9/11 refusal to use NATO for the initial phase of the campaign in Afghanistan, despite the symbolic gesture of NATO's first ever evocation of its collective defence Article 5, and the US 'coalition-of-the-willing' style operation in Iraq 2003, further reinforced the impression that the United States was indeed itself 'decoupling' from NATO. Combined with the tensions within the Alliance in the run-up to the Iraq War and the rise of the European Union's military dimension, NATO has come under increasing existentialist stress, which also partly explains its interest in a potentially face-saving, closer EU–NATO relationship in crisis management. NATO's post-9/11

112 *Johannes Varwick and Joachim Koops*

role in the international efforts against terrorism and its current engagement in Afghanistan provide both external opportunities for a strengthening of NATO's role transformation and prestige, but also – in the case of failure – a potential death-trap (Goldirova 2008). For the European Union, the Iraq War – despite the internal rift it created temporarily between those governments who opposed a US-led invasion of Iraq without a UN Security Council Mandate and those who supported it – nevertheless had a unifying long-term effect as it provided the external impetus for the European Union's ESS and the concept of effective multilateralism in the first place. Thus, these exogenous shocks affected the European Union and NATO almost in opposite ways: whilst the European Union's failure in the Balkans accelerated the strengthening of its military capacities, NATO's most important support-base slowly but surely decoupled from NATO since, and as a result of, its campaign in Kosovo. Whilst the Iraq War tarnished NATO's coherence and the 'war on terror' and NATO's first out-of-area mission in Afghanistan provide something of an existentialist test case for NATO, the European Union capitalized on the galvanizing shock of the Iraq War by making an important step towards the formulation of a putative common strategic identity that also links the European Union's activities in crisis management to the United Nations (see below). Overall, therefore, these external crises curiously facilitated the rise of the European Union's ESDP on the one hand, whilst contributing to the weakening of NATO on the other. For the evolution of the EU–NATO relationship, this has been an important external factor for the shift in the relative power distribution between both organizations, where NATO seems to be increasingly on the back foot. Finally, the conflict in Sudan and the subsequent request to both the European Union and NATO for the support of the African Union's mission has been an important external trigger for a rather explicit episode of interorganizational competition. Although NATO and EU military officials have lessened the impact of this rift by cooperating closely on the ground, the Sudan case will remain a key reminder of the competition inherent in the EU–NATO relationship and of the fact that 'mutual reinforcement' is a demanding goal, not an automatic given in EU–NATO relations.

'Significant Others': The role of the United States, United Nations and African Union

The influence of the United States has been as much a key external factor for the formation of the Cold War Euro-Atlantic Security structure as it has been for the post-Cold War evolution of the EU–NATO relationship. As we have seen, shifting US post-Cold War strategic interests away from Europe and towards Asia and the Middle East convinced Europeans, particularly the British, to build up their own defence capacities. Throughout the 1990s, the US positions on a more autonomous European role in defence ranged from outright opposition to conditional support. Once the EU Council Summits of Cologne and Helsinki affirmed in 1999 the development of the ESDP, it was above all US external pressure that pushed for a formalization of EU–NATO relations, thus representing a key external factor for the dense institutionalization of the EU–NATO relationship (Reichard 2006: 152; Howorth 2007: 163). In a more indirect way, the increasingly unilateralist and assertive foreign policy of the Bush administration since 9/11, particularly its ambivalence towards the United Nations in the context of the Iraq War and of the wider strategic interests in the 'war on terror', may have been an important factor in provoking a distinct EU strategic response with a conscious emphasis on multilateralism and the UN (Jørgensen 2006: 205). In the field of crisis management, the UN has become an important external focal-organization for the European Union's autonomous military crisis management activities, as exemplified by the European Union's missions *Artemis*, *EUFOR RD Congo* and *EUFOR Chad*, which were launched with the explicit goal of supporting the UN peace-keeping activities. Similarly, the EU Battlegroups were created with the express aim of supporting the UN, particularly on the African continent (Lindstrom 2007: 11; Koops 2007: 4). Thus, both the UN and the African Union provide an important strategic context for the European Union's autonomous military mission. Indeed, it could be argued that these missions provide a welcome external opportunity for the European Union to demonstrate both its role as a staunch UN supporter and for differentiating and distancing itself from both the United States and NATO in the field of crisis management. The UN thereby functions as an important legitimizer and receiver of the European Union's strive for more autonomy in the military realm and a key facilitator of the European Union's development of a more distinct international actorness and identity. These missions, arguably, not only provide the European Union with more visibility, but also with more independence vis-à-vis NATO. Thus, both the UN and the African Union, in effect, have been important external factors for the European Union's autonomization.[4]

Internal factors of change

Whilst external factors were at work for setting the overall structural preconditions that made an emerging EU–NATO relationship possible in the first place, and while exogenous shocks and the role of the United States and UN go a long way in explaining the changing EU–NATO power balance and the external context for a more UN-centred international identity, only internal factors can mainly explain the dynamics of EU–NATO interorganizationalism and the tendencies and dynamics of the European Union's Europeanized militarization.

Factors at the member state level

As we have seen, the Franco-British declaration on European Defence, announced by Jacques Chirac and Tony Blair on 4 December 1998 at St Malo, marked a fundamental break-through for the European Union's militarization, with crucial implications for the European Union's relations to and with NATO. Indeed, the agreement that 'in order to play its full role on the international stage [...] the European Union must have the capacity for autonomous action, backed by credible military forces [and] the means to decide to use them [...] where the Alliance as a whole is not engaged' (UK FCO 1998), was only made possible by Tony Blair's break with a 50-year-old British foreign policy veto on any multilateral military institutions that could potentially be autonomous from the United States or NATO. In contrast to French leaders, who have throughout the Cold War sought to build up the European Community as a counter-balance to the United States, Britain remained a staunch Atlanticist and something of a reluctant and weary European. The British concession to the French position on the issue of an EU military dimension was therefore ground breaking. The British prime minister did not, however, agree to use ESDP as a counterweight to the United States or as a tool to undermine NATO. For Blair, the prospect of assuming a leadership role in a major EU project – particularly after Britain had already been marginalized through its absence from the European Monetary Union – seems to have been part of the motivation behind the decision to give his blessing to ESDP (Deighton 2002: 725). Another reason, however, was his belief that – after the Europeans' failure to significantly improve their capabilities within either the WEU or NATO itself – the ESDP would provide a more compelling context for Europe's capability improvements, and would thereby strengthen the transatlantic Alliance and reduce the negative imbalances and lack of 'burden sharing' within the transatlantic relationship (Howorth 2003: 246–247). This is indeed why the St Malo Declaration explicitly stressed that the European Union's military project would be 'contributing to the vitality of a modernized Atlantic Alliance' (UK FCO 1998). Arguably, for the British Labour party, ESDP could be seen as the outward projection of the 'Third Way' to the foreign policy realm: a middle path between Atlanticism and Europeanism (Wallace and Oliver 2005: 162). St Malo did not mean, however, that the French and British positions did fully converge. Britain maintained its Atlanticist reflex, acting on many occasions as NATO's advocate, whilst France continues to interpret ESDP as a tool for a truly independent European international role. This explains the persistent French tendency to push for autonomous ESDP military missions, such as *Artemis* or *EUFOR RD Congo*, on the one hand, and, as we shall see, its veto on any initiative that could enhance NATO's role vis-à-vis ESDP, on the other. These tensions between the British and French positions have been seamlessly imported to the level of EU–NATO relations, highlighting the importance of these internal factors at the member state level for the evolution and dynamics of the EU–NATO relationship. Between the French and British poles, Germany was expected to play the role of a strong mediator (Varwick 2006: 16). From NATO's perspective, however, this hope has not materialized (interview with NATO Official, Public Diplomacy Division, November 2007). Instead, Germany has increasingly participated in and adapted to the ESDP's context and policies, epitomized by its eventual decision to take on the operational command of the European Union's mission *EUFOR RD Congo* in 2006 without recourse to Berlin Plus. Particularly in response to the more assertive US unilateralism under the Bush administration and in the wake of Iraq, the German government under Gerhard Schröder began a reorientation away from NATO and decidedly towards 'putting ESDP first' (Bornefeld-Ettmann *et al.* 2007: 138–139). This tells us as much about the shifting power balance between the European Union and NATO as it does about ESDP's Europeanizing appeal to and impact on key member states.

By Europeanization we refer to the complex integrative process by which the foreign policy interests, identities and security cultures of member states are both projected to and influenced by the European level (see also Wong 2005: 135–139). Thus, whilst key EU member states, such as France in particular, have managed to project their preferences to the ESDP domain, other member states, such as Germany, have used the ESDP context for a fundamental reorientation of their security identities. Most recently, even staunch, traditional NATOists, such as Poland, seemed to have progressively shifted their interests from NATO to the European Union as a result of participation in ESDP procedures and missions (Blaszczyk *et al.* 2007: 153). One explanation could be that member states perceive a greater degree of influence and ownership in the shaping of policies and institutional transformations of ESDP compared with their impact on a, however reluctantly, US-dominated NATO. The Europeanization of member states' foreign policies and military cultures also implies – with the exception of the 'Third Way Atlanticism' of Britain – that, on the member state level, preferences and organizational support bases are clearly shifting from NATO to the European Union, providing an important internal factor for increasing the power asymmetry between both organizations within the EU–NATO relationship.

Interorganizational and interpersonal factors

Dynamics at the interorganizational and interpersonal level have been important factors for the early phase of EU–NATO cooperation and the move towards the formalization of their relations. The early post-Cold War overlap of interests and competences between the European Union and NATO – with both organizations concentrating on newly emerging security concepts of 'crisis management' – created the potential for both cooperation and mutual reinforcement on the one hand as well as for inherent competition on the other.[5] As we have seen, after the European Union's decision to take over the WEU's tasks at the EU Council Summit in Cologne in 1999, external pressures by the United States pushed for a clarification and formalization of the relations between the European Union's emerging ESDP and NATO. Significantly, informal meetings already took place from 1997 between Javier Solana – NATO Secretary General at that time – the President of the EU Commission Jacques Santer and the Commissioner for Foreign Relations, Hans van den Broek (Reichard 2006: 122). This highlights that it was in fact the EU Commission, not the EU Council, which advanced EU–NATO informal exchanges in the early years. However, with the appointment of Javier Solana in October 1999 as the European Union's first High Representative for the Common and Foreign Security Policy the formalization and clarification of EU–NATO relations gained significant momentum within the ESDP context. In particular, the effective working relationship between Solana and his successor as NATO Secretary General, George Robertson – who previously as the former British defence minister had been a key architect of the St Malo agreement – proved to be a crucial factor for the rapid advance of EU–NATO relations. Under the Solana–Robertson leadership, a raft of EU–NATO cooperation channels was developed, such as the interim PSC–NAC meetings at ambassadorial and ministerial level. Most crucially, however, they were both instrumental for the eventual conclusion of the Berlin Plus agreement (ibid.: 123–125). This not only highlights the importance of the relationship between organizations' 'executive leaders' (Cox 1973) – acting as 'boundary spanners' (Biermann 2008: 166) – for the advancement and deepening of interorganizational relations, but also underlines the significance of the so-called alumni effect: the enabling impact of a leader switching from one organization to another and thereby facilitating interorganizational understandings and cooperation between the two organizations (Jönsson 1995: 2–3; Koops 2008: 27). Similar arguments about the importance of interpersonal relations have been made with reference to the initial establishments of closer cooperation between the WEU and NATO during the early 1990s, which, as William Wallace argues, were partly due to 'the excellent personal relations between NATO's German Secretary-General and his Dutch counterpart at the WEU' (Wallace 2005: 439). The actual practical application of Berlin Plus through the military missions *Concordia* and *Althea* was reportedly also facilitated by the good working relations between the military officers of both organizations in the field, particularly in the case of NATO's British Operation Commander John Reith and the European Union's British Force Commander David Leakey (Hofmann and Reynolds 2007: 5). Notwithstanding the current impasses at the political PSC–NAC level, the two Berlin Plus missions have also contributed to an overall consolidation and deepening of the EU–NATO relationship at the institutional level: whilst the European Union adopted NATO's military operational structures throughout both missions, both organizations also learned important interorganizational 'lessons' from their direct cooperation. As we shall discuss in more detail below, together with the European Union's learning from NATO's institutional design – particularly the European Union's replication of NATO's military committee – the interaction of both organizations in the field has led to a process of interorganizational assimilation on the part of the European Union. Whilst this facilitated cooperation, it was arguably also one factor for the European Union's increasing efforts to raise its own profile by launching its own autonomous missions and by making its NATO-dependent *Althea* mission more distinct from NATO's preceding SFOR operation (Leakey 2006: 59), thereby heightening the potential for image and identity rivalries. Indeed, in this context the role of Javier Solana has been crucial. Whilst having been a key driving force for the establishment of formal EU–NATO relations from 1999 to 2003, since the inception of *Concordia*, CFSP's High Representative was now increasingly pushing for the Europeanization of military activities and a more visible EU role (Barros-Garcia 2007). This, by implication, increased EU autonomy from NATO and competitive tensions between both organizations. In this context, the process of Europeanization of the European Union's military policies has been a crucial factor behind the European Union's moves towards greater autonomy and behind the increased potential for EU–NATO tensions as well as for the power shifts in the current phase of the EU–NATO relationship's evolution.

Overall, whilst external factors were important for setting the overall context and providing further stimuli that made the emergence of an EU–NATO relationship possible in the first place, internal factors – particularly the role of individuals – are better suited to explain the development of the relationship since the Franco-British decision on ESDP at St Malo. Indeed, similar to Blair's role in bringing about a fundamental shift of the British position on ESDP, analysts speculate that Nicolas Sarkozy could initiate a U-turn of the French stance towards NATO (Valasek 2007). A French rapprochement with NATO could signify a 'St Malo in reverse', as it were: strengthening NATO in return for further advances in ESDP. Finally, the role and influence of Javier Solana was important in promoting the formalization of Berlin Plus until 2003, followed by increased EU autonomy and visibility in the field from 2003 onwards, based on lessons learned from EU–NATO cooperation. Eventually, the internal twin processes of Europeanization and autonomization, facilitated by Solana's Council Secretariat, the European Union's independent military missions, and an effort to carve out a distinct identity vis-à-vis NATO and the United States, have contributed to the current interorganizational tensions and power shift within the EU–NATO nexus.

The EU–NATO relationship: Effective multilateralism or 'shrewd interorganizationalism' in the making?

In this final section, we seek to evaluate the EU–NATO relationship in the wider context of the European Union's interorganizational strategy of effective multilateralism. By applying our previous findings to a comparative analysis of the European Union's and NATO's impact on each other's policies, developments and institutional designs, we seek to assess what the empirical example of the EU–NATO nexus can tell us about the European Union's actual implementation and pursuit of its foreign policy concept of effective multilateralism in practice. As outlined in the ESS, effective multilateralism affirms the European Union's goal of strengthening other major international organizations and of equipping them with the necessary tools for fulfilling their respective roles and responsibilities in the international system (ESS 2003: 9). Thus, as Fraser Cameron (2005: 3) notes, 'if the EU wishes to promote "effective multilateralism" and ensure that conflict prevention and crisis management remain a priority, it must seek to strengthen its own role in the major international institutions as well as the institutions themselves'. Whether, how and with what impact this has been achieved through the EU–NATO relationship or to what extent it itself only reinforces an EU instrumental approach to effective multilateralism in the military realm forms the main focus of the final analysis below.

The European Union's limited impact on NATO

Despite the dense and highly institutionalized relationship between the European Union and NATO, the European Union's impact on NATO's policies, transformation

118   *Johannes Varwick and Joachim Koops*

or even institutional design has been rather negligible. Yet, it is important to note at the outset that unlike in other EU–IO relationships, where there is a strong EU Commission participation or a high degree of joint-voting discipline amongst EU member states (as is the case, e.g., in the EU–WTO or EU–UN General Assembly relationship, respectively), it is still inconceivable for the European Union to 'speak with one voice' within the Atlantic Alliance.

For one, it has been the long-standing attitude of US administrations and non-EU NATO members to vigorously oppose any idea of a unified European caucus within NATO (Biscop 2006: 9; Howorth 2003: 263). The prospect of being presented by a pre-negotiated, common EU position would not only pre-empt NATO's function as a decision-making and discussion forum in its own right, but would also seriously weaken the influence of the five remaining non-EU members within NATO. Thus, there is a considerable level of resistance amongst NATO members against even the suggestion of a common EU bloc within NATO (Valasek 2007: 5). Compared with other EU–IO relationships, the European Union's potential for impact may also be more limited due to the fact that the EU Commission and the EU Parliament are mostly marginalized in what is essentially an intergovernmental ESDP–NATO affair.[6] This might prevent a more comprehensive and also a more multifaceted EU impact, although, conversely, the absence of the usual EU inter-pillar turf wars should also be a positive, impact-enhancing factor.

More significantly, notwithstanding the Europeanization of EU member states' foreign policy preferences with respect to the European Union, the persistent difference in the key member states' positions on and strategies towards NATO – especially amongst the French and British governments – prevents a stable and common EU approach towards NATO at the member state level. Indeed, France's traditional NATO aversion and its regular opposition to initiatives that could significantly enhance NATO's role or transformation have been a reappearing trait of French foreign policy (Michel 2007; Soutou 2005). Unsurprisingly, France has also been one of the strongest opponents of an EU–NATO proposal with which the European Union could indeed have one of the most profound impacts on NATO, in the one area where the European Union has developed a distinct comparative advantage: in the realm of civilian crisis management and post-conflict reconstruction. Since the Feira EU Council summit of June 2000, the European Union has been developing effective tools for post-conflict stabilization and civil–military approaches to security governance, including capacities for police, rule of law and civil administration missions (Nowack 2006: 19). In the light of NATO's challenges to its reconstruction efforts in Afghanistan and its limited resources and complete absence of civil–military planning capabilities, the idea of a 'Berlin Plus in Reverse' has emerged and has found much support in US and NATO circles (Howorth 2007: 175–176; de Hoop Scheffer 2007). Such an arrangement, as the precise mirror image of the European Union's access to NATO's military assets under the existing 'Berlin Plus' agreement, would in turn allow NATO to draw on the European Union's highly developed civil–military resources and planning expertise (Flournoy and Smith 2005: 70). Yet, alongside France, several EU member states have voiced their opposition to such an arrangement, which, it is feared,

The EU and NATO   119

would allow NATO to venture into civil–military affairs and could thereby rival the European Union's distinctive approach to crisis management (Valasek 2007; Yost 2007: 89, 110–111).

In the context of effective multilateralism's aim of strengthening other international organizations and equipping them with the necessary tools to act, the lack of support for a 'Berlin Plus in Reverse' surely represents as much a missed interorganizational opportunity for mutual reinforcement as it does for a material EU impact on NATO's policies and reconfigurations.[7] The aversions to such new schemes, however, also highlight a more general malaise of the current EU–NATO relationship: the tendency – partly due to French and Turkish pressures – not to widen interorganizational cooperation or innovation beyond a strict and narrow interpretation of the existing EU–NATO arrangements under Berlin Plus. As a result, present formal EU–NATO meetings and exchanges and discussions are mostly confined to technical discussions of the ongoing EU–NATO *Althea* mission in Bosnia, whilst wider and potentially fruitful initiatives, such as EU–NATO collaboration on terrorism or EU–NATO civil–military cooperation in Afghanistan, are firmly kept off the agenda (Carp 2006: 40). Hence, as David Yost (2007: 94) points out, 'as currently interpreted, the Berlin Plus package functions to restrict cooperation, not to facilitate and promote it'. Similarly, in his much noted Berlin Speech, NATO Secretary General Japp de Hoop Scheffer might have jested about the NATO–EU relationship being a 'frozen conflict', but he rather accurately noted that 'some deliberately want to keep NATO and the EU at a distance from one another' (de Hoop Scheffer 2007: 3; see also Biermann 2008: 17). Taken together, these dynamics do not give encouraging signals, neither about the future of an effective EU–NATO multilateralism nor about a sizable EU impact on NATO.

However, beyond the issues surrounding Berlin Plus and direct, material impacts, there are arguments to be made about a more subtle, indirect EU impact on NATO in general, ideational terms. Hanna Ojanen, for example, points out that the European Union's own enlargement and institutional adaptation efforts contributed significantly to shaping NATO's own identity and post-Cold War transformation attempts (Ojanen 2004: 18). In terms of military capacity innovation and design, she also suggests that it was perhaps the European Union's decision to launch a European Rapid Reaction Force that has prompted NATO to follow suit with its own NRF (ibid.: 19). As we have seen above, similar arguments can be made about NATO's decision to launch a Maritime Security Strategy, not dissimilar to the EU Commission's proposal on a Maritime Directive, and, more fundamentally, to follow the European Union's decision on Eastern Enlargement at NATO's Brussels Summit in 1994 (Medcalf 2006: 131–132). With reference to enlargement, several commentators have also stressed, in a more explicitly constructivist fashion, the impact of the twin processes of EU and NATO enlargement towards the Central and Eastern European States on NATO's emerging role as a normative agent for democratization, stabilization and liberal socialization (Schimmelfennig 2003; Fierke and Wiener 2005). Taking their arguments a little further, one could argue that, within the framework of their parallel externalized Europeanization and stabilization process, the European Union contributed significantly to the shaping of NATO's emerging, highly politicized identity as a norm exporter. Arguably, this was aided by the fact that, although both enlargement processes were not formally coordinated, NATO membership was increasingly perceived by candidate states as a first step to EU membership, and thus as part and parcel of the same Europeanization process on the way to 'returning to Europe'. Thus, indirectly, the European Union could be seen as a co-sponsor of NATO's politicization and role diversification. In the same identity-shaping vein, it could also be argued that the European Union itself offered an important focus point and impetus for NATO's own identity 're-branding'. By associating itself and collaborating closely with the seemingly more dynamic security-newcomer European Union, it could be argued that NATO could shed, or at least diminish, its image as a Cold War relic in the process. Conceivably, the role as an EU-mentor could, at least in the short run, have also contributed to NATO's renewed sense of purpose. Considering the present EU–NATO problems and the lack of EU reciprocity, however, such a suggestion might seem rather cynical.

Whilst proving to be acutely difficult to verify empirically, these speculations about the European Union's indirect identity-shaping impacts on NATO raise crucial issues and aspects about the European Union's wider, ideational influence and form an important reminder of the wider 'soft issues' involved in evaluating interorganizational impact. Yet, they tell us little about the European Union's more direct impact on NATO's institutional design and strategic reforms. The truth on this matter remains that the lack of an overall more decisive EU impact on NATO's policies, institutions or reform process lies in the fact that it was mostly the United States, as NATO's most important internal and external factor, that almost single-handedly drove the organization's reform agenda. Indeed, with the exception of enlargement perhaps, the key changes in NATO's evolution, such as the decisions to transform it into a global alliance or an actor in the war on terror, were driven, and ultimately decided, by the United States (Medcalf 2006: 62; Lansford 2002; Varwick 2008: 164). It is thus perhaps not too surprising that the European Union's direct and more material impact and room for presenting reform initiatives were limited. Moreover, as we have seen above, the very fact that NATO has been a decidedly US-moulded and US-dominated organization caused EU member states to increasingly turn their attention towards the European Union in the first place, where they had hoped to increase their level of ownership and decision-making influence over European, and progressively globalizing, security policies. The European Union's key member states have had neither the means nor, increasingly, the interest in shaping NATO according to their preferences. Instead, as we have seen throughout this chapter, they focused on utilizing NATO for the build-up of the European Union's own structures. To this end, as we shall turn to in more detail below, NATO's impact on the European Union was crucial and far more pronounced than the European Union's impact on NATO.

NATO's 'enabling impact' on the European Union

NATO's impact on the European Union's institutional design, policies and actual experience gathering in the field of crisis management and wider security issues has been fundamental. Although NATO's own existence, role and function

The EU and NATO   121

represented throughout the Cold War a de facto veto on the European Union's development as an international actor in the military sphere, the post-Cold War period has reversed NATO's impact: from a constraint on the European Union towards becoming the key enabler and facilitator of the European Union's militarization. As soon as the European Union decided to develop the institutions deemed necessary for its European Defence and Security Policy in 1999, NATO officials had a decisive input in the creation of these institutions. As the vivid, albeit slightly hyperbolical, remark by a French Officer highlights:

> it was [...] rather as though the EU, having barely laid down the foundations for its own new construction, was being overwhelmed by consultants from the shiny glass and concrete NATO structures across the road, all proffering free advice on internal partitioning, electric wiring circuits, the positioning of water-pipes and the optimum number of floors.
>
> (Cited in Howorth 2007: 165)

However, even within EU circles it was clear that the institutional design of ESDP's key bodies would have to be modelled on NATO. Thus, the European Union's PSC was established as the equivalent of the North Atlantic Council and the ESDP's EUMC as well as the EUMS became a close replication of NATO's Military Committee and International Military Staff, respectively. Furthermore, the decision to appoint the former NATO Secretary General Javier Solana as the European Union's first High Representative was also, as we have seen, an instrumental factor in advancing the Europeanization of ESDP and the visibility of the European Union as an international actor. Beyond the institutional realm, and even before the creation of ESDP, NATO laid the fundamental ground work of a European military culture and the norm of multinational cooperation, which in effect provided the European Union with a vital head start for the development of its own military missions and multinational schemes. As Anthony Foster rightly notes, 'NATO has been influential in transmitting norms of professionalism, developing a common corpus of military doctrine, promoting interoperability and [...] minimising the fear of shared multinational command structures' (Foster 2006: 167).

NATO's most profound impact on ESDP has indeed been in the field. As we have seen above, NATO's operational support under Berlin Plus was indispensable for the European Union's first ever military mission, *Concordia*, and the ongoing mission *Althea* in Bosnia. In both missions, the European Union replicated and applied NATO's procedures and designs intimately (Kupferschmidt 2006; Juncos 2007). Indeed, applying the sociological concept of 'institutional isomorphism' to the EU–NATO relationship, Ana Juncos highlights how, by extensively learning and copying from NATO, ESDP has become strikingly similar to NATO in terms of institutional design, policies and performance in the field of crisis management (Juncos 2007). Most crucially, the European Union also continued to progressively transfer its learned NATO lessons to its own, autonomous missions, thereby increasing its own, independent actorness in the security realm. Indeed, for its first autonomous military mission, *Artemis* in the Democratic Republic of Congo, which was undertaken barely three months after

122   *Johannes Varwick and Joachim Koops*

the launch of *Concordia*, the European Union once again copied and adhered to NATO procedures throughout (Howorth 2005: 194). *Artemis* was not only a mission in support of the United Nations, thus heralding the European Union's shift from being a NATO consumer to becoming a UN provider, but also acted as the key inspiration for the European Union's Battlegroup Concept (Lindstrom 2007: 10). This was to further enhance its development towards an independent security actor. Thus, it has been one of the key ironies of the EU–NATO relationship that the institutional and operational 'lessons learned' from NATO have, ironically, aided the European Union's 'emancipation' from NATO in the end.

'Shrewd interorganizationalism' in the making

Indeed, the European Union's instrumentalization of NATO's enabling impact, coupled with the European Union's own limited impact on NATO, raises important questions about the European Union's adherence to the principles of its strategy of effective multilateralism and about the nature and function of the EU–NATO relationship therein. The evolution of the relationship so far suggests that the European Union has gained more than it has given. Indeed, the narrow implementation of the existing Berlin Plus package, and the absence of a 'Berlin Plus in Reverse' arrangement through which the European Union could reciprocate the access it has gained to NATO's assets, underlines the limited and asymmetrical impact between the European Union and NATO. More crucially, it also points to the fact that the EU–NATO relationship lacks one of the most fundamental features of multilateralism: 'diffuse reciprocity'. First coined by Robert Keohane (1985), 'diffuse reciprocity' describes one of the benefits of multilateral cooperation for participating actors who learn to shape their expectations and interests towards, in Caporaso's words, 'benefit[ing] in the long run and over many issues, rather than every time on every issue' (Caporaso 1992: 602). However, the narrow band-width and rather one-sided nature of the current EU–NATO relationship seem to still rather prevent long-term, mutual benefits.

Moreover, when it comes to a second, fundamental feature of multilateralism – cooperation based on 'generalized principles of conduct' (Ruggie 1993: 14) – the EU–NATO relationship does not seem to fare much better. As will be recalled, according to the EU–NATO Declaration on ESDP from December 2002, the EU–NATO relationship is founded on, *inter alia*, the general principles of 'partnership' – of 'ensuring that the crisis management of the two organizations are mutually reinforcing', of 'effective mutual consultation, dialogue, cooperation and transparency' and of 'coherent, transparent and mutually reinforcing development of the capability requirements common to the organizations, with a spirit of openness' (EU–NATO 2002). The lack of EU–NATO consultation prior to the launch of *Artemis*, the mutually restraining squabble over the African Union support mission in Sudan, the blocked dialogue in the NATO–EU Capability Group on mutually reinforcing capability developments and the inherent tensions between the EU Battlegroup scheme and the NRFs seem to undermine these general principles of conduct. Although, as we have highlighted, cooperation and mutual reinforcement seems to take place through informal

The EU and NATO   123

exchanges at the actual, operational level in the field, while the overarching political, formal relationship is unmistakably defunct. Arguably, the EU–NATO relationship's failure to meet two key requirements of multilateralism poses the question whether it actually deserves the label 'multilateralism', let alone 'effective multilateralism', at all.

What weighs far more heavily than the failure to adhere to scholarly definitions of multilateralism, however, is in this context the European Union's failure to adhere to its very own defining principles of effective multilateralism itself: namely, to strengthen international organizations and to equip them with the necessary tools (ESS 2003: 9). However, instead of strengthening 'its own role in the major international institutions as well as the institutions themselves' (Cameron 2005: 3), the European Union, at least in the case of its relations with NATO, seems to rather strengthen its own role through the partner institution. In the case of the EU–NATO nexus, this implies, as we have seen, a progressive autonomization and emancipation from NATO precisely as a result of drawing on the valuable and enabling experiences, institutional designs, learned lessons, capabilities and assets gained through EU–NATO cooperation in the first place. Hence, the European Union's approach to the EU–NATO relationship seems to highlight the European Union's essentially instrumental approach to multilateralism. It therefore leads us to the conclusion that the European Union's cooperation with NATO is less an example of altruistic 'effective multilateralism', than rather more an example of 'shrewd interorganizationalism' in the making: the European Union's tendency to use cooperation with other organizations for the enhancement and development of its own international actorness, capacities and strategic identity.

Conclusion

In this chapter, we sought to provide an evaluation of the EU–NATO aspect of the European Union's wider foreign policy strategy of effective multilateralism. We identified and analysed three key stages and principal changes in the post-Cold War evolution of the EU–NATO relationship. First, the beginning of a process of EU–NATO interorganizational convergence, particularly marked by the European Union's infringement on NATO's military domain. Second, the move towards a formalization of EU–NATO cooperation. Third, we concluded that the most recent and current phase in EU–NATO relations is characterized by the tensions between cases of effective EU–NATO cooperation in the field on the one hand, and the European Union's strive for military autonomy on the other, coupled with persistent EU–NATO political dysfunctions and rivalries.

We then analysed the key external and internal factors behind these changes and developments. Whilst external factors helped to set the overall structural preconditions and context for the emergence of the EU–NATO relationship in the first place, internal factors were better suited to explain the key developments and dynamics in the EU–NATO relationship since the St Malo Declaration. We identified in particular the crucial role of executive individuals at NATO and the European Union in furthering interorganizational cooperation, both at the political and military level.

124 *Johannes Varwick and Joachim Koops*

The former NATO Secretary General and current EU High Representative Javier Solana was identified as a key variable for facilitating the process of EU–NATO cooperation until at least 2004, and at the same time for fostering a Europeanization process through his work at the Council Secretariat and thus for decisively spurring the advance of the European Union's international actorness profile in the military field. Indeed, we highlighted that this process of Europeanization was an important internal factor for the European Union's autonomization by causing a slow but steady shift in the member states' strategic cultures and organizational preferences: away from NATO as the sole military agent, towards the European Union as an acceptable, and increasingly preferred, emerging alternative actor in crisis management. Overall, the analysis of the first two sections of this chapter showed that internal and external factors of change are intimately interlinked. External factors, such as the end of the Cold War or decisions by the US administrations, set the permissive parameters for subsequent developments that are mainly driven by internal processes and dynamics. Further exogenous shocks, such as external wars or international crises, might act as catalysts for hastening or re-channelling developments. But it is at the internal level where the external foundations and stimuli for change are either embraced and translated into historic advances or blocked and filibustered into lost opportunities. Again, the role of individuals and the socialization and Europeanization effects of ESDP institutions and missions were of crucial importance in the evolution of EU–NATO relations.

In the context of effective multilateralism, we sought to assess how exactly the European Union has used and translated the opportunity of the EU–NATO relationship into action. As we have seen, it has shrewdly used its interactions with NATO for its own institutional and operational advances in the military realm. Both the institutional structures, such as the PSC, EUMC and EUMS, and military procedures in the field have been replicated from NATO. Of course, this has not been done clandestinely against NATO's will and better judgement, but rather with the support of NATO officials. Yet, the EU–NATO relationship, as it currently stands, is characterized by mostly unidirectional impact and instrumentalization, where the European Union seems to be gaining more from its use of NATO than vice versa. Thus, the relationship's acute lack of 'diffuse reciprocity', which has long been agreed upon as the key feature of genuine multilateralism, leads us to question whether one could really regard the EU–NATO compact as an example of genuine 'effective multilateralism' between organizations. According to the ESS, effective multilateralism is pursued as a strategy to strengthen the key international organizations and the European Union's position within them. As we have noted at the outset, the EU–NATO relationship is one of the few examples where the European Union is structurally prevented from 'speaking with one voice' within NATO's North Atlantic Council. The other option, to strengthen the organization, in line with the European Union's espousal of effective multilateralism, would be by equipping NATO with the support and tools it needs to act as an effective organization. However, as we have shown, key EU member states prevent the European Union from providing NATO with access to the European Union's civilian instruments. Instead of viewing the EU–NATO relationship as an example of mutually reinforcing effective multilateralism, we have concluded that

The EU and NATO   125

it should rather be seen as an example of 'shrewd interorganizationalism' in the making, where the European Union relies on NATO in order to advance its own international actorness profile and assert its visibility and identity in the field of crisis management. This makes the European Union less and less a *sui generis* entity with a peculiarly inbuilt genetic code of altruistic foreign policy behaviour, but rather more and more like any other ordinary, interest-maximizing power in the international system.

However, the European Union's autonomization ambitions notwithstanding, for the future of transatlantic security relations, an effective cooperation system with NATO and the United States remains an indispensable imperative. Despite their differing views on the value and relevance of multilateralism, the European Union should continue to ensure that the United States remains a 'European power'. For the European Union, the strengthening of its own military capabilities will be as imperative as the strengthening of genuine links with NATO. To this end, the recent call by five former NATO generals for an 'EU–NATO steering directorate at the highest political level' indicates the will – albeit rather at the military level than at the political level – for revitalizing transatlantic security relations with a coordinated EU–NATO nexus at its core (Naumann *et al.* 2007: 144). For the foreseeable future, as the European Union's autonomous missions have highlighted – the European Union's current problems with the mission in Chad, in particular – the European Union might arguably remain an awkward 'civilian power with teeth' (Schmalz 2005: 57–59). NATO, despite facing severe existential problems of its own, might for the time being still remain better placed for high-intensity operations. In view of the European Union's ambitions in the military realm, the future relations between NATO and the European Union will, no doubt, continue to be dominated by rivalry and competition. However, in view of the broad congruence of membership in both organizations and the fact of a 'single set of forces' as well as the demanding international security policy agenda, it would be highly inefficient – politically and militarily – if both organizations were busy with themselves in some kind of beauty contest instead of giving effective impetus to the stabilization of the international system and to actively contributing to the solution of current and future security policy problems.

Notes

1 The first informal contacts between both organizations since were in fact held between Javier Solana – NATO Secretary General at that time – the President of the EU Commission Jacques Santer and the Commissioner for Foreign Relations, Hans van den Broek. These meetings took place at regular intervals from 1997 (Reichard 2006: 122) and highlight that it was in fact the Commission, not the EU Council, which advanced the EU–NATO coordination in the early years.

2 For an excellent and more detailed analysis of Berlin Plus, see Martin Reichard (2006), especially Chapters 4 and 8.

3 Similarly to the arrangements for *Concordia*, the very fact that NATO kept its own small 'back up' presence during the European Union's *Althea* missions implies a practical deviation from the operational situations originally envisaged under the Berlin Plus agreement.

126 *Johannes Varwick and Joachim Koops*

4 The United States's recent decision to establish an Africa Command (Africom) represents a major shift in its strategic interest and might heighten the future competition between NATO and the European Union on the African Continent.
5 Arguably, the emergence of the notion of crisis management was a response to the changing nature of security. The change from the Cold War monolithic and conventional threat of inter-state war, towards a more diverse post-Cold War threat of intra-state conflicts, ethnic genocide and civil war, also implied the need for different organizational responses and concepts. Whilst the concept of 'crisis management' was first mentioned in NATO's Strategic Concept of 1991 as a focus for NATO's strategic reorientation and military transformation (NATO 1991: para. 46), it was also taken up by the WEU in its Petersberg Task Declaration of 1992 (WEU 1992: Article II.4), which was subsequently taken over by the European Union and incorporated into the Treaty of Amsterdam in 1997.
6 Despite the fact that one representative of the EU Commission has been allowed to attend NAC–PSC meetings and several Commission representatives to attend the EU–NATO Capability Groups since November 2004, the EU Commission impact remains rather negligible (see Yost 2007: 91).
7 Yet, it has to be noted that there have also been reservations about a Berlin Plus Reverse agreement on the side of NATO officials, too, who fear the creation of an unnecessary dependence on the European Union (Yost 2007: 89).

References

Albright, M.K. (1998) 'The Right Balance will Secure NATO's Future', *Financial Times*, 7 December, p. 22.
Barros-Garcia, X. (2007) 'Effective Multilateralism and the EU as a Military Power: The Worldview of Javier Solana', EUI Working Papers 08, Robert Schuman Centre for Advanced Studies, Florence: European University Institute.
Barroso, J.-M. (2004) 'The European Union and the Emerging World Order – Perceptions and Strategies', speech delivered at the 7th ECSA World Conference, 30 November.
Biermann, R. (2008) 'Towards a Theory of Inter-organizational Networking: The Euro-Atlantic Security Institutions Interacting', *Review of International Organizations*, 3(2): 151–177.
Biscop, S. (2006) 'NATO, ESDP and the Riga Summit: No Transformation without Re-Equilibrium', *Egmont Paper*, 11, Brussels: Royal Institute for International Relations.
Blaszczyk, M.C., Jedrzejewska, A., Karasinska-Fendler, M., Pilichowska, A., Sobotka, K., Trzaskowski, R., Wypych, M. and Zurawski vel Grajewski, P. (2007) 'Security Cultures – "Poland"', in Institut für Europäische Politik (ed.): *EU-25/27 Watch*, September 5, 153–154.
Bornefeld-Ettmann, M., Brincker, G.-S., Göler, D., Delacor, M., Kuffel, P., Leppik, T., Lippert, B. and Sandawi, S. (2007) 'Security Cultures: "Germany"', in Institut für Europäische Politik (ed.) *EU-25/27 Watch*, No. 5, September,132–140.
Boyer, Y. and Quille, G. (2007) 'The Battlegroups: Catalyst for a European Defence Policy', paper for the European Parliament's Subcommittee on Security and Defence, Brussels: European Parliament, October.
Cameron, F. (2005) 'The EU and International Organisations: Partners in Crisis Management', *EPC Issue Paper*, 41, Brussels: European Policy Centre.
Caporaso, J.A. (1992) 'International Relations Theory and Multilateralism: The Search for Its Foundations', *International Organization*, 46(3): 599–632.
Carp, M. (2006) 'NATO Policy and Perspectives on Reconstruction Operations and NATO–EU Cooperation', in J. Dufourcq and D. Yost (eds) 'NATO–EU Cooperation in Post-Conflict Reconstruction', *Occasional Paper*, 15, Rome: NATO Defense

College. Online. Available HTTP: http://www.ndc.nato.int/download/publications/op_15.pdf (accessed 18 December 2007).

Clark, W. (2002) *Waging Modern War: Bosnia, Kosovo and the Future of Combat*, Washington, DC: Public Affairs.

Cornish, P. (2006) 'EU and NATO: Co-operation or Competition?', paper for the European Parliament's Subcommittee on Security and Defence, Brussels: European Parliament, October.

Council of the European Union (2003) 'A Secure Europe in a Better World: European Security Strategy (ESS)', Brussels, 12 December.

Cox, R.W. (1973) 'The Executive Head: An Essay on Leadership in International Organization', in L.M. Goodrich and D.A. Kay (eds) *International Organization: Politics & Process*, Wisconsin: University of Wisconsin Press.

Crisis Group (2005) 'EU Crisis Response Capability Revisited', *Europe Report*, 160, 17 January, Brussels.

de Hoop Scheffer, J. (2007) 'NATO and the EU: Time for a New Chapter'. Online. Available HTTP: http://www.nato.int/docu/speech/2007/s070129b.html (accessed 12 January 2008).

Deighton, A. (2002) 'The European Security and Defence Policy', *Journal of Common Market Studies*, 40(4): 719–741.

Dempsey, J. (2007) 'NATO Retreats from Establishment of Rapid-Reaction Force', *International Herald Tribune*, 20 September.

European Council Secretariat (2007a) 'Background: The EU Operations Centre'. Online. Available HTTP: http://www.consilium.europa.eu/uedocs/cmsUpload/070228-EU_OpsCentre.pdf (accessed 4 January 2008).

European Council Secretariat (2007b) 'Factsheet: EU Battlegroups', February 2007. Online. Available HTTP: http://www.consilium.europa.eu/uedocs/cmsUpload/Battlegroups_February_07-factsheet.pdf (accessed 4 January 2008).

European Union and NATO (2002) EU–NATO Declaration on ESDP, 16 December. Online. Available HTTP: http://www.nato.int/docu/pr/2002/p02-142e.htm (accessed 10 January 2008).

Fierke, K.M. and Wiener, A. (2005) 'Constructing Institutional Interests: EU and NATO Enlargement', in F. Schimmelfennig and U. Sedelmeier (eds) *The Politics of European Union Enlargement: Theoretical Approaches*, London: Routledge, 99–119.

Flournoy, M. and Smith, J. (2005) *European Defense Integration: Bridging the Gap Between Strategy and Capabilities*, Washington, DC: CSIS.

Foster, A. (2006) *Armed Forces and Society in Europe*, Basingstoke: Palgrave.

Gnesotto, N. (2004) 'European Strategy as Model', *Newsletter no. 9*, January, European Union Institute for Security Studies.

Goldirova, R. (2008) 'US Warns NATO may be "Destroyed" by Afghanistan Divisions', *Euobserver*. Online. Available HTTP: http://euobserver.com/?aid=25637 (accessed 15 February 2008).

Grevi, G., Lynch D. and Missiroli, A. (2005) *ESDP Operations*, Paris: EU Institute for Security Studies.

Hill, C. (1993) 'The Capability–Expectations Gap, or Conceptualising Europe's International Role', *Journal of Common Market Studies*, 31(3): 305–325.

Hofmann, S. and Reynolds, C. (2007) 'Die EU–NATO Beziehungen: Zeit für Tauwetter', *SWP Aktuell*, 37, July, Berlin: Stiftung Wissenschaft und Politik.

Howorth, J. (2001) 'European Defence and the Changing Politics of the EU', *Journal of Common Market Studies*, 39(4): 765–789.

Howorth, J. (2003) 'ESDP and NATO: Wedlock or Deadlock?', *Cooperation and Conflict*, 38(3): 235–254.

Howorth, J. (2005) 'From Security to Defence: The Evolution of the CFSP', in C. Hill and M. Smith (eds) *International Relations and the European Union*, Oxford: Oxford University Press, 179–204.

Howorth, J. (2007) *Security and Defence Policy in the European Union*, Basingstoke: Palgrave Macmillan.

Jönsson, C. (1995) 'An Interorganization Approach to the Study of Multilateral Institutions: Lessons from Previous Research on International Cooperation', Development and Multilateral Institutions Programme, *Working Paper No. 1.*

Jørgensen, K.E. (2006) 'A Multilateralist Role for the EU?', in O. Elgström and M. Smith (eds) *The European Union's Role in International Politics: Concepts and Analysis*, London: Routledge, 30–46.

Juncos, A. (2007) 'The Institutionalisation of EU Crisis Management Policies: The Case of EUFOR *Althea*', paper presented at the EU Crisis Management Conference, Brussels, June. Cited with the author's permission.

Kagan, R. (2003) *Paradise and Power: America and Europe in the New World Order*, London: Atlantic Books.

Kaim, M. (2007) *Die Europäische Sicherheits- und Verteidigungspolitik: Präferenzbildungs- und Aushandlungsprozesse in der Europäischen Union (1999–2005)*, Baden-Baden: Nomos Verlagsgesellschaft.

Keohane, R.O. (1985) 'Reciprocity in International Relations', *International Organization*, 40: 622–648.

Koops, J.A. (2004) 'Effective Multilateralism: The Future of the EU's External Identity in a System of Trilateral Security Governance', paper presented at the Conference 'New Europe 2020: Visions and Strategies for a Wider Europe', Turku, Finland, 27 August.

—— (2007) 'UN SHIRBRIG and EU Battlegroups', *OCGG Security Recommendation*, 6, Oxford: Oxford Council on Good Governance. Online. Available HTTP: http://www.oxfordgovernance.org/fileadmin/Publications/SR006.pdf (accessed 23 January 2008).

—— (2008) 'Towards Effective and Integrative Inter-Organizationalism', in K. Brockmann, H.B. Hauck and S. Reigeluth (eds) *From Conflict to Regional Stability: Linking Security and Development*, Berlin: German Council on Foreign Relations.

Kupferschmidt, F. (2006) 'Putting Strategic Partnership to the Test: Cooperation between NATO and the EU in Operation Althea', *SWP Research Paper No. 3*, April, Berlin: Stiftung Wissenschaft und Politik.

Lansford, T. (2002) *All for One: Terrorism, NATO and the United States*, Aldershot: Ashgate.

Leakey, D. (2006) 'ESDP and Civil/Military Cooperation: Bosnia and Herzegovina, 2005', in A. Deighton and V. Maurer (eds) 'Securing Europe? Implementing the European Security Strategy', *Zürcher Beiträge zur Sicherheitspolitik,* No. 77, Zürich: Center for Security Studies, 59–68.

Lindstrom, G. (2007) 'Enter the EU Battlegroups', *Chaillot Paper*, 97, Paris: EU-Institute for Security Studies.

Lundestad, G. (2003) *The United States and Western Europe Since 1945 – From 'Empire' by Invitation to Transatlantic Drift*, Oxford: Oxford University Press, Oxford Scholarship Online.

Medcalf, J. (2006) *NATO*, Oxford: Oneworld Publications.

Michel, L. (2007) *NATO's 'French Connection': Plus ça change...?*, Washington, DC: Institute for National Strategic Studies, National Defense University.

The EU and NATO 129

Naumann, K., Shalikashvili, J., Inge, P., Lanxade, J. and van den Bremen, H. (2007) *Towards a Grand Strategy for an Uncertain World: Renewing Transatlantic Relationship*, Noaber Foundation. Online. Available HTTP: www.csis.org/media/csis/events/080110_grand_strategy.pdf (accessed 10 February 2008).

North Atlantic Treaty Organization (NATO) (1991) *The Alliance Strategic Concept*, Rome, 8 November. Online. Available HTTP: http://www.nato.int/docu/basictxt/b911108a.htm (accessed 15 December 2007).

NATO (1999) *The Alliance's Strategic Concept, Washington*, 24 April. Online. Available HTTP: http://www.nato.int/docu/pr/1999/p99-065e.htm (accessed 15 December 2007).

NATO (2002) *EU–NATO Declaration on European Defence and Security Policy*. Online. Available HTTP: http://www.nato.int/docu/pr/2002/p02-142e-htm (accessed 30 November 2007).

Nowack, A. (ed.) (2006) 'Civilian Crisis Management: The EU Way', *Chaillot Paper*, 90, Paris: EU Institute for Security Studies.

Ojanen, H. (2004) 'Inter-organisational Relations as a Factor Shaping the EU's External Identity', *UPI Working Paper*, 49, The Finnish Institute of International Affairs.

Ortega, M. (2007) 'Building the Future: The EU's Contribution to Global Governance', *Chaillot Paper*, 100, Paris: EU Institute for Security Studies.

Reichard, M. (2006) *The EU–NATO Relationship: A Legal and Political Perspective*, Aldershot: Ashgate Publishing.

Ruggie, J.G. (ed.) (1993) *Multilateralism Matters: The Theory and Practice of an Institutional Form*, New York: Columbia University Press.

Schimmelfennig, F. (2003) *The EU, NATO and the Integration of Europe*, Cambridge: Cambridge University Press.

Schmalz, U. (2005) 'Die Entwicklung der Europäischen Sicherheits- und Verteidigungspolitik 1990–2004', in J. Varwick (ed.) *Die Beziehungen zwischen NATO und EU. Partnerschaft, Konkurrenz, Rivalität?*, Opladen: Budrich-Verlag, 45–59.

Shimkus, J. (2007) *NATO–EU Operational Cooperation*. Online. Available HTTP: http://www.nato-pa.int/default.asp?shortcut=1168 (accessed 17 January 2008).

Smith, H. (2002) *European Union Foreign Policy: What It Is and What It Does*, London: Pluto Press.

Soutou, G.-H. (2005) 'Three Rifts, Two Reconciliations: Franco-American Relations during the Fifth Republic', in D.M. Andrews (ed.) *The Atlantic Alliance under Stress: US–European Relations after Iraq*, Cambridge: Cambridge University Press, 102–127.

Touzkovskaia, N. (2006) 'EU–NATO Relations: How Close to "Strategic Partnership?"', *European Security*, 15(3): 235–258.

Treacher, A. (2004) 'From Civilian Power to Military Actor: The EU's Resistable Transformation', *European Affairs Review*, 9: 49–66.

United Kingdom Foreign and Commonwealth Office (UK FCO) (1998) *Joint Declaration Issued at the British–French Summit*, Saint Malo, France, 3–4 December. Online. Available HTTP: http://www.fco.gov.uk/servlet/Front?pagename=OpenMarket/Xcelerate/ShowPage&c=Page&cid=1007029391629&aid=1013618395073 (accessed 4 December 2007).

US State Department (2002) *The National Security Strategy of the United States of America*, Washington, DC: The White House.

Valasek, T. (2007) *The Roadmap to Better EU–NATO Relations, Briefing Note*, London: Centre of European Reform.

Varwick, J. (1998) *Sicherheit und Integration in Europa. Zur Renaissance der Westeuropäischen Union*, Opladen: Leske and Budrich-Verlag.

130 *Johannes Varwick and Joachim Koops*

—— (ed.) (2005) *Die Beziehungen zwischen NATO und EU: Partnerschaft, Konkurrenz, Rivalität?*, Opladen: Barbara Budrich Publishers.

—— (2006) 'European Union and NATO: Partnership, Competition or Rivalry?', *Kieler Analysen zur Sicherheitspolitik*, 18, June.

—— (2008) *Die NATO: Vom Verteidigungsbündnis zur Weltpolizei?*, München: Beck'sche Reihe.

Varwick, J. and Koops, J. (2007) 'Exporting Stability or Importing Instability? The EU at the Crossroads', in J. Varwick and K.-O. Lang (eds) *European Neighbourhood Policy: Challenges for the EU-Policy towards the New Neighbours*, Opladen and Farmington Hills: Barbara Budrich Publishers.

Wallace, W. (2005) 'Foreign and Security Policy: The Painful Path from Shadow to Substance', in H. Wallace, W. Wallace and M. Pollack (eds) *Policy-Making in the European Union*, 5th edition, Oxford: Oxford University Press, 429–456.

Wallace, W. and Oliver, T. (2005) 'A Bridge Too Far: The United Kingdom and the Transatlantic Relationship', in D.M. Andrews (ed.) *The Atlantic Alliance under Stress: US–European Relations after Iraq*, Cambridge: Cambridge University Press, 154–176.

Watanabe, L. (2005) 'The ESDP: Between Estrangement and a New Partnership in Transatlantic Security Relations', *Journal of Contemporary European Studies*, 13(1): 5–20.

Western European Union (WEU) (1992) *Petersberg Declaration*, Bonn, 19 June. Online. Available HTTP: http://www.assembly-weu.org/en/documents/sessions_ordinaires/key/declaration_petersberg.php (15 December 2007).

Wong, R. (2005) 'The Europeanization of Foreign Policy', in C. Hill and M. Smith (eds) *International Relations and the European Union*, Oxford: Oxford University Press, 134–153.

Yost, D.S. (2007) 'NATO and International Organizations', *Forum Paper*, 3, Rome: NATO Defense College.

7 EU–OSCE relations

Partners or rivals in security?

Peter van Ham[1]

Introduction

The story told on the European Union's website is both correct and endearing: The European Union as well as the Organization for Security and Co-operation in Europe (OSCE) 'were born out of the cold war, with a similar desire – to establish forms of co-operation in Europe which would defuse the tensions between former enemies and prevent further conflict on the Continent ... It is therefore natural that a degree of co-operation should have grown up' between these two organizations. Indeed, the European Union and the OSCE are both in the business of soft power, using economic and diplomatic instruments to reach political objectives.[2] Given that NATO is already engaged in Europe's collective defence, the European Union and OSCE lack military capabilities and have a particularly civilian take on dealing with security challenges.[3] Hence, both organizations share a comparable political pedigree, as well as a compatible strategic culture. In a way, they are therefore natural born partners (OSCE Press Release 2002).

This chapter outlines and analyses the EU–OSCE relationship. It asks how this partnership has developed during the last decade, and examines the opportunities and limits of cooperation between them. It studies the institutional interaction between both organizations, taking the European Union as the source institution from which influence originates, and trying to trace the causal pathway through which EU influence runs to the OSCE (as the target institution). Since international politics hardly resembles a laboratory, analysing institutional interaction is diffuse and difficult, and it is a challenge to investigate a long causal chain with a multitude of intervening variables. It should also be acknowledged that the systematic study of institutional interaction is in its infancy, which implies that much remains to be done to develop the conceptual toolkit to analyse this interface in international politics. Finally, it analyses the policy implication for the European Union of the changed patterns of influence in the EU–OSCE relationship.

This chapter assumes that the European Union may affect the OSCE by means of two mechanisms: knowledge and commitment.[4] Cognitive interaction is based on the premise that information, knowledge and ideas shape, or at least influence in a general way, the decision-making process of an international institution. Here, the European Union does not exert direct pressure on OSCE decision-making

132   *Peter van Ham*

fora, but the ideational interplay between both institutions supposes that inter-institutional persuasion and learning takes place (Schram Stokke 2001). Cognitive interaction suggests that the European Union, as the source institution, changes the order of preferences of actors relevant to the OSCE (as the target institution), not by political pressure per se, but by new information, insights, reports, initiatives, and so on. Such a direct, and occasionally causal, relationship may be difficult to trace and prove, and is by no means unidirectional. Source and target institutions may swap places, and the normative interplay between the European Union and OSCE may result in mutual and even balanced cross-fertilization. For example, the OSCE's approach towards security, linking human, military and economic aspects closely together, has been an inspiration as well as a model for the European Union, which has acquired a security identity rather late in its development as an international actor.

At the same time, the European Commission makes no bones about its role as a model which other international institutions might – perhaps even should – emulate. In its report *Shaping the New Europe* (of 2000), the European Commission argues that 'Europe's model of integration, working successfully on a continental scale, is a quarry from which ideas for global governance can and should be drawn' (European Commission 2000). The European Union does not merely stand for 'good governance' (encompassing the rule of law, transparency, democracy, etc.), but also for an alternative to the classical norms of Westphalian statehood. As Ben Rosamond argues, 'the EU stands – self-consciously sometimes – as a beacon of what it might mean to engage in the post-Westphalian governance of globalization. It is in this sense a normative transmitter to the rest of the world' (Rosamond 2005).

The other mechanism to be considered is centred on (political) commitment. Institutional interaction through commitment is premised on the reality that EU member states coordinate their preferences, policy stances and decisions within OSCE fora. If EU member states are bound by a commitment made within the EU framework, politically or otherwise, interaction through commitment has a serious and noticeable impact on the OSCE as a target institution. This concept assumes that member states prefer to harmonize their political stances in institutions with overlapping agendas and areas of obligation. Analytical uncertainty and cognitive dissonance influence member states to honour commitments made in the source institution by collectively pushing them in the target institution. The question of commitment is closely related to the level of 'actorness' of the European Union: Is the European Union capable of determining and carrying out an effective and efficient foreign policy, in this case within the OSCE?

This chapter also makes a judgement whether the institutional interaction between the European Union and the OSCE can, on balance, be considered beneficial, adverse or neutral for the source as well as for the target institution. Interaction may be considered beneficial when there is synergy between the European Union and OSCE, and when both institutions gain from the relationship; adverse interaction occurs if one of the institutions (or even both) is affected negatively, if policies are disrupted, and credibility – or even its very existence – is questioned. Neutral interaction obviously assumes that mutual effects are indeterminate or negligible.

EU–OSCE relations 133

Without losing sight of the inevitable elements of competition and institutional sibling rivalry giving the relationship its edge, this chapter concludes that the European Union and OSCE are most likely to develop an informal – and potentially formal – strategic partnership. The main driving force for such a partnership is the European Union. Over the past few years, the European Union has intensified its commitment to a strong and efficient OSCE and has taken several steps to re-enforce the performance of the European Union in the OSCE itself.[5] This does not come out of the blue since, for Brussels, the OSCE has several important assets and advantages. For example, the OSCE's institutional reach includes the Caucasus and Central Asia, regions which the European Union had paid scant attention to until recently. However, with the European Union's eastward enlargement (in 2004) and the new security environment after 9/11, the European Union had to adjust its geostrategic focus. Countries which had hitherto not shown up on the European Union's political radar screen – such as Moldova and Georgia – re-appeared with a vengeance. In order to catch up, the European Union has tried to piggyback on the OSCE's long-standing agenda to develop good governance in the whole Euro-Atlantic area. The OSCE's presence, knowledge and contacts in Europe's new 'near abroad' are highly valued in Brussels, and considered an important strategic asset which the European Union should use to strengthen its own security objectives.

EU–OSCE interaction therefore knows a wide variety of functional and political linkages (Young 2002). Both institutions overlap significantly in their approach to security, membership and geographical area of responsibility. Since this chapter takes the European Union as the source institution, most attention goes to the question of how the European Union affects, influences and drives OSCE affairs. Significant consideration will be given to the normative interplay between both institutions, where the European Union seems to consider the OSCE as being nested inside the European Union's strong multilateral framework.[6] The European Union's security strategy ('A Secure Europe in a Better World', adopted in December 2003) calls for an effective multilateral system, including the development of a strong international society, well-functioning institutions and a rule-based international order. This obviously implies backing the UN and other universal political institutions and treaties. But for the European Union, supporting the OSCE (as well as the Council of Europe) has particular significance. Obviously, 'good governance' begins at home, and for the enlarged European Union its extended strategic habitat now includes areas where the OSCE can be of great use.

It is against the backdrop of the overall objective of 'effective multilateralism' that this chapter analyses the EU–OSCE relationship, arguing that the ensuing strategic partnership has much to offer, not only for the European Union, but for Europe at large.

The European Union's historical footprint in the OSCE

The European Union (and its predecessor – the European Community) has been actively involved in setting up the OSCE's forerunner: the Conference on

134 *Peter van Ham*

Security and Co-operation in Europe (CSCE). The process to develop the CSCE goes back to the 1950s, when the Soviet Union pushed the idea to develop a Pan-European Security Conference which would legitimate and consolidate the boundaries of the Cold War European state system.

During the final preparations for the CSCE (or 'Helsinki Final Act' of 1975), the then nine European Community member states announced that they would operate as a group. They also consolidated their diplomatic efforts in the nascent European Political Cooperation (EPC), the forerunner of the European Union's Common Foreign and Security Policy (CFSP). The European Commission conducted negotiations on economic issues within the OSCE's so-called second basket. The Helsinki Final Act was adopted not only by member states, but Italy's Prime Minister Aldo Moro, then President of the European Council, also stated that he signed on behalf of the European Community. During the CSCE follow-up meetings until 1989, the European Community was recognized by an official nameplate (reading 'Member States, Presidency/EC'). From 1990 onwards, the EC/EU role within the OSCE process became more recognizable, as well as more important. As President of the European Commission, Jacques Delors signed the OSCE's 'Charter of Paris for a New Europe', in November 1990 (Pijpers 1990, especially Chapter 4).

All this sounds utterly undramatic from today's perspective. However, the institutional roots of the European Union's efforts to coordinate the foreign and security policies of its members can be traced back to their participation and role within the CSCE. With the joint preparations and negotiations of the Helsinki Accords, the EPC kick-started itself, with the current CFSP as the outcome. Few will be familiar with the historical background of the OSCE's impact on the process of European political integration. Still, it is good to realize that EU–OSCE relations have a long track record, and that both organizations have benefited from each other's active involvement.

One could also reasonably claim that the European Union has used the OSCE framework as a rather low-key, low-risk learning ground to gradually solidify an initially brittle culture of political cooperation. Over the decades, the EU member states have tried out and consolidated mechanisms of harmonizing their political positions and security attitudes, and hence developed its EU 'actorness'. Actorness can be defined as the level of external recognition (the ability of an actor to negotiate with other actors), external authority (the legal competence to act externally) and autonomy (the institutional distinctiveness and independence from other actors) as well as internal cohesion. It has therefore been within the sheltered OSCE environment that the European Union could develop a habit of political cooperation and develop a more mature security culture. In a way, this has set the tone of this liaison, which resonates in today's calls for a strategic partnership.

The European Union and its member states have been actively engaged in the OSCE since its inception. Over the decades, the European Union has been instrumental in the institutional reform of the OSCE and its metamorphosis from a political *salon de thé* (starting with the Multilateral Preparatory Talks for the Helsinki Accords, and the subsequent CSCE) to a real international organization with a Secretariat, a Permanent Council, as well as multiple subsidiary bodies like the High Commissioner on National Minorities, and the Office for Democratic Institutions and Human Rights (ODIHR). One could therefore argue that the cognitive interaction from the European Union (and former European Community) to the CSCE/OSCE has been significant, in particular during the first phase of their institutional relationship. This cognitive interaction was also based on the commitment of the European Union and its member states, which has in turn developed and solidified the European Union's actorness.

It should, however, also be noted that NATO has played an equally active role in the OSCE's institutional development. John Borawski even argues that it is 'no exaggeration to state that from the very beginning of the Helsinki process the NATO "caucus" has provided a decisive input into the work of the CSCE, including the evolution of CSCE structures' (Borawski 1994: 39). NATO as well as the NATO-centric North Atlantic Cooperation Council (NACC) which was created in 1993 and included many Central European states formerly under Soviet influence have contributed directly to the development of the CSCE/OSCE as a crisis manager and stabilizer. The so-called Ad Hoc Group on Cooperation in Peacekeeping (set up in 1994) gave NATO a means to influence CSCE/OSCE *modus operandi*. Since the European Union was nigh invisible as a security actor in the early 1990s, NATO influence on the OSCE was more significant.

After the accession of ten new member states, mostly from Central Europe, the European Union's role inside the OSCE has been strengthened further. The European Union (and its member states) now provides almost half of the OSCE's membership (of 55 participating states); it is the main funder of the OSCE's annual budget (about 75 per cent), as well as the provider of the majority of personnel for its field missions. Especially EU support, politically as well as financially, of OSCE field missions is important, since these long-term missions have become its core business. These missions are recognized as one of the most effective tools of the OSCE aimed at conflict resolution and stabilization in areas like the Balkans (Kosovo, Bosnia-Herzegovina), the Caucasus (Georgia, Nagorno-Karabakh), as well as Moldova. These missions account for around 85 per cent of the OSCE budget, which implies that the European Union's financial and material impact on the OSCE is very significant (Huber 2003). The European Union has, however, consistently failed to make effective use of this lever to steer the OSCE's activities. As Martina Huber concludes in her study on OSCE long-term missions: 'The lack of EU–OSCE co-operation in the Balkans has been both inexplicable and inefficient ... Also in Central Asia, the EU would be able to build much better on OSCE assets whereas the OSCE would benefit from the political and financial weight of the EU' (Huber 2003: 133).

The EU–OSCE relationship indicates that EU foreign policy pursues what Alfred Wolfers has called 'milieu goals', rather than 'possession goals'. Possession goals are based on a narrow reading of the national (or European) interest, whereas milieu goals aim to shape the strategic environment in which Europe operates (Wolfers 1962: 73–76). The European Union is especially interested in supporting (financially and politically) the so-called human dimension of security, which is considered one of the OSCE's strong suits. The European Union is therefore the key supporter of the OSCE's ODIHR (based in Warsaw), and many ODIHR

136 *Peter van Ham*

programmes in Central Asia. ODIHR is especially active in election monitoring, always strongly backed by the European Union. In this way, ODIHR, and the OSCE in general, is used by the European Union as a lever to encourage good governance in Europe's neighbourhood. For example, the European Union made it clear that '[c]ompliance by Belarus with the international commitments it has entered into in the context of the OSCE would be likely to contribute to the subsequent development of its relations with the European Union'.[7] Hence, for many countries the OSCE has become a stepping stone, or purgatory, towards strengthening ties with the European Union itself (Sporrer 2003: 17). This obviously makes the European Union one of the OSCE's most important multilateral partners (together with NATO).

As a sub-conclusion, one can argue that it is beyond doubt that the European Union has significant financial clout, voting power and political weight. This offers the European Union ample opportunities to shape the OSCE agenda and its policy priorities and activities. The European Union could, in principle, block financial support for the OSCE's institutions and activities, it could block decisions, or steer the OSCE's political course in a certain direction by influencing its agenda. Brussels has, however, not fully taken advantage of its hegemonic role in the OSCE, although it is gradually waking up to the reality that it could – and perhaps should – do so. Within the OSCE process, the European Union is the key player together with Russia (or, prior to 1991, the Soviet Union). Although the United States is a member of the OSCE, from Washington's perspective this institution is a side show of marginal importance. Given America's low profile, the European Union has positioned itself as the driving force behind the OSCE and its policies.

The European Union's actorness in the OSCE is most pronounced if there is an agreed political position among EU member states. On most cases of substance, EU member states follow the lead of the EU Presidency (which rotates every six months) which speaks for the Union in the OSCE's Permanent Council. The Permanent Council convenes weekly in Vienna to discuss current developments and to take appropriate decisions. Generally, the European Union speaks with a single voice (of the rotating Presidency) in OSCE fora when there is an agreed position. The basic guidelines of EU policies are derived from the European Council conclusions, reached in Brussels. All too often, however, EU Delegations take into account last-minute instructions from their capitals, and ambassadors from EU member states have to coordinate and de-conflict positions amongst themselves and under the guidance of the EU Presidency.

Political guidance is therefore important. But in bureaucratic terms, the main mechanism for the European Union to achieve consensus and a joint commitment is the so-called system of 'chef de file' – individual EU member states being responsible for a specific dossier, giving them the responsibility to develop expertise and credibility, and offering them the lead in swaying the European Union as a whole to adopt a certain position. As a result, EU positions within the OSCE Permanent Council are generally derived from national initiatives agreed upon in EU coordination meetings. Since the European Union acts as a caucus within the OSCE, it is usually difficult to renegotiate EU positions that are already the result of sometimes intricate compromises. The small delegation of the European Commission functions as the institutional memory of the European Union. On economic and environmental matters, it is the European Commission which acts for EU member states, for example by preparing EU positions for the annual OSCE Economic Forum.

This EU unanimity is, therefore, the general norm within the OSCE (in 95 per cent of cases). Critics (often non-EU member states) argue that EU unanimity results in watered-down statements which also limit the debate in the OSCE Permanent Council. EU positions within the OSCE tend to be lowest common denominators, and are thereby less influential since they tend to be both predictable and – with only few exceptions – unexciting. Proponents argue that a common EU position is beneficial to the OSCE since it gives the organization a head start in fleshing out a broader consensus. As Austrian ambassador to the OSCE, Margit Waestfelt, argued in July 2006: 'The EU is working ahead, so to speak. It doesn't mean that the EU works in isolation, draws up its position and says, "That's it, take it or leave it!" On the contrary, we consult in a variety of ways' (Lööf 2006: 14–15). Ambassador Waestfelt argued that the EU Presidency during a regular week holds numerous meetings with the European Union as well as non-EU countries for an exchange of views, and that, 'taken together, these regular encounters provide a wide reservoir of knowledge and opinions which the EU presidency takes into account. So the relationship is much more interlinked than it might appear' (Lööf 2006: 14–15).

Since this practice of coordination and joint commitment is now well established, other OSCE states have come to expect the European Union, together with aspirant EU member states who tend to associate themselves with the emerging EU consensus, to act unanimously. It should, however, be noted that this good habit of a European harmony shows some signs of erosion since the European Union's 2004 enlargement, and it is now all too often that other EU member states take the floor to air a dissenting opinion, which of course tends to dilute the European Union's overall message. But despite this counteraction, the norm of a single EU position within the OSCE implies that expectations are raised, and EU Presidencies are expected to deliver accordingly.

The European Union's political commitment remains one of the main sources of the Union's influence in its interaction with the OSCE. But here, too, much depends on imponderables, such as the commitment of the EU Presidency to take its role within the OSCE seriously. Some EU Presidencies have little love lost for the OSCE, others give it their full attention. Austria, which held the EU Presidency in the first half of 2006, certainly falls in the latter category. In an effort to strengthen EU–OSCE relations, Austria put forward the proposal to arrive at an *EU–OSCE Joint Declaration on Common Fields of Cooperation*. This document – which is still in the draft stage and discussed in more detail below – will be of special importance since it covers practical cooperation between both institutions as well as an effort to effectively coordinate policies on a more strategic level.[8]

Change over time: Institutional ties and practical cooperation

The overlap in membership and the communality of interests and objectives between the European Union and the OSCE makes institutional cooperation indispensable.

138　*Peter van Ham*

With the adoption of the 1999 Platform for Cooperative Security, the OSCE declared its firm intention to cooperate with other security institutions, the European Union and NATO included. With its 1999 *Charter for European Security*, the OSCE aimed to set up 'a flexible coordinating framework to foster cooperation, through which various organizations can reinforce each other drawing on their particular strengths. We do not intend to create a hierarchy of organizations or a permanent division of labour among them.'[9] To map out the possibilities for institutional interaction, the OSCE prepares detailed reports on its cooperation with other international organizations working on issues within its remit.

The European Union and OSCE have institutionalized political contacts at the Ministerial and Ambassadorial level. At the political level, the European Union is represented at most OSCE meetings by the delegation of the member state that holds the EU Presidency. The European Commission has its own delegation to most international organizations based in Vienna, the OSCE included. The first formal working group level exchange between both organizations took place as late as May 2003, which may explain why the EU–OSCE dialogue is not very intensive until now. The Troikas of both the European Union and OSCE meet twice annually and there is staff-to-staff contact on most levels. The two Troikas (of current, previous and incoming Presidency and Chairman-in-Office [CiO]) generally discuss issues of shared interest (ranging from Moldova and Kosovo, to racism and anti-Semitism), and prepare for the EU–OSCE meetings at Ministerial level.

Since 2003, EU–OSCE relations have been further intensified. Apart from the regular political exchanges at Ministerial level, the Troika at the European Union's Political Director level (of its Political and Security Committee – PSC) regularly meets with the OSCE Troika and the European Union's Heads of Missions. Similarly, the PSC and the EU Working Group on the Council of Europe and the OSCE frequently come together with the OSCE's Secretary General and other OSCE representatives. Moreover, headquarter working contacts between the EU Council's Secretariat, the European Commission, and the OSCE Secretariat have intensified over the years.

Despite these strengthened and formalized contacts, the exchange of information between both organizations leaves much to be desired. The European Union and OSCE have committed themselves to improve the flow of information, especially since cooperation on a practical level is increasing. In order to address these problems, suggestions have been made to establish a permanent EU mission to the OSCE and to strengthen the EU Council OSCE Working Group in Brussels. The OSCE still lacks an official delegation or office in Brussels. The country holding the OSCE CiO represents the organization also in its relations with the European Union. This means that the effectiveness and visibility of the OSCE are highly contingent upon its CiO, and the minister of foreign affairs in particular. It also implies that the OSCE CiO may be more effective when held by an EU member state. In that case, it is easier to smooth over divergences between both institutions, and to filter EU foreign and security policies into the OSCE agenda.

A February 2003 EU Council publication called *Draft Conclusions on EU–OSCE Cooperation in Conflict Prevention, Crisis Management and Post-Conflict Rehabilitation* identified four areas where inter-institutional cooperation should be enhanced: exchange of information and analyses, cooperation on fact-finding missions, coordination of diplomatic activities as well as statements and communiqués and, finally, training and cooperation during field missions. In that document, numerous other suggestions were made to improve EU–OSCE cooperation, of which meetings between the EU Troika, OSCE Troika and the OSCE Secretary General during EU Presidencies, as well as more openness and frequent contact between both bureaucracies, were the most important.

EU–OSCE cooperation in the field has developed gradually since the early 1990s. Both institutions have gathered experience and expertise in the wide spectrum of conflict prevention and post-conflict rehabilitation, most notably in Southeast Europe. For example, the OSCE was actively involved in the implementation of the Brioni Accords of July 1991, as well as with the European Union's subsequent Monitoring Missions in the Balkans. The European Union and the OSCE also worked closely together in implementing UN sanctions imposed on the former Republic of Yugoslavia and the Republika Srpska. For Albania, both organizations initiated a so-called 'Friends of Albania' group (in September 1998) which coordinates the international efforts to support Albania in its development aspirations. Moldova offers another example of successful EU–OSCE cooperation, since the OSCE Mission collaborated with the EU TACIS programme to encourage the Government of Moldova and the Trans-Dniestrian authorities to begin reconstruction projects.

The European Union and the OSCE have also worked closely and effectively together in implementing the 2001 Ohrid Agreement which works towards the stabilization of Macedonia. In 2004, the European Commission even lauded

> the excellent cooperation which the EU has enjoyed over the years with the OSCE Spillover Monitoring Mission in Skopje. The work of the OSCE Mission has been a decisive factor in promoting stability and democracy in the country and complements the Union's own efforts in this field. We remain confident that in the future this mutually reinforcing cooperation will continue.[10]

Areas of close cooperation have been election monitoring, police matters, as well as media and inter-ethnic issues. The OSCE Mission has hosted the European Union and has had daily relations with European Commission officials, mainly to exchange information.

The European Union and the OSCE also work closely together in Croatia and Kosovo. Especially in Kosovo, the European Union has taken over many tasks from the OSCE with the strengthened EU Mission there in 2006. Prior to that, the EU–OSCE relationship has been symbiotic: the OSCE Mission in Kosovo received funding for its activities (mainly in institution building) from the European Union's European Agency for Reconstruction, and the OSCE–EUMM (EU Monitoring Mission) relationship has been more than adequate. Another recent example of EU–OSCE cooperation is the border assistance mission for Ukraine and Moldova, where the European Union has established an operation (of some 150 staff) supporting the border authorities of both countries in improving their capabilities. The OSCE mission in Chisinau has advised the European Union and offered practical support, and has been in place since December 2005.

140　*Peter van Ham*

All these examples illustrate that both institutions work closely together on the ground, most notably in the Balkans and the southern Caucasus. EU and OSCE programmes, projects, missions and other policy ventures largely overlap in their objectives as well as in their methods (Burghardt 1999; Otte 2002). The OSCE's activities in Central Asia give it a specific security niche, since this is an area where the European Union has little experience and expertise. In 2006, the OSCE had seven field missions, and eight centres and offices in the Balkans, Eastern Europe, the Caucasus, as well as in Central Asia. This OSCE presence offers the organization 'eyes and ears' and hands-on competences. Rather than seeing the OSCE as a direct rival, the European Union is actively involved in developing this OSCE expertise. For example, at the OSCE's Istanbul Summit (November 1999), the European Union supported the establishment of REACT (Rapid Expert Assistance and Co-operation Teams), which includes a database of experts who can be used during crisis situations.

But due to – or should one say despite of – the overlapping objectives and policies, there have been occasional hitches between both institutions. Within the European Union (European Commission and European Council) and the OSCE Secretariat, the possibilities for improving inter-institutional cooperation remain on the agenda, without, however, making much progress. Areas of specific attention are cooperation in civil crisis management and the modalities of the European Union's contribution to OSCE-led missions, joint selection and training programmes for field staff and cooperation in the planning of new operations. Since both organizations focus on conflict prevention and stabilization, seeking more synergies would seem commonsensical, but have proved to be difficult to achieve.

Inter-institutional dynamics: EU–OSCE competition

Since the 1990s, we have witnessed the 'OSCE-ing' of European security, in the sense that attention has shifted from classical collective defence to collective (and societal) security. The comprehensive approach of the OSCE has gradually been adopted by other security-related actors, like NATO and the European Union. This implies that the European Union has been the target institution, susceptible to the flow of ideas in which the OSCE has been the spring and inspiration. Paradoxically, however, the OSCE-ing of European security has increasingly marginalized the OSCE itself, rather than strengthened it.

For example, the European Union currently develops its own policies and capabilities in areas where the OSCE has been active for many years. In the Balkans, the European Union seems to ignore the OSCE's missions. The European Union's *Althea* operation has made it more difficult for the OSCE to call upon EU member states to assign staff for other civilian crisis management missions. Moreover, in the context of its new European Neighbourhood Policy (ENP), the European Union has appointed special representatives for Moldova, the southern Caucasus as well as Central Asia. These are regions where the OSCE has developed much expertise based on its long-established missions.

Another example is the launch of the European Union's first rule of law mission to Georgia (known as EUJUST *Themis*) in July 2004. *Themis* involves some ten international civilian experts plus local staff to support the local authorities in reforming the Georgian criminal justice system. This EU mission clearly overlaps with the OSCE's REACT mechanism, which aims to pool civilian experts for rapid deployment. It has therefore been suggested that the European Union should coordinate its contribution of national experts to OSCE missions via an EU pool, or that the European Union could function as a sub-contractor to the OSCE and start EU missions under EU command at the OSCE's request (Biscop 2005). Whatever solution will be chosen, the scarcity of civil crisis management experts simply requires more and closer EU–OSCE cooperation.

The European Union decided in December 2004 to develop so-called *Civilian Headline Goals 2008*, committing member states to a more effective and rapid capability for civilian crisis management. Several EU member states are drawing upon their experience within the OSCE, arguing that the European Union should look for lessons to be learned and the best practices for civilian crisis management as they have been developed within the OSCE. The OSCE has successfully reorganized its asset management system, which now includes a data base for available equipment, the deployment of procurement experts for all missions and the establishment of framework contracts. The OSCE is also considering establishing warehouses as well as readily available standard equipment packages (so-called rapid deployment – or start-up – kits). These kits could differ depending on the mission, but most likely contain laptops, mobile phones, cars and documentation.

The European Union is also looking at proposals for pooled cooperation between coalitions of EU member states, for example gendarmerie-type forces, which would allow burden sharing in the equipment and deployment of civilian forces. The European Union also considers the OSCE's practice of reimbursing personnel in its crisis management missions a sensitive issue within the Union since EU member states still have to pay their own way, rather than getting compensated by a flat monthly rate. The European Union's elaborate election monitoring mechanism follows the methods of ODIHR, which enables the European Commission to participate in election observation missions outside of the European continent.

The European Union's increased interest in Central Asia was recently illustrated by the new *Central Asia Initiative* launched under the German EU Presidency (in February 2007), which should bundle together the EU security and energy interests in the region. In this *Initiative*, the European Union aims to outsource the humanitarian dimension to the OSCE, mainly to leave its own hands free to deal with its own political and energy agenda. Within the OSCE, this emerging division of labour is seen with concern since it is realized that this would seriously undermine the comprehensive security concept which forms the very basis of the organization. It does seem, however, an almost inevitable and unstoppable trend. If the European Union would indeed crowd out the OSCE, one could argue that the OSCE has become a victim of its own success.

The European Union's primacy also extends to the important area of soft power, or the power of attraction. It is generally acknowledged that as long as a country

142   *Peter van Ham*

has a realistic prospect to accede to the European Union, the pull of membership offers Brussels a significant lever to steer this country towards democracy and a market economy. In this respect, the European Union has more soft power than the OSCE. But for some countries, EU membership is not on the cards, at least not for the foreseeable future. To assure cooperation with these countries, the European Union has introduced its ENP, in May 2004. The European Union will now focus more political attention (and limited financial resources as well) on countries such as Moldova, Belarus, Ukraine as well as the southern Caucasus.[11] Some countries (such as Belgium, which held the OSCE Chair in 2006) see this as an opportunity for the European Union to serve as a bridge between the United States and Russia within the OSCE.[12] Indeed, the European Union recognizes that, for the ENP to be successful, close cooperation with the OSCE is important. European Commissioner Chris Patten therefore argued (in July 2004) that 'EU enlargement inevitably means that we need to develop a very close and co-operative relationship to make the best of what the EU and regional organizations like the OSCE can bring to security and co-operation in Europe' (OSCE News 2004). Monika Wohlfeld, the OSCE's Head of Mission Programme, even claims that 'the EU's new neighbours initiative is in fact a very important test case, also for the EU's relations with the OSCE' (Wohlfeld 2003: 54).

The ENP's impact on the OSCE remains unclear. But there is certainly a visible tendency for the European Union to 'reproduce itself' in its relations with non-members, and with aspirant EU member states in particular (Lavenex 2004; Bicchi 2006). The European Union uses its power of attraction and its influence within the OSCE to project its policy solutions on its direct neighbourhood, using the overlapping EU–OSCE policy agenda as a preferred platform and vehicle. It remains undecided, however, what impact EU enlargement will have on the OSCE itself. As Andrej Zagorski has argued, 'arithmetics do not make a great difference. The OSCE is not a voting machine, and the fact that the majority of its participating states are going to come from NATO, and/or the EU, would only strengthen the reluctance of non-members of the two groups to deviate from the consensus rule' (Zagorski 2002: 222–223). It could be argued that EU enlargement will gradually marginalize the OSCE, whereas one could equally contend (and hope) that both organizations will remain 'natural-born partners' (Wohlfeld 2003; Dunay 2006: 72–73), even despite growing pressures.

Given the developments outlined above, it is obvious that the OSCE needs to reconsider its role and place in Europe's dynamic security architecture. In an influential report *Common Purpose: Towards a More Effective OSCE* (published in June 2005), a 'Panel of Eminent Persons' argued that the OSCE 'should focus on what [it] does best and where its value added lies'.[13] Since the European Union and OSCE have similar security visions, a more strategic partnership between both organizations would be politically pertinent. With Romania and Bulgaria having joined the European Union in January 2007, the European Union's influence in the OSCE has increased accordingly. What is more, three EU member states will be holding the OSCE chairmanship in a row (between 2006 and 2008): Belgium, Spain and Finland. This offers a unique opportunity to strengthen the

EU–OSCE relationship, for example, by holding regular meetings between the EU Presidency, the European Union's High Representative for CFSP, the European Union's External Affairs Commissioner and the OSCE's CiO. The logical focus of cooperation would be to incorporate the OSCE in developing the European Union's Neighbourhood Policy.

Policy implications: Strengthening the European Union's role *vis-à-vis* the OSCE

At the General Affairs Council (GAERC) of 13 December 2004, the EU Foreign Ministers approved an assessment report (drafted by the Dutch EU Presidency) to strengthen the relationship between both organizations and to enforce the performance of the European Union inside the OSCE.[14] The Report strikes a very positive and constructive tone towards the OSCE, arguing that both organizations have great communality of interests and objectives. It is based on the assumption that the European Union and OSCE have mutually reinforcing roles in maintaining the security and stability in and around Europe. It is recognized that the European Union in its Security Strategy has identified similar threats (terrorism, WMD proliferation, failed states and organized crime), as has the OSCE in its 'Strategy to Address Threats to Security and Stability in the Twenty-First Century' (adopted in December 2003). The European Union pays tribute to the OSCE's *acquis*, which covers a full range of norms on politico-military, economic and human rights dimensions. Based on the EU Report and interviews with EU officials (in Brussels and Vienna), a clearer picture emerges of how the Union sees the OSCE's future.

Given the political invisibility of the United States inside the OSCE, the European Union now finds itself on the opposite side of the political fence from Russia and its shifting coalition of followers. The European Union therefore stresses the importance of a coordinated EU stance inside the OSCE, since Russia and its Commonwealth of Independent States (CIS) allies express growing doubts of the OSCE role and relevance. Time and again, the European Union stresses that the OSCE's comparative advantage in the European security field is to support core principles of democracy, good governance, the rule of law and respect for fundamental human rights. The other dimensions of the OSCE (politico-military and economic) are given relatively short shrift compared with the OSCE's human dimension. The Russian government issued a statement in July 2004, criticizing the OSCE for its selective approach in human rights and election monitoring. This was followed by an appeal of CIS states in September 2004.

The European Union recognizes in its 2004 assessment report that a 'well-coordinated policy of the EU *vis-à-vis* the OSCE appears to be all the more important in a period when Russia and some CIS states express doubts on the role of the OSCE'. In several public statements, these CIS states have argued that the OSCE does not strike the right balance between its traditional three dimensions, complaining that the promotion of democratic values and human rights (mainly in the CIS region) are too much in the forefront of the OSCE's activities. OSCE Secretary General Marc Perrin de Brichambaut has formulated Russia's criticism clearly:

144 *Peter van Ham*

members of the Commonwealth of Independent States criticized the OSCE in 2004 for applying double standards, paying too much attention to human rights and the internal affairs of a select group of states, and thus departing from its traditionally co-operative approach. It seemed that Russia and some of its allies were losing their sense of ownership in the OSCE.

(Brichambaut 2006: 52–53)

This CIS criticism is not surprising since the OSCE's human dimension mechanisms were first and foremost designed to address the human rights and security problems of the former Soviet-dominated part of Europe. Western Europe already had the Council of Europe and the European Union to at first encourage, and later assure, good governance and democracy. Hence, OSCE missions and activities concentrated on the Balkans, Central Asia, the southern Caucasus and Eastern Europe; no mission or major activity has taken place in Western Europe or North America. Therefore, the OSCE offers the European Union a valuable security forum in which Russia and other CIS states can be engaged and where the human dimension can be addressed. The existing EU–Russia bilateral relationship is considered less suitable for these debates, especially since energy security has risen to the top of the agenda since early 2006. The OSCE framework is preferred since it offers a crucial system of peer review of existing human rights and good governance norms and standards. The European Union often reiterates that security challenges in the post-Soviet space have economic, environmental and political causes, rather than traditional armed conflict. This makes the OSCE such a valuable partner for the European Union in this region.

The constructive approach of the European Union was clearly expressed in a statement by Austria's Foreign Minister Ursula Plassnik, who spoke for the EU Presidency at the OSCE's Permanent Council in February 2006.[15] Mrs Plassnik sees the OSCE mainly as a community of states based on shared values, and with the ultimate goal to strengthen mutual confidence and cooperation. It is in this area where EU–OSCE cooperation could be strengthened, especially in the light of the growing pressure on values such as tolerance and non-discrimination. The European Union's Fundamental Rights Agency (the successor of the EU Monitoring Centre on Racism and Xenophobia) is a key partner of the OSCE's ODIHR. Both the European Union and OSCE emphasize the need for cultural dialogue, especially with Muslim states and communities, to build bridges and remove misunderstandings. Since 1998, ODIHR has already carried out joint programmes with the European Union, mainly funded by the European Community's European Initiative for Democracy and Human Rights. The European Union and OSCE also started joint programmes in Central Asia, in summer 2004, focusing mainly on human rights issues.

The *EU–OSCE Joint Declaration* (still only available in draft form) testifies to the willingness of both the European Union and OSCE to bring their cooperation to a different level. The *Joint Declaration* is to include civilian crisis management, international terrorism, organized crime, as well as relations with Russia. Although this is not the first lofty declaration of its kind (both the European Union and the OSCE have these in abundance), the *Joint Declaration* will set a first, and potentially important, step towards a real strategic partnership between both organizations. As we have seen, such a document is long overdue.

Finally, the European Union's complex institutional set-up in the security area requires attention. The European Union's pillar structure has made it at times difficult for the European Union to speak with one voice, also inside the OSCE. Since the EU–OSCE relationship is especially close in the area of civilian crisis management, cross-pillar coordination within the European Union is called for, but has proved to be hard to achieve. The dispersal of competences within the European Union makes cooperation an intricate matter, especially since conflict prevention and post-conflict rehabilitation thrives on a mixture of economic, financial and diplomatic tools, which often-times find themselves in different hands within EU institutions. Rivalry between the European Commission and the European Council, sometimes turning into turf battles, has complicated relations with the OSCE (Stewart 2006). At times, the OSCE receives different and conflicting signals and demands from the European Council, the European Commission, the EU Presidency, the EU Troika, the European Union's PSC, and the wide array of Council Working Groups. This has been a problem for the OSCE, more than for the European Union, especially since the European Union has undertaken more and more of the OSCE's original tasks.

Concluding remarks

This chapter has outlined the EU–OSCE relationship and traced the patterns of cooperation and competition between both institutions. As argued at the outset, international politics does not resemble a clear-cut laboratory and hence does not generate equally clear-cut answers. What has become evident, however, is that the European Union has gradually strengthened its hold over the OSCE since its inception in the mid-1970s. The two mechanisms of influence – knowledge and commitment – have been instrumental in the strengthened EU grip over the OSCE. The OSCE has always made the case to avoid a hierarchy of institutions in Europe since it feared to end up on the bottom of the pile. But EU enlargement and the widened scope of EU security interests and operations has resulted in the marginalization of the OSCE.

It is clear that the European Union has taken many leafs out of the OSCE's security book, and basically incorporated the OSCE's philosophy of collective and human security into its own strategy. A strong commitment within the OSCE's decision-making fora, and a political commitment to the institutional development of the OSCE, has in turn been beneficial for the advance of the European Union's actorness. This implies that the OSCE has, from the outset, influenced the European Union more than the other way round; cognitive interaction has been a one-way street.

But since the end of the Cold War, the European Union has gradually strengthened its role as a security actor in Europe and beyond and has pushed the OSCE to the sidelines. The European Union's collective weight inside the OSCE has increased, also because the United States and Russia have both given the OSCE

146　*Peter van Ham*

the cold shoulder. The European Union's commitment in the OSCE's Permanent Council and other OSCE institutions (such as ODIHR) and field missions and activities has over the years turned the organization into a sidekick and outpost of Brussels. Nothing could be done in the OSCE without the European Union, and this asymmetrical power relationship has turned the EU–OSCE relationship into *de facto* dependency.

The conclusion has, therefore, to be drawn that the institutional interaction between both organizations has been beneficial for the European Union, but increasingly negative for the OSCE. If imitation is the highest form of flattery, the European Union has flattered the OSCE out of business, or limited the OSCE to these security tasks (i.e. the human dimension of security) which it has no time and need to be involved itself. The European Union now leaves a few security crumbs to the OSCE, such as human security matters in Central Asia. The OSCE has become an instrument of the European Union to project good governance in those regions in its direct vicinity where it has other direct interest (e.g. energy and other resource concerns). An EU–OSCE strategic partnership is still on the cards, and is a serious option to keep the OSCE relevant as a security actor.

One can further conclude that the EU–OSCE relationship has offered the European Union opportunities to sharpen the contours of its 'European interest', mainly *vis-à-vis* Russia and the former Soviet Union. Within the OSCE, the European Union basically stands alone against Russia, since the US role is rather marginal. Michael Smith was therefore correct when he argued that the European Union is developing a postmodern foreign policy, although 'the reality is that power and resources are and will remain diffused, and that the search for the holy grail of a "European interest" will never be rewarded' (Smith 2003: 569; see also van Ham 2001). But the OSCE has been a useful forum for the European Union to develop its soft power and its policies of persuasion.

Notes

1 Dr Peter van Ham (*pvanham@clingendael.nl*) is director of the Global Governance Research Programme at the Netherlands Institute of International Relations 'Clingendael' in The Hague, and Professor at the College of Europe in Bruges (Belgium). He is a member of the Advisory Council on International Affairs to the Dutch Government.
2 For a more historical overview of EU–OSCE relations, see Cameron (1995). See also Bloed (1993).
3 Although the European Union is developing its European Security and Defence Policy, the foreign policy identity of the European Union remains markedly civilian.
4 This taxonomy is derived from Oberthür and Gehring (2006).
5 The most notable document which testifies to the European Union's changed attitude towards the OSCE is the Assessment Report on the EU's Role vis-à-vis the OSCE, approved by the European Union's GAERC on 13 December 2004.
6 For the concept of nestedness, see Young (1996).
7 'Presidency statement on behalf of the European Union on monitoring of the elections in Belarus, Brussels on 27 July 2001', *Bulletin EU 7/8-2001, Common Foreign and Security Policy*, 14/34.
8 Ambassador Waestfelt has argued that this document is important since 'anything can change, so I think to confirm something that is already happening naturally is always an advantage', ibid., p. 15.

EU–OSCE relations   147

9 *OSCE Charter for European Security*, 1999, p. 4.
10 'EU statement in response to the Address by Minister of Foreign Affairs of the former Yugoslav Republic of Macedonia made in the Permanent Council of the OSCE', 5 February 2004. Internet: http://www.eu2004.ie/templates/news.asp?sNavlocator=66, 402,404& list_id=17
11 See the European Union's ENP website: http://europa.eu.int/comm/world/enp/index_ en.htm
12 Speech by Belgium Minister of Foreign Affairs Louis Michel in Prague, 2 March 2004. Internet: http://www.diplomatie.be/nl/press/speechdetails.asp?TEXTID=15925
13 *Common Purpose: Towards a More Effective OSCE, Final Report and Recommendations of the Panel of Eminent Persons*, June 2005.
14 Assessment Report on the EU's Role vis-à-vis the OSCE, approved by the European Union's GAERC on 13 December 2004. This document was circulated with restrictions and is not in the open domain.
15 Statement by Foreign Minister Ursula Plassnik at the meeting of the Permanent Council of the OSCE, 2 February 2006, Vienna.

References

Assessment Report (2004) Assessment Report on the EU's Role vis-à-vis the OSCE, approved by the EU's GAERC on 13 December.
Bicchi, F. (2006) '"Our Size Fits All": Normative Power Europe and the Mediterranean', *Journal of European Public Policy*, 13(2): 286–303, March.
Biscop, S. (2005) 'The EU, the OSCE and the European Security Architecture: Network or Labyrinth?', *Helsinki Monitor Conference*, Vienna, 9 September.
Bloed, A. (1993) *The Conference on Security and Cooperation in Europe: Analysis and Basic Documents, 1972–1993*, Leiden: Martinus Nijhoff Publishers.
Borawski, J. (1994) 'Forging the NATO–CSCE Partnership', *Helsinki Monitor*, 5(2): 39–47.
Brichambaut, M.P. de (2006) 'How Things Turned Nasty for the Nice Guys of the OSCE', *Europe's World*, 1(3): 52–3 (summer).
Burghardt, G. (1999) 'Frühwarnung und Konfliktprävention als Aufgaben der Europäischen Union und der Zusammenarbeit zwischen EU und OSZE', in IFSH, *OSZE-Jahrbuch*, Baden-Baden.
Cameron, F. (1995) 'The European Union and the OSCE: Future Roles and Challenges', *Helsinki Monitor*, 6(2): 21–31.
Dunay, P. (2006) *The OSCE in Crisis*, Paris: Chaillot Paper, No. 88, April, pp. 72–73.
European Commission (2000) 'Shaping the New Europe', Brussels, 9.2. COM, 154 final.
European Council (2004) 'EU statement in response to the Address by Minister of Foreign Affairs of the former Yugoslav Republic of Macedonia made in the Permanent Council of the OSCE', Brussels, 5 February.
EU's ENP website (2004) Online. Available HTTP: http://ec.europa.eu/world/enp/index_ en.htm (accessed 2 September 2008).
EU Presidency (2001) Presidency statement on behalf of the European Union on monitoring of the elections in Belarus, Brussels on 27 July 2001, *Bulletin EU 7/8-2001, Common Foreign and Security Policy*, 14/34.
Huber, M. (2003) 'The Effectiveness of OSCE Missions', *Helsinki Monitor*, 14(2): 125–135.
Lavenex, S. (2004) 'EU External Governance in "Wider Europe"', *Journal of European Public Policy*, 11(4): 680–700, August.
Lööf, S. (2006) 'The OSCE and the EU: Complementing Each Other's Strengths', *OSCE Magazine*, July, 14–16.

148 *Peter van Ham*

Michel, L. (2004) Speech by Belgium Minister of Foreign Affairs in Prague, 2 March. Online. Available HTTP: http://www.diplomatie.be/nl/press/speechdetails.asp?TEX TID=15925 (accessed 2 September 2008).

Oberthür, S. and Gehring, T. (2006) 'Conceptual Foundations of Institutional Interaction', in S. Oberthür and T. Gehring (eds), *Institutional Interaction in Global Environmental Governance: Synergy and Conflict among International and EU Politics*, Cambridge, MA: The MIT Press.

OSCE (1999) *OSCE Charter for European Security*, p. 4.

OSCE (2005) *Common Purpose: Towards a More Effective OSCE, Final Report and Recommendations of the Panel of Eminent Persons*, June.

OSCE News (2004) 'EU External Relations Commissioner Patten Praises Level of Co-operation with OSCE', 15 July.

OSCE Press Release (2002) 'Javier Solana Describes the OSCE as a "Natural-Born Partner" of the EU', 25 September.

Otte, M. (2002) 'ESDP and Multilateral Security Organisations: Working with NATO, the UN, and the OSCE', in E. Brimmer (ed.), *The EU's Search for a Strategic Role: ESDP and Its Implications for Transatlantic Relations*, Washington DC: Center for Transatlantic Relations, pp. 35–56.

Pijpers, A.E. (1990) 'The Vicissitudes of European Political Cooperation', PhD thesis, Leiden University.

Plassnik, U. (2006) 'Foreign Minister, Statement at the meeting of the Permanent Council of the OSCE', 2 February, Vienna.

Rosamond, B. (2005) 'Conceptualizing the EU Model of Governance in World Politics', *European Foreign Policy Review*, 10(4): 478 (winter).

Schram Stokke, O. (2001) 'The Interplay of International Regimes: Putting Effectiveness Theory to Work', *FNI Report 14*, Lysaker, Norway: Fridtjof Nansen Institute.

Smith, M. (2003) 'The Framing of European Foreign and Security Policy: Towards a Post-Modern Policy Framework?', *Journal of European Public Policy*, 10(4): 556–575, August.

Sporrer, W. (2003) 'The OSCE and the Stability Pact for South Eastern Europe: Can a New Relationship Improve Performance?', *Helsinki Monitor*, 14(1).

Stewart, E.J. (2006) *The European Union and Conflict Prevention: Policy Evolution and Outcome*, Münster: LIT Verlag.

van Ham, P. (2001) *European Integration and the Postmodern Condition*, London/New York: Routledge.

Wohlfeld, M. (2003) 'EU Enlargement and the Future of the OSCE: The Role of Field Missions', *Helsinki Monitor*, 12(1): 52–64.

Wolfers, A. (1962) *Discord and Cooperation: Essays on International Politics*, Baltimore: Johns Hopkins University Press, pp. 73–76.

Young, O.R. (1996) 'Institutional Linkages in International Society: Polar Perspectives', *Global Governance*, 2(1): 1–23, January.

Young, O.R. (2002) *The Institutional Dimension of Environmental Change: Fit, Interplay, and Scale*, Cambridge, MA: The MIT Press.

Zagorski, A. (2002) 'The OSCE in the Context of the Forthcoming EU and NATO Extensions', *Helsinki Monitor*, 13(3): 222–223.

8 The European Union at the ILO's International Labour Conferences

A 'double' principal–agent analysis[1]

Peter Nedergaard

Introduction: The framework about coordination and delegation

How does the European Union coordinate its policies in international organizations? Based upon detailed information from participating officials and numerous documents, in this chapter I analyse the policy coordination among the EU member states before and during the International Labour Organization's (ILO) three-week International Labour Conferences in Geneva that are held every year in June. These conferences are by far the most important activities as far as the ILO is concerned and I see them as the best proxies for an overall analysis of the European Union's relationship to the ILO.

As mentioned by Jørgensen in Chapter 1 of this book there is very little scholarly work on the relationship between the European Union and international organizations. As it also seems clear from the introduction there are many approaches from which this relationship could be studied. I have chosen to analyse the coordination aspects of the EU–ILO relations because they clarify the relationships between the member states and the ILO as well as the relationships between the European Union and ILO. At the same time, when analysing the relationship *as* coordination, it also becomes possible to measure changes in the relationship.

Coordination problems in a narrow sense have been analysed as coordination games, which include various conventions about social behaviour; however, it is not possible to analyse most practical coordination problems as games (Mueller 2003: 14–16). Coordination problems in a broader sense have been dealt with by a few scholars who have also developed a general coordination framework as a body of principles about how activities can be coordinated (e.g. Malone and Crowston 1991; Malone *et al.* 1993). In an attempt to structure this chapter and to bring the general study of practical coordination further as well as to come up with new insights about the relationship between the European Union and international organizations, I use the framework proposed by these researchers. In general, there seems to be a need for more research in coordination problems in the broad sense of the word.

The choice of approach also means that I leave other and more policy-oriented approaches aside that could also have been very interesting to investigate: Which

150 *Peter Nedergaard*

Table 8.1 Components of coordination

Components of coordination	Associated coordination processes
Goals	Identifying goals (e.g. goal selection)
Activities	Mapping goals to activities (e.g. goal decomposition)
Actors	Mapping activities to actors (e.g. task assignment)
Interdependencies	'Managing' interdependencies (e.g. resource allocation, sequencing and synchronizing)

Source: Malone and Crowston (1991).

overall policy strategy (if any) does the European Union pursue through the ILO? How does the European Union promote its own 'model of social partnership' in the ILO, which is the UN 'social partnership' organization par excellence?

The questions that the proposed coordination framework tries to answer are the following concerning the European Union's relationship *vis-à-vis* the ILO: How are overall goals subdivided into activities? How are resources allocated among these activities? How are activities assigned to groups or to individual actors? How is information shared among different actors to help achieve the overall goals?

According to a broad definition, coordination means 'the act of working together'. Thus, there must be one or more actors, performing some activities that are directed towards some goals. By the word 'together', the definition implies that the activities are not independent. Instead they must be activities by actors that in a way help achieve the goals. These goal-relevant relationships between the activities are called interdependencies.

In Table 8.1, the relevant components and the coordination processes associated with them are summarized.

According to the proposed framework, all four components – goals, activities, actors and interdependencies – are necessary for a situation to be analysed in terms of coordination. However, there are also important power relations between these four components, which are handled through bargaining and delegation processes. Both bargaining and delegation processes must thus be included in order to analyse coordination processes in the political world.

Bargaining takes place in connection with power distribution among the different decision-making units at the same hierarchical level, whereas delegation takes place in connection with power distribution across different hierarchical levels. There is a huge collection of political science literature on delegation (and an even more voluminous literature in economics), for example Evans *et al.* (1993) and Moravcsik (1993), as well as on the principal–agent theory on delegation in political systems, for example Thatcher and Sweet (2002), Kiewiet and McCubbins (1991), Tallberg (2002) and Pollack (2003). However, as mentioned in the introduction to the book, only very little scholarly work has been conducted on delegation to supranational institutions (an exception is Tallberg 2002), and little research has been done on delegation to supranational institutions acting within the framework of international organizations except in the area of trade policy (Dür 2006; Meunier 2005; Young 2002).

The EU at the ILO 151

In accordance with mainstream political science, bargaining at the same hierarchical level is studied in this chapter both in the institutional context within which bargaining occurs and with the focus on the values of the actors involved, the method of communication of bargaining moves and the methods of completion of the bargaining process (cf. Roberts and Edwards 1991). However, I will also consider other forms of bargaining where bargaining takes place through an intensive discussion and information about the 'acceptable' argumentative logics and story-lines (e.g. also Hajer 1995; Nedergaard 2007b). In other words, I try to find out who has got the role of 'discursive coordination' in the sense of Hajer on the side of the European Union (Hajer 1995, 2002).

Delegation is conceptualized within the principal–agent framework where delegation is assumed to be inherently problematic because of agents' opportunistic behaviour (i.e. agents want to maximize their own interests despite the preferences of their principals). However, in order to test the quality of the delegation process, it is not enough to analyse the sanctioning measures of the possibility of strategic behaviour. Instead, one should also (and rather) be investigating the conditions under which delegation takes place and the level of discretion allocated to the agent.

At the same time, the principal–agent framework applied in this chapter is a 'double' principal–agent framework that covers both delegation from member states to the Commission and/or the Presidency as well as delegation from the European Union to the ILO.

This chapter is structured as follows. In the section below, the institutional context of EU coordination in the ILO is put in place with regard to goals, activities, actors and interdependencies as far as the European Union is concerned. The specific institutional set-up of the International Labour Conferences of the ILO is analysed in the third section of the chapter. In the fourth and fifth sections, the goals and activities of the two 'first-order' agents (the Commission and the Presidency, respectively) are analysed with respect to other relevant actors (and not least their principals) and their interdependencies. The sixth section contains an evaluation of the development of the European Union as a principal *vis-à-vis* its 'second-order' agent, the ILO. In the seventh section, the coordination during the ILO International Labour Conferences among the EU member states is compared with the coordination among the OECD (Organisation for Economic Co-operation and Development) countries at the same conference in IMEC (which is the other important ILO coordination arrangement) because IMEC is a strong rival *vis-à-vis* the European Union when it comes to analysing the European Union as a principal in relation to its agent, the ILO, and finally the eighth section contains the conclusion of the chapter.

EU coordination in the ILO is an area full of institutions and organs. Hence, in Table 8.2 all institutions and organs mentioned in the chapter are presented and described.

EU coordination in the ILO

One of the organizational strengths of the European Union is that many of its goals and activities of its various actors are very well defined when facing an event like the ILO International Labour Conferences due to both a flexible and strong judicial

Table 8.2 Institutions and organs in the chapter

Name	Description
International Labour Conference	The yearly three-week conference held in Geneva by the ILO
Commission	The central executive organ of the European Union
DG Energy and Transport	The General Directorate for Energy and Transport in the Commission
DG Employment and Social Affairs	The General Directorate for Employment and Social Affairs in the Commission
DG Justice, Liberty and Security	The General Directorate for Justice, Liberty and Security in the Commission
Presidency	The rotating presidency of the Council of Ministers
Council of Ministers	The primary legislative organ of the European Union
European Court of Justice	The primary judicial organ of the European Union
Council of Ministers Working Group for Social Affairs	The working group on social affairs that prepares initiatives for the Council of Ministers on Employment, Social Policy, Health and Consumer Affairs
European Union's Tripartite Advisory Committee for Labour	The committee carrying out discussion on labour policy in which government, employer and worker delegates are included
Council of Ministers Working Group for Maritime Transportation	The working group on social affairs that prepares initiatives for the Council of Ministers on Transport, Telecommunications and Energy
Committee of Experts	The Committee of Experts is an ILO organ that evaluates the state of application of international labour standards
Committee on Freedom of Association	The Committee on Freedom of Association is responsible for complaints submitted to the Governing Body alleging violations of freedom of association and for representations that concern such issues
Governing Body of the ILO	The Governing Body is the executive body of the International Labour Office (the Office is the secretariat of the Organization). It meets three times a year in March, June and November. It takes decisions on ILO policy, decides the agenda of the International Labour Conference, adopts the draft Programme and Budget of the Organization for submission to the Conference and elects the Director General

Table 8.2 (Continued)

Name	Description
Committee on the Application of Standards	The Conference Committee on the Application of Standards is made up of government, employer and worker delegates. It examines the report in a tripartite setting and selects from it a number of observations for discussion
UN's Commission on Human Rights	Commission on Human Rights procedures and mechanisms are mandated to examine, monitor and publicly report on human rights situations in either specific countries or territories
UN's Economic and Social Council (ECOSOC)	The principal organ to coordinate economic, social and related work of the 14 UN specialized agencies, ten functional commissions and five regional commissions
IMEC	The coordinating organ in the ILO consisting of the Industrialized Market Economic Countries (in practical terms, the OECD countries)

Source: Compiled by the author.

system (Nedergaard 2007a). The Commission and the Presidency of the Council of Ministers act as agents on behalf of their principals (Pollack 2003). The respective roles of the Commission and the Council are defined in the Treaty. In the ILO outside the yearly International Labour Conference, the Commission represents the European Union in areas that affect the European Union.[2] In other areas and due to the special constitution of the ILO,[3] it is necessary for close cooperation between the Commission and the Presidency. In various issues under the Common Foreign and Security Policy that are especially relevant, the Presidency acts on behalf of the Council of Ministers. For example, in the context of the ILO International Labour Conference in 2005, this required the issuing of EU opinions in cases regarding Burma/Myanmar, Zimbabwe and Colombia, for example.

However, the Presidency does not always have a clear mandate from the Council of Ministers. The time factor determines whether or not a reading in the Council is possible before the International Labour Conferences take place. The documents for the International Labour Conferences are usually ready in March at the earliest, which makes formal preparations in the EU system more difficult. The schedule for the Working Group for Social Affairs of the Council of Ministers is, moreover, often very busy from March to May in connection with the preparations for the June meeting in the Employment, Social Policy, Health and Consumer Affairs Council. Hence, most often, for practical reasons, the Presidency is allowed a high level of discretion during the International Labour Conferences, which is also due to the fact that its principals on the spot most often can control the Presidency during the conference.

154 *Peter Nedergaard*

On the other hand, if an issue at the International Labour Conference is prognosticated to concern significant aspects of EU competency or EU policies, or when there is a clear and apparent danger for conflicts between ILO and EU regulations or policies, it may necessitate urgent and extensive coordination meetings in the Working Group for Social Affairs of the Council of Ministers or in other relevant working groups of the Council of Ministers in order to identify common goals among the EU member states before the International Labour Conference takes place.

The practice of involving the Council of Ministers before the International Labour Conference stems from the early 1990s. In 1992 and 1993, the Council discussed the upcoming International Labour Conferences based on a recommendation from the Commission regarding Conference negotiations on the prevention of major industrial accidents and part-time work.[4] However, the Council of Ministers failed to reach any conclusions before the International Labour Conference.

Therefore, on 12 January 1994, the Commission presented a proposal for a decision by the Council of Ministers regarding the exercise of external Community competencies at the International Labour Conference with the areas that are within the scope of shared competencies between the European Union and the member states (cf. COM(94)2 final). In other words, once and for all, the Commission wanted rules of delegation with regard to the yearly ILO International Labour Conference.

The proposal should be seen in the context of the European Court of Justice's 19 March 1993 opinion (opinion 2/91), which obliges the Commission and the member states to closely cooperate on issues within the shared and exclusive competencies of the European Union, that is, in cases where there is a need to manage their interdependencies. The Council of Ministers did not conclude its discussions on the Commission's proposal. However, according to the Commission officials, the Commission finds that today the proposal is used in practice in EU coordination at the ILO.

The impact of both the proposal from the Commission and from the European Court of Justice signifies the importance for EU coordination in international organizations of both the Court and the Commission – the two EU institutions where the European Union's 'multilateral genetic code' is probably most significant – as actors in the EU decision-making processes, and also in instances of non-decision-making by the Council of Ministers. In practice, COM(94)2 finally outlines the goals, activities, actors and interdependencies of the European Union's coordination during the International Labour Conference.

Later on, the Commission unsuccessfully proposed to strengthen EU coordination in the ILO (cf. COM(2003)526/F). However, Spain and Greece have expressed particular resistance to the Commission's proposal to the Council for strengthened competencies for the European Union during the International Labour Conference. This is due to the fact that, in the case of strengthened competencies, various issues concerning fishing and maritime transportation[5] – where Spain and Greece have strong national interests – would then have to be coordinated at the EU level. Essentially, this shows the conditions under which delegation takes place during the ILO International Labour Conferences, that is, that delegation to the Presidency and the Commission are being kept within tight limits due to the Treaty obligations and the Court of Justice's interpretations.

However, in the phase leading up to the negotiations, EU coordination has a far greater role to play. In this phase before the ILO International Labour Conference, issues are presented at meetings between national experts who concern themselves with ILO issues that are summoned and funded by the Commission itself pending approval by the Presidency or by meetings summoned by the Presidency via the Council of Ministers in close cooperation with the Commission.

As can be seen, in the European Union, the Commission and the Presidency almost act as twin agents *vis-à-vis* their principals, the member states, where, however, the Commission plays the role as leading agent until the International Labour Conference starts and the Presidency takes over as the leading agent. Hence, EU coordination *vis-à-vis* the ILO International Labour Conference is to a large extent a question of managing interdependencies between the Presidency and the Commission. However, this is not so different from the daily 'agent coordination game' in Brussels (Nedergaard 2007a).

The ILO International Labour Conferences

Ahead of the International Labour Conferences, general coordination among the EU member states regarding the overall execution of the Conferences as well as coordination in the areas of the different activities of the Conference takes place. The goal of the ILO International Labour Conference may be divided into three activities:

1   Procedural activities: Procedural questions regarding, for example, methods for selection of critical country cases,[6] the rules of procedure of the Conference and elections for the Governing Body of the ILO.
2   Professional or technical activities: For example, occupational health and safety, work in the fisheries sector, promoting youth employment, and the Committee on the Application of Standards.
3   Political activities: The budget of the ILO and concrete country cases selected by the ILO's independent mechanisms of monitoring international labour market issues (e.g. the Committee of Experts and the Committee on Freedom of Association).

A number of preparatory meetings are held regarding each of the three Conference activities. In these meetings, there are orientations on the relevant decisions by the Council of Ministers and relevant EU regulations and especially on possible issues regarding the European area in the background reports to the committees at the International Labour Conference. The meetings are especially occupied with the professional or technical activities of the ILO International Labour Conference. The meetings are summoned and funded by the Commission according to an agreement with the Presidency.

Furthermore, there are informal exchanges on other relevant issues, such as political issues, conventions, and so on. Normally, the Commission prepares an informational note with the intent of contributing to and facilitating EU coordination at International Labour Conferences on these issues.

156 *Peter Nedergaard*

In addition, the branches of the Commission stay in contact with the EU social partners[7] regarding ILO issues. Relevant sectors with a functioning EU Sector *Social Dialogue* Committee have been formalized, such as fisheries and the exchange of information regarding ILO issues. By doing so, according to Commission officials, the Commission deliberately took the special set-up of the ILO into consideration. First and foremost, the Commission considers the tripartite set-up, which implies that ILO issues are to an increasing extent relevant to the social dialogue of the European Union, as in, for example, the *Social Dialogue* sector committees. In order to coordinate, the Commission also has contact with the social partners in the European Union as well as other international actors before the International Labour Conference and other relevant ILO meetings. The purpose of this intensive information from the Commission's side before the Conference is to ease the bargaining processes at the Conference itself where the representatives of the social partners are present. The intensive information process *vis-à-vis* the social partners contributes to a common understanding of the challenges facing the European Union at the Conference according to the Commission. In other words, the intensive meeting and information activities arranged by the Commission before the ILO International Labour Conference is a kind of 'discursive coordination' through the creation of a community of participants in the ILO International Labour Conference who adhere to the same argumentative logic (Hajer 1995, 2002).

The Commission at the International Labour Conferences

EU coordination in the ILO is conducted in a special context compared with other UN organizations. Other international instruments that are discussed in the UN or other UN organizations are negotiated and adopted using a framework that, in principle, has been established and approved before negotiations are initiated. This coordination framework identifies and recognizes relevant parties such as the European Union, when EU competencies are involved (cf. COM(2003)526/F). This is not the case for the ILO.

Hence, the Commission does not play any formal role during the ILO International Labour Conferences. However, in later years the Commission has lobbied with a view to achieving an independent status for the European Union in the context of the ILO, without much success. As mentioned in footnote 3 of this chapter, the ILO's Constitution (Article 2) still allows only states to be members of the organization. The Commission thus lacks legal competence to champion EU interests during the Conferences, which has had an impact because of resistance from certain member states on stronger coordination within the group of member states itself, cf. the section about EU coordination in the ILO above in this chapter.

In relation to EU coordination at the Conferences themselves, the Commission provides the member states' representatives with information on overall EU policies in the relevant areas as it did before the Conferences. The Commission assists coordination efforts with information on Council of Ministers' decisions and conclusions in order to make the bargaining process among member states as frictionless as possible and in order to create a common understanding on the nature of the problems at the table of the International Labour Conferences. The Commission also offers its interpretation of relevant EU regulation in relation to legal questions. A minor Conference task for the Commission's Representation in Geneva is to print and distribute EU submissions at the Conference. In general, the Commission acts as the cement of EU coordination at the ILO International Labour Conferences, which is, of course, not different from the role played by the Commission in other settings (Dinan 2005: 217–219).

The current Treaty basis includes a number of provisions regarding the European Union's powers to enter into agreements with third countries and international organizations. None of these are applicable to the ILO. However, the case law of the European Court of Justice has established a principle of parallel competencies in the internal and external aspects of the European Union. This implies that the European Union has the competence to enter into an agreement, if the agreement regulates an area that internally falls within the scope of EU legal acts. Conventions within the ILO framework will thus typically be included in the European Union's area of competence.[8] Hence, member states do not enter into agreements if the participation of member states will affect common internal EU legal acts. As mentioned above, specifically regarding the ILO, the European Court of Justice has stated in Opinion 2/91 that there will be no exclusive EU competence if and when EU directives are in the shape of minimum standards, as ILO Conventions themselves typically provide for minimum standards. Conversely, the European Union is assumed to have exclusive competence if European Union directives are to take the form of total harmonization.

Even though, as mentioned, the Commission does not play any formal role during the International Labour Conferences, it is still highly visibly present, and, normally, 15–25 officials from the Commission take part in the Conferences. Also, most often the Commissioner for Employment, Social Affairs and Equal Opportunities attend the International Labour Conferences. Usually, the Commissioner and/or the Director-General for Employment, Social Affairs and Equal Opportunities participate in part of the Conference's second week (the 'ministerial week') when the ministers of employment and labour are present at the Conference as well.

In short, the Commission and Commission officials have no formal role during the International Labour Conferences, but the Commission is nevertheless represented by a relatively high number of officials at various levels who seek to help and 'smooth out' the bargaining processes using their expertise if needed in order to improve the lines of information and coordination and, if possible, thereby enhancing the common EU position.

The Presidency at ILO International Labour Conferences

The Presidency is the formal representative of the European Union during the ILO International Labour Conferences. The Presidency leads EU coordination and acts as agent on behalf of the EU member states during the three weeks of the Conference.

158   Peter Nedergaard

EU coordination of the Presidency consists of preparing and initiating EU policy statements based on elements of overall EU policies, such as the Lisbon declaration. The Presidency also handles all logistics and practical tasks: summoning meetings, exchanging information and chairing meetings. The intensity and quality of coordination at the Conference largely depends on the Presidency member state.

Normally, the Presidency keeps in touch with the European Union's ILO office and keeps it informed of latest developments, especially on political issues.[9] Finally, the Presidency tries to create good connections with the additional ILO decision makers, *employers* and *employees*, thereby being on top of opinions and strategies. The ILO Constitution implies that labour market parties may form a majority versus governments in the decision-making process, except when it comes to questions regarding the ILO budget. Hence, the formal and informal contacts between the Commission and the social partners of the European Union before the yearly ILO International Labour Conference are not only to accommodate the employers and employees, but also to improve the manoeuvrability of the European Union and the EU member states when negotiating during the Conference if and when they are in accordance with their 'own' social partner representatives. In other words, the social partners are deliberately exploited (and are most often willing to be exploited) by EU institutions in order to enhance EU coordination so that the European Union can act as a 'second-order' principal (i.e. the European Union *vis-à-vis* the ILO) to be reckoned with *vis-à-vis* its 'second-order' agent, the ILO.

EU coordination meetings during the ILO International Labour Conferences are either executed in the Council of Ministers' Geneva representation, in the UN mansion or in the ILO building. If member states require interpretation, the meetings are held in the Council's representation, where interpretation services are available. With an increasing Conference workload in latter years the options for leaving the Conference are limited. As a consequence, there is an increasing tendency to hold coordination meetings in English without any interpretation.

There are no formal requirements for EU coordination at the ILO International Labour Conferences. Some Presidencies prefer that their permanent UN Ambassador preside over the initial and general meetings, that is, on political issues where the UN delegations can utilize their significant expertise and the possibility of regarding the cases in connection with cases brought up before the Human Rights Commission or the UN's Economic and Social Council.

Due to the relatively dated logistics at the Conference where access to electronic devices is scarce, ongoing communications between the Presidency and the member states' embassies in Geneva are established. When the European Union criticizes individual countries, coordination takes a draft statement from the Presidency as a starting point. The Presidency collects input for the draft policy statement from the Commission that updates the Presidency on any possible former EU statements on the same issues. During the coordination process, the representatives of the member states clear the draft policy statements with the national authorities. Through the ongoing dialogue a consensus regarding the contents of the EU statement is established that can be interpreted in no other way than the Presidency being a 'first-order' agent under strict control and permanent surveillance of its 'first-order' principals on the spot during the International

The EU at the ILO 159

Labour Conference. The Presidency then makes the policy statement in the committee/in plenum on behalf of the European Union.

Professional or technical activities such as working environment, labour law, social law and maritime affairs are usually covered by representatives from the Ministries of the Presidency. The coordination of these issues differs to some extent from the coordination of political activities. The background is that the relevant national experts are present in Geneva and thus do not require the same degree of close contact to national ministries. The working routines of the technical committees thus make larger requirements on the discretion of the EU coordination, however, most often with experts from the member states present in the committees, which, again, limits the actual discretion of the EU coordination. It is often difficult to predict, for instance, which concrete parts of a draft convention are discussed on a specific day of the Conference. Therefore, several daily EU coordination meetings are often scheduled concerning professional or technical activities during the ILO International Labour Conference.

With respect to professional or technical issues, the first priority is to establish the areas where member states have the same positions, that is, with a relevant EU regulation as a starting point. The Commission's representatives at the Conference contribute information on relevant regulations as well as EU policies in other multilateral fora in order to help the bargaining processes to run as smoothly as possible.

The development of EU coordination *vis-à-vis* the ILO

The EU Treaties of Amsterdam and Nice have expanded the scope of issues that are relevant for the ILO and the European Union's internal and external policies. This, for instance, applies to the strategy for employment and social inclusion, social dialogue, working conditions and fundamental rights including non-discrimination (Hix 2005: 256–258). Hence, one could expect a demand to an increasing extent of pre-emptive EU coordination of ILO issues. This could also imply facilitating contacts to third countries and regions (industrialized as well as developing) via the ILO International Labour Conferences and other relevant meetings. However, many member states see or act differently, and the increased relevance of the ILO for the European Union is only reflected to a certain extent in their position *vis-à-vis* a strengthened European Union coordination during the Conferences.

On the other hand, the Commission *has* in later years strengthened its efforts in preparing for the Conferences. However, as mentioned, the intensity of EU coordination before the Conferences depends on the issues on the International Labour Conference's agenda. Issues that affect overall EU policies and strategies require extensive EU coordination. This is, for example, the case of occupational safety, gender equality and non-discrimination – issues that affect the free movement of labour, informing and consulting employers, collective dismissals and corporate takeovers as well as sector elements such as working conditions in the fisheries and maritime areas.

The same applies to issues of growing importance for EU policies of various ILO policies, such as the ILO's *social dimension of globalization* (i.e. interdependencies

160   *Peter Nedergaard*

between economic, employment and social policies, trade as well as external relations and cooperation) and the connection between the European Union's employment strategy and the ILO's strategy for 'Decent Work'.

At the same time, also the European Union in general is in the process of strengthening its cooperation with the ILO.[10] The 14 May 2005 exchange of letters between the ILO and the Commission, the European Social Agenda documents and other relevant documents in the area of development policy, including the Commission's 13 July 2005 Communication (cf. COM(2005)311 final), and the July 2004 strategic partnership in the area of development cooperation that is implemented through the 2001 exchange of letters, are all examples of this.[11] On the other hand, more cooperation between the European Union and ILO does not necessarily lead to a strengthened EU coordination *vis-à-vis* the ILO at the yearly ILO International Labour Conferences. As noted earlier in this chapter, EU coordination *vis-à-vis* the ILO International Conference mainly (but not only) takes place when either the Treaty or the European Court suggests it.

In general, judging from information from government representatives from the various member states, it is clearly a shared experience that the intensity in the shape of increased scope and quality of the EU coordination is increasing. Participants with long historical experience point out that a similar development was experienced at the beginning of the 1990s, but that conditions changed in the mid-1990s due to resentment on the part of some member states. In other words, it seems that the demand for EU coordination during the ILO Labour Conference, to a certain extent, swings like a pendulum.

In short, there has been a real increase in EU coordination activities – at least since the mid-1990s – as well as a stronger need for such coordination. Obviously, the Commission has also strengthened EU coordination in the run-up to the ILO International Labour Conferences, and all actors seem to be satisfied with that. However, due to the specific characteristics of the ILO Constitution, EU coordination at the Conference itself is officially left to the Presidency and its willingness and ability to coordinate at the Conference. At the same time, the Presidency as an agent is under strict control by its principals during the Conference. Still, the Commission plays a strong role as a behind the scenes coordinator at the Conference.

One thing is that there has been some increase in EU coordination activities. Another thing is whether this increased coordination has been successful or not.

Evaluating whether or not a specific EU coordination has been successful depends on the criteria selected for evaluation. Member states in favour of the potential EU consensus position on ILO issues will presumably experience an intensive and detailed coordination as successful, whereas member states that prefer a strong national base for ILO agreements will most often prefer less extensive and less substantial EU coordination.

A criterion for success is when member states succeed through the bargaining processes in getting EU regulations, basic EU values or core EU issues that have most often been promoted by the Commission before and, informally, at the Conference reflected in ILO instruments (Conventions and Recommendations) or internal/external ILO policies. Any such success will usually require that the Presidency establish close contacts and cooperation with ILO labour market parties and also potentially with the IMEC group. In general, according to most observers, the ILO is willing to act as an agent for the European Union in most of the 'soft' policy areas where the European Union's 'social market economy' approach and the European Union's recognition of the role of the social partners is seen as an admirable way forward by the ILO officials and a great number of the ILO member states (although not necessarily the most important ones).

The 2004 Conference's deliberations on the topic of 'migrant workers' (migration) are an example of this type of successful coordination. The European Union succeeded to a large extent in finding common ground for determining the ILO's goals and mandate in relation to migrant workers. There are numerous examples where the European Union has been a less successful 'second-order' principal *vis-à-vis* the ILO. In its extreme consequence, this has sometimes meant that the EU coordination has been reduced to an exchange of information on the respective member states' national positions, or that all attempts at any further coordination have been abandoned. An example of such a 'failure' is the inability of the EU member states in agreeing on a common approach for the treatment of the 'Employment relationship' topic in 2003.

The European Union and IMEC

Some of the difficulties of EU coordination stem from the fact that the European Union is not the only (want to be) principal during the International Labour Conferences where all EU member states participate. Traditionally, the so-called IMEC group has been the strongest coordinator during the Conferences. How is the relationship between EU coordination and IMEC coordination at the International Labour Conferences? IMEC is the agent for a group of countries consisting of the *Industrialized Market Economic Countries*. The composition of the group more or less corresponds to the make-up of the OECD. With the accession of the new EU countries to the IMEC group in the autumn of 2004, the IMEC group is less homogeneous than the EU group. As coordination happens by consensus at the very conference,[12] it is a logical consequence that the scope of areas susceptible to IMEC coordination is smaller than for the EU coordination also because the IMEC does not have an organizational and 'discursive' driver like the Commission.

IMEC coordination is, as a starting point, only carried out in relation to *formal activities*: procedural questions, working methods, elections for the ILO's Governing Body, and so on. Submissions may frequently be framed only in general terms based on common goals regarding transparency, efficiency, decentralization and a result-oriented solving of tasks. In other words, the IMEC as an agent is probably under even stricter control by its principals than the European Union.

Concrete political cases related to specific countries are discussed in the IMEC framework, but common submissions are rarely produced. Yet, on the other hand, general IMEC submissions on political cases are produced, for example, when defending the monitoring system of the ILO (Committee of Experts and the

162   *Peter Nedergaard*

Committee on Freedom of Association), where criticism from groups of countries that feel targeted on an unreasonable basis is countered. Similarly, general submissions on the ILO budget are produced, encouraging increased efficiency, more focus on the ILO's core areas and decentralization of the organizational structure.

What are the advantages of coordination in the IMEC compared with EU coordination? According to participants in both settings, first, the geographical dispersion of the IMEC countries commands respect. The IMEC group also finances more than 90 per cent of ILO activities. Due to this fact, IMEC submissions are also awarded special interest and attention on the part of the ILO office, other member states and social partners. Second, the informal tone and character of meetings under permanent Canadian auspices contribute to a good and efficient social and professional climate for cooperation. According to participants in the IMEC meetings, the 'power of the argument' is perceived as dominant during the coordination. It is of less importance (however, not unimportant) if a large country, such as the United States or Japan, supports the argument.

Conversely, the relative general character of the content of IMEC submissions weakens the significance of IMEC, as it leaves the ILO bureaucracy with relatively large room for manoeuvre when following up on submissions. The IMEC, on the other hand, wields great influence over the formal activities of the ILO.

Especially in relation to budgetary questions, there are real differences between large IMEC countries and the general position of the EU member states. A large majority of EU countries thus supports a zero-growth budget regulated according to the inflation rate, whereas the large IMEC countries (the USA, Japan, Canada and Australia) want a nominal zero-growth budget. For this reason, the budget area is not included in IMEC coordination.

What are the advantages of coordination in the European Union compared with the IMEC? First, the European Union's intensive coordination (more frequent and of longer duration than the coordination in the IMEC because EU coordination starts several months before the Conferences) implies that the ILO International Labour Conference activities are frequently addressed earlier and more thoroughly under EU than under IMEC auspices. At the same time, as agents of the European Union, EU Presidencies sometimes have had the habit of not informing the IMEC group of planned and delicately balanced EU submissions. A number of times this has led IMEC members to express frustration – after an EU submission – over not being able to support a motion as well as over the fragmentation of the government group the European Union thereby causes.

Second, outside of the ILO International Labour Conferences and meetings of the Governing Body, the Commission in particular has close professional contacts with the ILO office. This is frequently reflected in the draft proposals the ILO produces for the deliberation on the activities of the International Labour Conferences where Commission submissions are often integrated.

Third, the fact that the European Union in a number of areas has implemented basic ILO policies (i.e. the Decent Work Agenda) in policies, strategies and external relations with third countries (i.e. the GSP system's requirement for third countries' adherence to the eight basic ILO Conventions as a prerequisite for achieving easier access to the European market) may be seen as an example of mutual influence in the relationship between the European Union and the ILO. Concurrently, the European Union and the EU member states' concrete implementation of and adherence to ILO standards entail a high degree of respect and responsiveness from ILO labour market parties. This reflects the fact that, to a lesser extent than the IMEC, EU coordination aims at formal activities and conversely has great significance for the general political and technical activities. In other words, when applying a 'double' principal–agent framework, the ILO is a more willing agent for the EU principal than for the IMEC principal. There is also no doubt that the majority of member states of the ILO prefer a strong EU coordination to a strong IMEC coordination.

On the other hand, in general, with the exception of policy differences concerning the ILO budget, there are no serious or 'fundamental' conflicts between the European Union and the IMEC. However, increasing pressure from the Commission and some member states for increased independence and prioritization of EU coordination at the expense of IMEC coordination sometimes causes some frustration among leading IMEC countries. This frustration is related to formal rather than actual issues. There are thus no significant divergences between the European Union and the IMEC on the most important political or procedural questions.

EU member states generally maintain the same position within the IMEC framework as with the EU framework. However, some divergences may be inferred from the different levels of enthusiasm EU member states display when it comes to participating in coordination in the two fora.

There *is* a group of EU member states that emphasizes strengthened EU position in the ILO and has occasionally expressed the opinion that the EU member states should withdraw from the IMEC, unless it is solely used for the exchange of views and information. The opposite is of course true for less eager ILO common position member states. A large majority of EU member states find that the choice of coordination forum should be made based on a concrete informed strategy for achieving the optimal result for the European Union's member states. In this context, the view that the larger group of countries behind any given common position will achieve the most impact is frequently put forward. At the same time, the position by most EU member states that one should choose the agent (the European Union or IMEC) that produces the optimal result also reflects that when applying a 'double' principal–agent framework to the European Union in the ILO it becomes clear that the 'first-order' principal–agent relationship (EU member states *vis-à-vis* the European Union) is much more important than the 'second-order' relationship (the European Union *vis-à-vis* the ILO).

Conclusion

The coordination framework and the concepts from the 'double' principal–agent framework proposed at the beginning of the chapter has proved itself useful in order to structure the analysis of the EU coordination before and during the yearly ILO International Labour Conferences. On this basis, the analysis of practical EU policy coordination can be understood and explained in context.

The quality of EU coordination overwhelmingly depends on the initial preparations of the Presidency and the Commission as well as the Presidency representatives' ability to work for and achieve consensus during the ILO

164   *Peter Nedergaard*

International Labour Conferences. In this connection, the Presidency must be able to coordinate and manage the interdependencies stemming from the quite divergent views of the Commission and the member states.

It is important, furthermore, that the Presidency and the Commission working in concert succeed in delivering a high degree of service when managing logistics and practical tasks in relation to the location and planning of meetings as well as efficient preparations and quickly updating drafts for EU submissions. In many respects, the Commission and the Presidency almost act as twin agents *vis-à-vis* their principals, the member states, where, however, the Commission plays the role as leading agent until the International Labour Conference starts and the Presidency takes over as the leading agent.

In addition, the analysis of the chapter has shown that there is a sharp difference between EU coordination before the ILO International Labour Conferences and EU coordination during the Conferences. In general, both the Presidency and the Commission are being kept within tight limits by the principals due to the Treaty obligations and their interpretations by the Court of Justice. However, in the phase leading up to the Conferences, the EU coordination has a greater role to play. In this phase, the Commission summons experts from the member states to meetings in Brussels in order to discuss activities at the Conferences relevant to the European Union and in order to inform about already adopted EU positions on the various issues. This phase of coordination is characterized by what could be called discursive coordination with the Commission as the driving force.

In order for coordination to be a success, it is important that the Commission is in close contact with the labour market parties *before the Conferences*. It is also central that the Presidency understands the significance of keeping in close contact with labour market parties *at the Conferences* and utilizes these contacts. An EU initiative would be devoid of any real significance if it had not been cleared with at least one of the parties in advance.

When the European Union is analysed as a principal *vis-à-vis* its agent, the ILO, there are relatively large problems of control. First, because the European Union is not the only agent as the IMEC is a strong competitor. Second, because the European Union as an agent is suffering from coordination difficulties due to differing member states' interest in the ILO issues. On the other hand, also outside the Treaty obligations, the European Union seems to be successful *vis-à-vis* its principal on the 'soft' policy areas as well as in the European Union's general approach to social partnership.

In sum, when applying a 'double' principal–agent framework to the European Union in the ILO it becomes clear that the 'first-order' principal–agent relationship (EU member states *vis-à-vis* the European Union) is much more important than the 'second-order' relationship (the European Union *vis-à-vis* the ILO).

Notes

1 I have received help from many sides in preparing this chapter. Not least Klaus Pedersen from the Danish Ministry of Employment has been a great help in gathering data about EU coordination before and during the ILO International Labour Conference in 2005. Monica Thurmond and Thomas Horn have helped to translate some of the material into

The EU at the ILO   165

proper English. Commission and government officials have also contributed with information to the analysis of this chapter. For a number of years, the author himself participated in the International Labour Conferences and their preparation.

2 In the following, I write 'EU' or 'European Union' also when I am referring to the 'European Community', that is, the first pillar of the European Union.

3 The ILO's 1919 Constitution is significant for the relations between the European Union and the ILO. The ILO's conventions and recommendations are prepared, negotiated and adopted according to the 1919 rules. However, this fact creates problems, as regional organizations such as the European Union did not exist in 1919. The closest approximation is the special challenges of federal states.

4 Cf. Commission: COM(92)473 final; Commission, SEC(93)766 final; Council 6757/93 of 26 May 1993.

5 The ILO has adopted conventions and recommendations concerning working conditions in the fishing industry as well as in the maritime transportation sector.

6 Critical country cases are cases that could be subject to official criticism from the ILO.

7 'Social partners' is 'euro-speak' for employers' and employees' representatives.

8 Still, there is significant room for manoeuvre if and when the European Union has to take part in the drafting of conventions. The Commission has lobbied for increasing the European Union's influence on the current drafting of the new and extensive ILO Maritime Convention to be decided upon primo 2006. The maritime area does to some extent differ from other ILO issues, that is, due to the inclusion of transportation as a trans-border element.

9 The Presidency carries out EU coordination during the International Labour Conference with practical assistance from the Council of Ministers' representation in Geneva.

10 Even today, there are many common EU–ILO projects, especially concerning labour conditions in the developing countries. For an overview, check www.google.com using 'EU' and 'ILO' as keywords in the search process.

11 Cf. exchange of letters. Online. Available HTTP: http://europa.eu.int/comm/employ ment_social/news/2001/jun/131_en.html (accessed 1 May 2006).

12 EU decision-making is also inclined toward consensus, yet after a lengthy and reiterated negotiating process.

References

Dinan, D. (2005) *Ever Closer Union. An Introduction to European Integration*, Houndmills, Basingstoke: Palgrave Macmillan.

Dür, A. (2006) 'Assessing the EU's role in international trade negotiations', *European Political Science*, 5(4): 362–376.

Evans, P.B., Jacobson, H. and Putnam, R. (1993) *Double-Edged Diplomacy: International Bargaining and Domestic Politics*, Berkeley: University of California Press.

Hajer, M. (1995) *The Politics of Environmental Discourse – Ecological Modernization and the Policy Process*, Oxford: Oxford University Press.

—— (2002) 'Discourse analysis and the study of policy making', *European Political Science*, 2(1): 61–65.

Hix, S. (2005) *The Political System of the European Union*, New York: Palgrave Macmillan.

Kiewiet, D.R. and McCubbins, M.D. (1991) *The Logic of Delegation*, Chicago, IL: University of Chicago Press.

Malone, T.W. and Crowston, K. (1991) 'Toward an interdisciplinary theory of coordination', *Working Paper No. 120*, MIT Center for Coordination Science.

Malone, T.W., Crowston, K., Lee, J. and Penland, B. (1993) 'Tools for inventing organizations: Toward a handbook of organizational processes', 2nd IEEE Workshop on Enabling Technologies Infrastructure for Collaborative Enterprises (WET ICE), Morgantown, WV, USA.

166 *Peter Nedergaard*

Meunier, S. (2005) *Trading Voices: The European Union in International Commercial Negotiations*, Princeton: Princeton University Press.

Moravcsik, A. (1993) 'Introduction: Integrating international and domestic theories of international bargaining', in P.B. Evans, H. Jacobson and R. Putnam (eds) *Double-Edged Diplomacy. International Bargaining and Domestic Politics*, Berkeley: University of California Press.

Mueller, D.C. (2003) *Public Choice III*, Cambridge: Cambridge University Press.

Nedergaard, P. (2007a) 'European Union administration: Legitimacy and efficiency', *Nijhoff Law Special Series No. 69*, Leiden/Boston: Martinus Nijhoff Publications.

—— (2007b) 'Blocking minorities. Networks and meaning in the opposition against the proposal for a directive on temporary work in the Council of Ministers of the European Union', *Journal of Common Market Studies*, 45(4): 695–717.

Pollack, M.A. (2003) *The Engines of European Integration*, New York: Oxford University Press.

Roberts, G. and Edwards, A. (1991) *A New Dictionary of Political Analysis*, London and New York: Edward Arnold.

Tallberg, J. (2002) 'Delegation to supranational institutions: Why, how, and with what consequences?', *West European Politics*, 25(1): 23–46.

Thatcher, M. and Sweet, A.S. (2002) 'Theory and practice of delegation to non-majoritarian institutions', *West European Politics*, 25(1): 125–147.

Young, A. (2002) *Extending European Cooperation: The European Union and the 'New' International Trade Agenda*, Manchester: Manchester University Press.

9 The European Union and the International Criminal Court

The politics of international criminal justice[1]

Martijn Groenleer and David Rijks

Introduction

On 17 July 1998, 120 states decided to create a permanent International Criminal Court (ICC) in order to try the perpetrators of genocide, crimes against humanity and war crimes when states are unwilling or unable to carry out investigation or prosecution.[2] Upon the 60th ratification of the Statute of the ICC on 1 July 2002, the Court became a reality. Only a year after its judges had been sworn in and the prosecutor had been appointed, it started its first investigations, leading in 2006 to the arrest of the first suspect and his subsequent transfer to The Hague, the seat of the Court. The ICC started its first trials in 2008.

Over the years, the European Union has played a significant role in the creation and development of the ICC. Ever since the creation of an ICC was put on the agenda of the UN General Assembly in the late 1980s, EU member states were involved in negotiating its tasks and designing its structure. Once the Statute of the ICC had been agreed upon, EU member states were among the first to become Parties to the Statute, and they have provided the majority of funding for the ICC to perform its tasks.[3] Hence, the ICC has sometimes been called an 'EU Court'. Moreover, to support and assist the ICC in its activities, the European Union has adopted Common Positions and Action Plans and has concluded a cooperation and assistance agreement with the ICC.

This chapter examines the relationship between the European Union and the ICC. It aims to answer three types of question. The first asks how the European Union's support for an ICC has evolved throughout the years. The chapter demonstrates that, during the preparatory stages of the Court, national policy positions were divergent rather than similar. But, over time, EU member states as a collective have seemingly escaped the logic of diversity, which has proven such an oft-cited impediment to coherence and effectiveness in many areas of EU foreign policy.

The second type of question asks why the European Union supports multilateral institutions such as the ICC and the international legal order of which the ICC is part. The chapter identifies a number of specific factors that have contributed to the formation of a highly visible EU policy in support of the ICC that is greater than the sum of its constituent parts. Some of these pertain to specific characteristics of the development of the ICC policy area within the European Union itself.

168   *Martijn Groenleer and David Rijks*

Others relate to the importance of external pressures and demands on the European Union, in particular the strong American opposition to the ICC, which have helped to shape European policies and to raise their profile.

The third type of question asks what the consequences of EU support for the ICC are both for the EU member states and the European Union. The chapter shows that, on the one hand, the ICC has developed into an important theme in EU foreign policy. Central to our argument is the significance of the Common Foreign and Security Policy (CFSP) as a platform through which member states coordinate their positions and channel their support for the ICC. On the other hand, the establishment of the Court as a milestone in the evolution of international criminal law, and the global political controversy it has sparked, have left their mark on both the European Union and its member states. For the European Union in particular, itself a hybrid of an emerging polity and an international organization, the development of the ICC as an issue of foreign policy has enhanced its role as an international actor in its own right.

The chapter concludes with the (policy) implications of these patterns of influences for the European Union and the challenges that the European Union faces in its relationship with the ICC.

The European Union's policy towards the ICC: Rome and beyond

The ICC as an issue of EU foreign policy can broadly be divided into three analytically distinct categories. These categories developed according to different logics, their dynamics having different impacts on political outcomes. The first category concerns the position of EU member states in the negotiations over the Rome Statute. The influence of the European Union on the ICC's design and structure before and during the Rome Conference was limited; member states only occasionally made use of the European Union to coordinate their positions. The second category includes initiatives relating to the promotion of ratification and implementation of the Rome Statute. The European Union has in this area been able to successfully develop a consistent and proactive set of policies on its own account through which it has had an impact on the development (and change) of the ICC. Policies in the third category relate to the preservation of the integrity of the ICC Statute and the effectiveness of the Court in the face of actions of third states to curtail its powers. In this area, the European Union has experienced much more difficulty in formulating common positions and strategies.

Negotiating the Rome Statute

The European Union has not always operated as a bloc in favour of a strong and independent ICC. Early EU support was much more a reflection of the support already expressed – albeit to different degrees – by individual member states. Yet, informal meetings, both in New York and in Brussels, and in between and during the official negotiations, have certainly brought member states closer together.

In the period leading up to the Diplomatic Conference held in Rome in 1998 support for the ICC was primarily 'bilateral'. Although member states actively participated in the Ad Hoc Committee (1995), the Preparatory Committee (1996–1998) and the UN General Assembly's Sixth Committee, coordination within the EU framework was limited. EU involvement consisted of broad statements of the Council Presidencies merely welcoming the proposed establishment of the ICC.[4] The European Union as such did not have clearly stated preferences as regards the design and structure of the ICC and did not put forward proposals or respond to initiatives of others. If one at this stage could speak of negotiations at all (for talks were still exploratory and often did not concern substantive issues), member states negotiated on their own behalf.

During the negotiations on the Statute for an ICC, the Union was essentially split. The 'EU 13', part of the so-called Like-Minded Group (LMG), actively lobbied for the creation of a strong and independent ICC in the Preparatory Committee's negotiations. As members of the LMG, the 'EU 13' had agreed on several broad principles, the so-called cornerstone positions, that set out the minimal requirements for an ICC on particularly controversial design issues, notably the role of the UN Security Council. On the basis of these positions, the LMG coordinated their negotiating strategies and organized working groups (Edgar 2002; Nel 2002). The two permanent members of the UN Security Council, the United Kingdom and France, however, allied with the United States and the other permanent members of the Security Council.

In their efforts to create a strong and independent ICC, the 'EU 13' and eventually also the British and the French were ready to abandon the United States (and the other permanent members), all voting in favour of the Statute of the ICC at the end of the Rome Conference.[5] Within four years, all fifteen member states had signed and ratified the Statute.

Ratification and implementation of the Statute

The adoption of the Statute in Rome was only the first step towards an operational ICC; a subsequent Preparatory Commission had to work out the arrangements essential to the operation of the Court. EU involvement in this area has seen a slow start, but gathered pace as internal coordination further increased and member states were gradually drawn in to an expanding range of policy initiatives.

The first CFSP common position on the ICC was adopted on 11 June 2001, which mainly served to reiterate the positions already taken by member states.[6] On instigation by a resolution of the European Parliament,[7] an Action Plan was drawn up to give effect to this common position and agreed by the Council's Public International Law Working Group (COJUR)[8] on 28 May 2002. The Action Plan, however, remained a legally unbinding, political document.[9]

When it had become clear that the Statute would enter into force already in 2002, much faster than anyone could have foreseen, EU efforts focused on the practical arrangements for the actual establishment of the Court. To that effect, individual member states were actively involved in the preparation of the first meeting of the Assembly of States Parties and the draft budget for the first financial year of the ICC, as well as in the election of the judges, the appointment of the prosecutor and the recruitment of staff.

The European Union as such became more involved with the adoption of a revised common position on the ICC by the Council on 20 June 2002. Member states agreed to jointly support a worldwide ratification campaign for the Court to attain a universal character and to assist third countries in the implementation of the Statute.[10] National governments were free to determine the details for this assistance, but an effort was made to coordinate policies and to arrive at a rough division of labour.

A third common position on the ICC on 16 June 2003[11] did not entail major changes, but a revised Action Plan adopted in 2004[12] brought a number of new initiatives, most notably the creation of an EU Focal Point for the ICC and the possibility of the deployment of member states' legal experts under the 'EU flag' to countries requesting assistance with the investigation of crimes under the Statute.[13] Another direct consequence of the Action Plan was the enhanced cooperation in the organization of seminars and workshops to assist third countries with the implementation of the Statute into their national legal systems. Furthermore, diplomatic demarches to third countries got to be planned jointly to further the universal acceptance of the Court. Since the adoption of the first Action Plan in 2002, the various EU Presidencies have carried out over 275 demarches to more than 110 countries and international organizations.[14] Finally, better planning and coordination allowed the ICC to be brought up in treaty negotiations or political dialogues with third countries, such as Russia, China and India.

In addition to the cooperation under the CFSP, the Council also adopted several decisions in the area of Justice, Freedom and Security (formerly Justice and Home Affairs) that demonstrate EU commitment to the ICC and the principle of complementarity.[15] By creating a European network of contact points with respect to persons responsible for genocide, crimes against humanity and war crimes, member states sought to strengthen the internal coordination and coherence with regard to investigations and prosecutions. The network thus increased the capacity of member states to deal with international crimes at the national level.

As a consequence of this enhanced coordination and increase in strategic planning, the European Union became more cohesive in its support for the Court. EU policy-making on the ICC had taken firm shape, and the Union could pull more weight in its discussions with third parties. The accession to the Rome Statute of Japan in 2007, is for instance partly thanks to the tireless efforts of the European Union and its member states.

Unexpected problems arose with the entry into the European Union of the ten new member states. Whereas most of them had been signatories to the Statute and had swiftly ratified it, the Czech Republic by May 2004 had not – and still has not – ratified the Statute. In 2001, the Chamber of Deputies of the Czech Parliament rejected a bill for ratification of the Statute, because of its precarious relationship to the Constitution of the Czech Republic. The Government, on several occasions, has expressed its commitment to submit a proposal for ratification as soon as the Parliament passes a constitutional amendment. While the Rome Statute is not formally part of the *acquis communautaire*, failure of one or more member states to ratify may undermine the EU Common Position on the ICC and is detrimental to the European Union's credibility as a supporter of the ICC. A situation where the Czech Presidency is to lead demarches to encourage third states to ratify the Statute, in the first half of 2009, would be awkward at best.

Once the Court had become operational and started to investigate the first situations, it became clear that the relationship between the European Union and the ICC was in need of legal footing. As the European Union as such cannot become a party to the Statute, an Agreement between the ICC and the European Union on cooperation and assistance was therefore concluded in 2005.[16] The agreement completes the EU framework for support of the ICC by laying down the legal obligation for the European Union to cooperate with the Court, and as such is the first ever legally binding agreement of this kind between the European Union and another international organization.

In accordance with the agreement, the European Union and the Court have to exchange information and documents of mutual interest, for instance pertaining to information the European Union acquires in the course of its missions in third countries.[17] In addition, the Court can make use of facilities and services, such as satellite images from the field, and the expertise of gratis personnel offered by the European Union.

Preserving the integrity of the Statute

Despite growing internal agreement on how to foster the universal acceptance the Court, the ICC had become a bone of major political contention between the European Union and the United States. Other large states such as China, India and Russia also abstained from ratification of the Court's Statute, yet the United States had taken a very strong position against the ICC.[18]

The new Bush administration withdrew the US signature on 6 May 2002.[19] The European Union reacted with a statement expressing its disappointment with this action and its hope that the United States would not foreclose future cooperation with the Court.[20] Barely three months later, the American Service-members Protection Act (ASPA) was enacted, aimed at shielding American military personnel from ICC jurisdiction. It provided the legal basis for the State Department's initiative to negotiate legal safeguards, which have become known as bilateral 'non-surrender' (or, less neutral, 'immunity') agreements, against the transfer of American service-members to the ICC with as many countries as possible. In these agreements, the contracting state agrees not to surrender a broad scope of persons including current or former government officials, military personnel and US employees (including contractors) and nationals to the ICC without the express prior consent of the United States.[21]

Shortly after the Rome Statute entered into force on 1 July 2002, EU member states were individually approached by the United States with the request to conclude bilateral agreements. In marked contrast to policies aimed at the promotion of the ratification of the Rome Statue, the European Union found itself having to respond to new circumstances impacting on the integrity of the Rome Statute in a very short timeframe. COJUR concluded on 5 September that the US request was not acceptable. This conclusion was endorsed unanimously by the Political and Security Committee at its 10 September meeting. Due to differences of opinion on how to deal with the request, a decision of the Council was postponed until the end of the month. On 30 September 2002, the EU foreign ministers agreed on a set of guidelines for member states to observe when considering the necessity and scope of a bilateral non-surrender agreement with the United States, known as the 'Guiding Principles'.

The Council Conclusions and Guiding Principles, adopted as non-binding political documents, have been criticized for a number of reasons. Non-Governmental Organizations (NGOs) in particular have pointed to legal shortcomings in the Guiding Principles. The most important inadequacy, they claim, lies in their purpose.[22] Most legal experts have concluded that the Guiding Principles do not rule out the conclusion of *any* agreement between member states and the United States that limits the jurisdiction of the ICC in any way; however, opinions differ.[23]

Notwithstanding the legally non-binding character of the documents, compliance is remarkably high. All current 27 member states have been approached by Washington to sign a bilateral non-surrender agreement with the United States, yet only Romania has signed such an agreement, on 1 August 2002, virtually immediately after the American request. In response to harsh criticism from EU countries, the Romanian parliament postponed ratification, initially until agreement on the matter was reached between the United States and the European Union. The agreement has not been ratified since. Concerns have also been raised about the US–UK extradition treaty, which includes a 'Side Letter' affirming the UK commitment not to extradite US citizens to the ICC.[24] However, British as well as other EU diplomats are keen to reiterate publicly that this does not amount to a bilateral non-surrender agreement 'in disguise'.

Another threat to the integrity of the Court's Statute surfaced in June 2002, when Washington insisted that a UN Security Council resolution be adopted to permanently exempt all Americans participating in UN-sanctioned peacekeeping operations from ICC jurisdiction and enabling the United States to veto a prosecution indefinitely.[25] Opponents of the resolution have argued that, under such a resolution, States Parties to the Rome Statute would be obliged to breach their obligations under the Statute by not extraditing a potential American suspect of crimes against humanity, war crimes or genocide to the ICC.

An open debate on the US proposed resolution took place on 10 July 2002, during which France, Germany, Ireland and The Netherlands made statements against the adoption of the resolution. The EU declaration by the Danish Presidency, by contrast, failed to explicitly denounce the draft resolution. The United Kingdom swung to support the United States and voted in favour of the resolution. The only other member state in the Security Council, France, was left isolated and abstained from the vote. Eventually, on 12 July, the US draft resolution was adopted unanimously as resolution 1422/2002.

In the spring of 2003, it became clear that Washington was aiming for renewal of resolution 1422. A number of member states, most notably Germany, France and The Netherlands, opposed the renewal of resolution 1422, and made separate statements in which they voiced their concerns, in addition to the EU declaration by the Greek Presidency. France and Germany (together with Syria) abstained. By contrast, the United Kingdom and Spain conceded to the United States and voted in favour, leaving the European Union split on the issue. On 12 June 2003, resolution 1422 was renewed by the Security Council by vote of 12–0 and became resolution 1487/2003.

On 20 May 2004, the United States tabled a resolution to renew resolution 1487 for another 12-month period. This time the United States was unsuccessful at mustering support and eventually had to withdraw the resolution, which was widely regarded as a diplomatic defeat. With the United Kingdom as the only supporter of the renewal of resolution 1487, the European Union has ostensibly come a step closer to a common position on immunity for UN peacekeepers.

The conclusion to be drawn from the experiences of the European Union in preserving the integrity of the Rome Statute is that policies have been predominantly reactive rather than proactive, and that coordination among member states has been problematic. Remarkably enough, the EU response has proven effective in containing some of the potentially most damaging US policies to undermine the ICC. The next section will analyse why the European Union supports the ICC and how variations in support can help explain policy outcomes.

From domestic support to international opposition: Explaining the European Union's policy towards the ICC

Two initial remarks about the attempts to explain the EU support for the ICC are in place. First, the European Union as such is not a party to the Statute of the ICC. Any account of EU support therefore needs to start with explaining why its member states have signed and ratified the Statute. Second, explanations of EU support also need to take into account the differences over time, particularly before and after the Rome Conference was held, and before and after the Bush administration entered office. We analyse both internal and external factors that help explain why and how the European Union has come to support the ICC.

Internal developments

Until Rome, the support of the European Union for the ICC can mainly be explained by specific characteristics of the development of the ICC policy area within the European Union itself (cf. Cowhey 1993; Finnemore 1996a; Risse *et al.* 1999).[26] Most EU countries felt they had nothing to fear from a strong Court. They considered it unlikely that the human rights situations in their countries would ever sanction the Court's involvement (cf. Moravcsik 1995). Supporting the ICC was associated with benefits for member states' international and domestic reputation. It allowed them to champion the curbing of human rights violations and the promotion of international criminal justice, while additional constraints were minimal

174 *Martijn Groenleer and David Rijks*

(cf. Strange 1982). Some member states had specific additional reasons to support the Court. The cases of The Netherlands and Germany deserve brief mention.

Germany was one of the most ardent supporters of the creation of an ICC. After the Second World War, the allied countries created the Nuremberg tribunal, prosecuting Nazi leaders for the crimes committed. It is difficult to maintain that this tribunal has rendered truly universal justice. This historical legacy made Germany refuse what was called an 'alibi court' (Pace 1999). Instead it pleaded for universal jurisdiction and limitations on immunity of political and military leaders. During the Rome Conference, Germany's commitment to a strong Court materialized as it resisted alleged US pressure. Reuters reported that the Pentagon had sent a letter to the German government stating that it would reconsider its military assistance if Germany would not reverse its position on the ICC.[27]

The Netherlands had its own specific reasons to support an ICC. In an effort to strengthen its reputation as an active promoter of the international legal order (which is a duty even laid down in the Dutch Constitution) and to further develop the image of The Hague as 'international legal capital', The Netherlands in 1998 announced its candidature for hosting the ICC (Bevers *et al.* 2003). The Netherlands already hosted the International Court of Justice, the Permanent Court of Arbitration and the International Criminal Tribunal for the former Yugoslavia. Although there were other candidates, the Dutch bid was accepted by other countries without much discussion.

Most EU member states were part of the LMG of countries that coordinated their negotiating strategies on contested provisions of the Rome Statute (Edgar 2002; Nel 2002). The concept of the LMG was based on a new approach to the negotiation of international treaties, also referred to as the 'New Diplomacy' (Cooper *et al.* 2002; Fehl 2004). This approach had been effectively applied during the Ottawa landmines conference in December 1997. There, a similar group of like-minded countries, in unprecedentedly close cooperation with civil society, had successfully negotiated a convention banning anti-personnel mines, yet lacking the support of the United States (Anderson 2000; Harpviken 2002).

The only two EU countries initially not part of the LMG were the United Kingdom and France. Although they were not opposed to the idea of creating an ICC – indeed they publicly supported it – they had serious reservations as to its powers. They therefore tried to slow down the process of creating an ICC by, for instance, opposing the setting of a date for the Diplomatic Conference.[28] Both countries objected to a Court that could investigate and prosecute their citizens without their prior approval. With soldiers engaged in military operations across the globe, they feared politically motivated referrals to the Court. Siding on this point with the United States and in contrast to other EU countries, they therefore insisted on the necessary safeguards to protect their citizens from an overactive prosecutor.

In 1997, when the Labour Government of Tony Blair took office, the United Kingdom dramatically changed its position in favour of a strong ICC. As part of Labour's 'ethical dimension' to foreign policy, the United Kingdom announced that it rejected the Security Council's ability to control the Court's docket. The United Kingdom was subsequently accepted into the LMG. Although the United Kingdom had officially reversed its stand, now allying with the other EU countries, it faced intense pressure during the Rome Conference, both from outside and inside its government. The UK speech, on behalf of the European Union, at the opening of the conference, was criticized as 'weak' by NGOs.[29] Moreover, the UK delegation to the Rome Conference was internally divided. Ministry of Defence delegates reportedly clashed with their colleagues at the Foreign Office on the independence of the Court's prosecutor, a dispute that was quickly settled in favour of the latter by the then UK Foreign Minister, Robin Cook.[30]

France, the only EU country not yet part of the LMG at the start of the Rome Conference, changed its position on the independent position of the prosecutor in the course of the negotiations. It also reversed its position on the Security Council's veto power over the ICC. However, France – apparently also under pressure from the Ministry of Defence – only joined the other EU countries in support of the draft Statute after it had negotiated a proposal allowing states the possibility of blocking prosecution of their citizens for war crimes for a period of seven years after the entry force of the Statute.[31] France became a member of the LMG in the last week of the Rome Conference.

In the background, broad parliamentary commitment to a strong ICC has been instrumental in fostering governmental support throughout the European Union. Members of Parliament, such as Herta Däubler-Gmelin (Germany) and Emma Bonino (Italy), brought initiatives before their legislatures to support the creation of an ICC. Earlier, as a Commissioner for Humanitarian Affairs, Bonino had successfully secured Italy's bid to host the Diplomatic Conference. The ICC was also a central theme of the Parliamentarians for Global Action, a world-wide network of legislators developing initiatives to promote international law and human rights.

Since the adoption of the Rome Statute, there has been a gradual increase in volume and scope of common EU policies that aim to promote the ratification and implementation of the Rome Statute by third countries. Over time, planning has become increasingly strategic and the number of EU-wide initiatives has proliferated significantly, suggesting that the more reluctant states have also been drawn into the policy-making process and at least a minimal level of 'Europeanization' of member states' policies towards the ICC has occurred. Two factors in particular are likely to have contributed to a harmonization of member states' positions in this area: the background of the actors involved and the special relationship with non-state actors.

First, Groenleer and van Schaik (2007) point to the common background and experience of the officials participating in the Council Working Group dealing with the ICC. Most national 'ICC units' are staffed by legal experts in international criminal justice. Some of them had participated in the 1998 Rome Conference, while others had been involved in the establishment of other international tribunals. Not only is the character of their work pioneering, it is also of a highly technical-legal nature. This provides representatives with some autonomy from their administration's scrutiny and enhances the potential for the acquisition of new insights (Christiansen *et al.* 2001; Checkel 2003; Lewis 2005).

Second, a remarkable symbiosis has developed between member states and NGOs.[32] Member states benefit significantly from the information provided by NGOs and, in return, NGOs are regularly invited to present their views in the

176   *Martijn Groenleer and David Rijks*

margins of the regular COJUR Sub-area meetings, which is exceptional under the CFSP framework. NGO lobbying has produced concrete results, as at least several of their proposals were incorporated into the 2004 Action Plan and into the three common positions. In that sense, NGOs have acted as so-called norm entrepreneurs (cf. Finnemore and Sikkink 1998; Fehl 2004).

External pressures and demands

In addition, explanations for the EU policy towards the ICC after Rome follow primarily from external pressures and the demands on the European Union, in particular the strong US opposition to the ICC. Whereas the adoption of the Rome Statute had increased the intensity of interaction in the EU framework, it was not until the US position changed from benign abstention to fierce opposition that the European Union took a marked stance on the ICC. The US position necessitated, it was felt by member states, a European response.

Where bilateral agreements were concerned, member states faced a dilemma. Governments were confronted with a direct choice between two interests: a strong basic commitment to the Court, which is enshrined in the common positions on the ICC, as well as a good relationship with Washington, albeit the latter's importance differed across member states. In an address to the European Parliament, the Danish Presidency declared that the proposed agreements by the United States were not in conformity with member states' obligations under the Rome Statute. Despite this apparent incompatibility, 'having regard to transatlantic relations, flatly rejecting the US proposal is absolutely no solution'.[33]

The member states of the European Union differed vastly in their opinion of the legality of bilateral non-surrender agreements, as well as on the question of how the integrity of the Court is best guaranteed. The key question therefore is why none of the member states has signed a bilateral agreement with the United States, especially since some countries had indicated considering doing so in 2002. More importantly, what is the influence of cooperation through the CFSP on national positions in this regard? Can we speak of a 'Europeanization' of member states' foreign policies on this point?

Member states' positions on immunity for American nationals can be divided into two categories.[34] The first group consists of states that were declared opponents of bilateral agreements that may undermine the Court's integrity. This group includes The Netherlands, France, Germany, Sweden, Belgium and Austria who had all publicly indicated that they did not intend to sign a bilateral agreement with Washington on the ICC.[35]

At the other end of the spectrum, three member states had declared to seriously consider granting immunity to US nationals. It is no secret that the UK government had been sympathetic towards US immunity deals. Early in September 2002, it even made proposals to other EU member states for an amended bilateral agreement, purportedly backed by Italy and Spain.

At first glance, it was the strongest supporters of the ICC that in comparison paid the highest price for the final consensus in the form of the Council Conclusions and

Guiding Principles. Ironically, for the states that had had to compromise the most, conceding that the Conclusions were indeed a compromise to the United States would only worsen the situation.[36]

The consequences of the EU compromise are, however, more complex. In the short term, the Guiding Principles reflected an adequate balance for Italy, Spain and the United Kingdom between their commitment to the ICC and their allegiance to Washington as a lowest common denominator.[37] In the longer run, other factors are likely to have contributed to European governments consistently declining to sign bilateral 'non-surrender' agreements with the United States. First, prolonged participation in the European Union's framework for common policy-making on the ICC has fostered a shared normative consensus about the appropriateness of such agreements (Christiansen *et al.* 2001; Checkel 2003; Lewis 2005). We argue that the close interaction with representatives from different member states and NGOs is likely to have fostered a certain degree of collective understanding in the COJUR ICC Sub-area (cf. Finnemore 1996b; Finnemore and Sikkink 1998). There is, however, little conclusive evidence to support the claim that the United Kingdom, Italy and Spain as a result have lost their sympathy towards a bilateral agreement with the United States.

Second, in responding to US requests for immunity, European governments faced additional complexities. The conclusion of an immunity agreement would, just as any international treaty in most countries, not only require a signature by the executive, but also parliamentary ratification. As parliaments in most member states, supported by NGOs, have consistently taken a strong stance in favour of an effective and independent ICC, signing a 'non-surrender' agreement by a government was thus likely to be met by severe domestic political criticism. Most governments were therefore seeking a common 'European response' which would accommodate US concerns and forestall new US requests to individual member states.

Third, calls for a common EU position did not only originate from the Union itself. The governments of many third states (such as Japan) had been anxiously awaiting the position of the European Union on this issue. The European Union, as the main proponent of the Court, was expected to provide moral and political guidance to which third states could align themselves. Aspiring EU members in particular expressed a keen interest in a common EU position.[38]

The European response to US requests for UN Security Council resolutions to permanently exempt all Americans participating in UN-sanctioned peacekeeping can claim considerably less success. It was clear to all member states that outright rejection of such resolutions would be politically unfeasible. After the political rift over the war in Iraq and the ongoing tensions surrounding the bilateral non-surrender agreements, even the most ardent supporters of the Court were reluctant to engage in yet another political conflict with Washington.

Furthermore, concerted EU action has proven exceptionally difficult. Discussions in the COJUR meetings were mostly limited to brief exchanges of views, typically followed by the conclusion that 'continuation' of the dialogue with the United States is important. More substantive coordination took place

178 *Martijn Groenleer and David Rijks*

through the COREU network, which has been used to devise EU statements, yet it fell short of harmonizing national votes in the Security Council (cf. Laatikainen and Smith 2006; K.E. Smith 2006).

Much more significant for the eventual lack of support for renewal of the resolution in 2004 is the different political context at the time of the US request. The revelations about prisoner abuse in the Abu Ghraib prison in Iraq by American military personnel had angered opponents and proponents of resolution 1422 alike.[39]

Consequences of the European Union's ICC policy: Evaluating its effects on the European Union

The consequences of the European Union's ICC policy can be evaluated in two ways. First, the European Union's initiatives have had an effect on both the formal and informal institutions of the Union. Second, and perhaps most importantly, the European Union's actions have had a significant impact on the European Union's profile as a global actor.

The European Union as an institution: 'Institutionalization' of formal structures and informal practices

The materialization of the European Union's policy towards the ICC has had a considerable impact on the structures and practices of the European Union as an institution (Stone Sweet *et al.* 2001; M.E. Smith 2004). We identify three key changes across the main EU institutions.

First, a special sub-area has been added to the COJUR. COJUR deals with issues relating to international law and is formally responsible for the ICC, but due to the complex nature of the issue and for reasons of efficiency, a separate ICC sub-area was created in mid-2002. As a subsidiary body of the COJUR working group, the ICC sub-area's main task is to advise COJUR on legal issues relating to the Court. The sub-area usually meets four times a year in Brussels; once a year it meets in The Hague in order to prepare for the Court's Assembly of States Parties. Sessions of the sub-area are closed and in principle only attended by representatives of the member states (mostly senior diplomats or legal experts), a senior official of the Council Secretariat (since the 2004 Action Plan designated as the so-called EU Focal Point), a representative of the Commission, and an expert from the Council Legal Service.

Second, while the Commission is formally only 'associated' with the foreign policy-making process, its role in the European Union's effort to promote ratification and implementation of the Statute has been enhanced considerably over time. The Commission – as the representative of the European Communities – participated in the Rome Conference as an observer. Although it did contribute financially to the Trust Fund for the participation of the least developed countries in the meetings of the Preparatory Committee and the Rome Conference, the Commission did not play a major role in the process leading up to Rome and during the conference itself.

Within the framework of the European Initiative for Democracy and Human Rights, however, the Commission has provided over € 17 million of funding to the ratification and implementation campaigns carried out by civil society organizations such as the Coalition for an International Criminal Court (CICC).[40] Commission representatives furthermore frequently take part in troika demarches on ratification of the Statute. In a number of cases, this has indeed enhanced the potential effectiveness of demarches, especially of those to countries aspiring EU membership.[41] Although some see in this involvement a subtle attempt to 'communautarize' the ICC as a human rights issue and to transfer it in part to the first pillar, it has significantly increased the number of occasions at which the ICC is routinely brought up during high-level contacts, both in the work of other Council preparatory bodies and between the European Union and (groups of) third states (cf. Pollack 2003). The Commission has, for instance, introduced an 'ICC' clause in the revised Cotonou Agreement, which applies to 79 African, Caribbean and Pacific countries and the European Union. The clause is supposed to serve as the standard clause to be inserted when negotiating other agreements with third countries.[42]

Finally, the involvement of the European Parliament in the policy-making process on the ICC is limited though consistent and firm. Particularly through its informal group of Friends of the ICC, it has supported budget allocations for activities in support of the Court and has always taken a very active stance on the ICC, typically more activist than that of member states' governments. In addition to a significant number of oral and written questions, the European Parliament has adopted a number of resolutions on the ICC and the ASPA.[43]

The European Union as an international actor: Cohesion, autonomy, authority and recognition

Over time, the European Union can be said to have increasingly operated as a genuine actor, not merely being the sum of its individual member states. On a number of occasions, it has functioned both actively and deliberately in the international arena, as an international actor (Sjöstedt 1977; K.E. Smith 2003).[44]

Indeed, Groenleer and van Schaik (2007) argue that the European Union's ability to function as an international actor on matters relating to the ICC is a function of both the congruence and convergence of individual member states' preferences and interests in the field of human rights and international law. This has not only resulted in a high degree of agreement on basic values and distinct institutional practices, but also in a high degree of acceptance of EU authority and recognition by other actors. The recognition of the European Union as an international actor has been demonstrated by the interaction with both non-state actors, notably NGOs and of course the ICC itself, and third states, in particular the United States.

The EU Council Conclusions on bilateral agreements and the Guiding Principles appear to have been welcomed as an important policy direction by many third countries. Although the Guiding Principles were originally intended for internal policy coordination, their use in external relations has become

180   *Martijn Groenleer and David Rijks*

common practice. The promotion of the ICC and its principles and the preservation of the Statute's integrity have developed into EU foreign policy objectives in their own right (Manners 2002; cf. Lucarelli and Manners 2005).

Whereas the United States initially tried to drive a wedge between EU member states seeking to conclude bilateral agreements with individual member states that were supportive of US policy objectives, it has later shifted approach by attempting to conclude an EU–US bilateral agreement. EU member states, as was mentioned above, until now have been able to close ranks in the face of US pressure to compromise on the ICC.

In addition, a US demarche carried out with the Council Secretariat in June 2003, complaining about the European Union's diplomatic efforts to prevent third countries from concluding a bilateral agreement with the United States, suggests that the United States was hindered considerably by the common EU standpoint expressed in the Council Conclusions and Guiding Principles in its efforts to conclude bilateral agreements with certain third states.[45]

In recent years, the US administration has gradually softened its approach towards the ICC. President Bush waived restrictions on military and economic aid to a large group of countries that refused to sign a bilateral agreement. While the United States still considers the ICC to be flawed, it has expressed agreement with the objectives of the Court and its role in certain cases. The United States did not reject the adoption of a UN Security Council resolution referring the situation in Darfur to the ICC. It also supported the use of the ICC facilities in The Hague for the trial of Charles Taylor by the Special Court for Sierra Leone.[46]

Determining the extent to which the EU position has helped to bring about the change in the US approach is problematic, as other, geopolitical, considerations have been equally important. Many policy-makers within the administration came to realize that the United States was 'shooting [itself] in the foot' with its anti-ICC campaign: not only did it damage its reputation as a supporter of human rights, but by denying military or economic assistance to countries unwilling to sign a bilateral non-surrender agreement, it also moved these countries closer to China.[47]

Conclusion: Implications and challenges for the European Union

This chapter set out to examine the relationship between the European Union and the ICC. It has presented an explanatory account of why the European Union and its member states support the ICC and how the Union and the Court influence each other.

The preceding analysis suggests that it is imperative to account for developments in international politics over time, as well as to distinguish between different policies pertaining to distinct aspects of the functions of the Court. Taking a temporal perspective, initial EU support was limited to general declaratory statements in the absence of a united standpoint by its member states. With the enactment of the ASPA and subsequent US initiatives to obstruct the successful operation of the ICC, the European Union found itself having to step up both the scope and intensity of its support for the Court in order to match Washington's diplomatic efforts. Many third states, confronted with persuasive requests to grant immunity from ICC jurisdiction to US nationals, turned to the European Union for guidance and political support. Within the Union itself, member states needed to overcome internal differences on the admissibility and desirability of a compromise with the Bush administration on these bilateral 'non-surrender' agreements. Paradoxically enough, the American opposition to the Court has proven instrumental in raising the external profile as well as the internal coherence of EU foreign policy with regard to international criminal justice.

Efforts to increase the number of ratifications of the Rome Statute worldwide and to encourage third states to implement the provisions of the Statute into their national legislation have proliferated steadily, as cooperation in this field institutionalized. Initiatives have become increasingly comprehensive and have come to involve virtually all member states. We argue that this can, at least in part, be explained by the dynamics of cooperation in the Council, as well as by the influence of the European Commission and other NGOs on the decision-making process.

By contrast, the European Union's commitment to the preservation of the integrity of the Rome Statute has manifested itself in much more haphazard policy responses. The European compromise on US requests for bilateral immunity agreements was in essence strongly reactive. Unity hinges on a delicate balance between commitment to the practice and principles of the ICC on the one hand, and a perceived interest in transatlantic relations on the other. Whereas the European Union has successfully closed ranks on bilateral agreements, concerted European action has proven much more problematic in the UN Security Council, when responding to American requests for resolutions to exempt military personnel participating in UN-sanctioned peacekeeping operations from ICC jurisdiction.[48]

What are the implications of the relationship between the European Union and the ICC? Although at first glance the EU leadership in the field of human rights and international law may have important drawbacks relating to both universal acceptability and effective functioning of the ICC. The question is whether an international legal order can be created, let alone function effectively, when some of the major powers do not support an important institution of that order.[49]

The challenges for the future relation between the European Union and the ICC are therefore daunting. Two bear particular importance. First, the member states will need to cooperate with the ICC and assist in its operations in terms of financial resources, investigations and trials, and enforcement of orders and sentences, because the ICC is heavily reliant on state cooperation. This could, at the same time, bring about new policies and legislation at the national level. As a platform through which member states coordinate their positions and channel their support for the ICC, the European Union could play an important role in strengthening national prosecutions and investigations.

While cooperating with the ICC, the European Union and its member states will, however, have to remain wary of interfering too much with, for instance, the training and selection of its staff, judges and prosecutors in view of the ICC's independence. As the ICC's reputation as a fair, effective and independent institution is growing, the US government – although this is publicly denied by US officials – has seen its fears of politically motivated charges to be unwarranted.[50]

Second, and closely related, the European Union will need to maintain a dialogue with the United States.[51] This does not mean that the European Union and its member states will have to compromise on the core principles and values underlying the ICC, but rather that it takes the US position, its concerns and its interests seriously. As suggested in 2005 by Javier Solana, High Representative for the CFSP, the European Union should seek practical solutions trying to establish a *modus vivendi* between supporters of the ICC, notably the EU member states, and the United States, based on common goals such as ending impunity for the most heinous international crimes. This view has been endorsed by John Bellinger, the State Department's chief legal adviser: 'We believe that divisiveness over the ICC distracts from our ability to pursue these common goals, and hope that supporters of the Rome Statute will join us in constructive efforts to advance our shared values.'[52]

Notes

1 The authors are grateful to Hans Bevers and Adriaan Bos for useful comments on an earlier version of this chapter.

2 The Court only deals with cases when a State is unwilling or unable to carry out the investigation or prosecution. This is referred to as the principle of complementarity.

3 Up to the accession of Japan in July 2007, EU member states' assessed contributions amounted to 75.6 per cent of the total assessed contributions to the Court. See the Council's information brochure on the European Union's policies on the ICC, 'The European Union and the International Criminal Court', November 2007, p. 18.

4 Consider, as an example, the statement by the Spanish Presidency on behalf of the European Union in the UN General Assembly's Sixth Committee: 'An International Criminal Court should be an independent permanent institution with the widest possible participation, and closely linked to the United Nations.' Statement by the Permanent Representative of Spain Mr Juan Antonio Yanez-Barnuevo on behalf of the European Union, New York, 30 October 1995.

5 For more detailed yet largely descriptive accounts of the negotiating process and the Rome Statute, see Arsanjani (1999), Bassiouni (1998), Kirsch (1999), Kirsch and Holmes (1999), Lee (1999a, 1999b) and von Hebel *et al.* (1999).

6 Council Common Position 2001/443/CFSP of 11 June 2001 on the International Criminal Court.

7 European Parliament Resolution on entry into force of the Statute of the International Criminal Court, P5_TA(2002)0082.

8 The acronym refers to the French designation 'Comité Juridique'.

9 Action Plan of 15 May 2002 to follow up on the Common Position on the International Criminal Court.

10 Council Common Position 2002/474/CFSP of 20 June 2002 amending Common Position 2001/443/CFSP on the International Criminal Court.

11 Council Common Position 2003/444/CFSP of 16 June 2003 on the International Criminal Court.

12 Action Plan of 4 February 2004 to follow up on the Common Position on the International Criminal Court.

13 The proposal for this initiative originated from NGOs. It appeared in one of the draft versions almost unnoticed, and was adopted by the member states without much discussion.

With the support of several EU member states, including Germany, Sweden, Finland and the United Kingdom, and EU funding, the idea has been further developed into the 'Justice Rapid Response' initiative. For more information on the initiative, see http://www.justicerapidresponse.org

14 Council of the European Union, 'The European Union and the International Criminal Court', November 2007, p. 10.

15 Council Decision 2002/494/JHA of 13 June 2002 setting up a European network of contact points with respect to persons responsible for genocide, crimes against humanity and war crimes; Framework Decision 2002/584/JHA of 13 June 2002 on the European Arrest Warrant and the Surrender Procedures between Member States; Council Decision 2003/335/JHA of 8 May 2003 concerning the investigation and prosecution of genocide, crimes against humanity and war crimes.

16 Council of the European Union, 'Agreement between the International Criminal Court and the European Union on Cooperation and Assistance', 14298/05, Brussels, 6 December 2005.

17 The European Union and the ICC have negotiated separate implementing agreements concerning the exchange of classified information, a sensitive issue during the negotiation of the agreement on cooperation and assistance.

18 For more detailed discussions of the reasons behind the US opposition to the ICC, see, for instance, Wedgwood (1998, 1999), Scheffer (1999, 2002), Sewall and Kaysen (2000), Bolton (2001) and Mayerfield (2003).

19 When authorizing the signature, the Clinton administration had, however, made clear that it had no intention to submit the Statute as such to the Senate for ratification. Public Papers of the President, 'Statement on the Rome Treaty on the International Criminal Court', 8 January 2001.

20 Council of the European Union, 'Statement of the European Union on the position of the United States towards the International Criminal Court', 8864/02, Brussels, 14 May 2002.

21 The United States claims that these bilateral agreements are in conformity with Article 98.2 of the Rome Statute, which stipulates that a state does not have to meet a request by the Court to surrender a person to the ICC when this would constitute a breach of other international agreements.

22 As the Council Conclusions note, 'The Council has developed the attached set of principles to serve as *guidelines for member states when considering the necessity and scope of possible agreements* or arrangements in responding to the United States' proposal' (emphasis added). See Council Conclusions on the International Criminal Court, 30 September 2002, p. 1.

23 Many civil society organizations and institutions, as well as the European Parliament, had advocated a principled rejection of any bilateral agreement between member states and the United States, especially after a leaked analysis of the Commission Legal Service qualified bilateral non-surrender agreements as 'illegal'. Hence, in theory, the European Union paved the way for agreements that would allow for *partial* immunity for a *limited class* of US nationals.

24 The Extradition Treaty was signed on 31 March 2003 and entered into force on 26 April 2007.

25 On the Security Council Resolution granting immunity for UN peacekeepers, see, for instance, Weller (2002) and Jain (2005).

26 In addition to such general factors as the fall of the Berlin Wall and the end of the Cold War, and the establishment of *ad hoc* tribunals for the conflict in the former Yugoslavia and the genocide in Rwanda.

27 Human Rights Watch, 'World Report 1999'. Online. Available HTTP: http://www.hrw.org/worldreport99/special/icc.html (accessed 22 December 2007).

28 Interview with government official.

29 Human Rights Watch, 'E.U. Split Produces Weak Position on International Court', Rome, 15 June 1998.

30 Human Rights Watch, 'HRW disappointed by U.K. Stand on International Court', 9 July 1998; interview with NGO representative.

31 Upon ratification, France subsequently made a declaration under Article 124 in which it stated that 'it does not accept the jurisdiction of the Court with respect to the category of crimes referred to in article 8 when a crime is alleged to have been committed by its nationals or on its territory'.

32 For a more detailed yet slightly biased account of the role of NGOs before and during the Rome Conference, see Pace (1999) and Pace and Thieroff (1999). For a discussion of the relationship between NGOs and the ICC, see Pearson (2006). More in general about the role of NGOs in global governance, see Willetts (1996), Weiss and Gordenker (1996), Keck and Sikkink (1998) and Cooper *et al.* (2002).

33 See Foreign Minister's statement, on behalf of the Council, at the European Parliament's plenary sitting on 25 September 2002 on the state of play regarding the International Criminal Court following the informal meeting of Foreign Ministers in Elsinore on 29 and 30 August 2002.

34 Those countries that are not included have not issued an official public position on US requests for a bilateral agreement.

35 The Netherlands are an important strategic target for the United States to secure immunity for its nationals. Under ASPA, the President of the United States has the discretion to use 'all means necessary and appropriate' to free from captivity any US or allied personnel held by or on behalf of the ICC. Since this theoretically includes the use of force against The Netherlands, ASPA has been dubbed 'The Hague Invasion Act'.

36 Germany, one of the most ardent supporters of the Court, even issued an unusual 'ICC-Supportive Interpretation of and Commentary on [the EU Council Conclusions]' in which it gives a positive spin to the political and legal content. See 'Non-paper from the German ICC Task Force: ICC – Supportive Interpretation of and Commentary on the EU General Affairs Council Conclusions on the International Criminal Court of 30 September 2002', p. 2.

37 For a comprehensive discussion on how this agreement came about and what its function was, see Thomas (2005).

38 By that time, Romania – then a candidate to join the Union – had already signed a bilateral immunity agreement, for which it was severely criticized by the European Union and NGOs. In response, president Ion Iliescu publicly declared that Romania 'will wait for a joint position of the European institutions before ratifying [the bilateral agreement] in parliament', *Financial Times*, 27 September 2002.

39 For a comprehensive analysis of the role of national, transnational and EU actors on the EU response to US requests for bilateral non-surrender agreements, see Rijks (2004) and Thomas (2005).

40 Council of the European Union, 'The European Union and the International Criminal Court', November 2007, p. 16. The CICC – covering over 2,000 NGOs worldwide – is the largest NGO solely directed towards the promotion of the ICC. The Coalition has an office in Brussels.

41 For example, when a demarche was made in Ankara, the Commission explicitly linked ratification of the Statute to Turkey's record on human rights, an important criterion for EU membership.

42 Council of the European Union, 'The European Union and the International Criminal Court', November 2007, p. 13; interview with Commission official.

43 See on the ICC on 19 November 1998 (OJ C 379, 7.12.1998, p. 265), 18 January 2001 (OJ C 262, 18.9.2001, p. 262), 28 February 2002 (P5_TA(2002)0082), 26 September 2002 (P5_TA(2002)0449) and 24 October 2002 (P5_TA(2002)0521). On ASPA on 4 July 2002 (P5_TA(2002)0367).

44 Other more elaborate studies of the European Union as an international or global actor include Meunier (2000), Ginsberg (2001) and Bretherton and Vogler (2006).

45 Interview with Council official.

The EU and the ICC 185

46 U.S. Department of State, 'International Courts and Tribunals and the Rule of Law', speech by John Bellinger, Legal Adviser to the Secretary of State, Washington, DC, 11 May 2006.
47 *Economist*, 'International Criminal Court: Let the Child Live', 25 January 2007.
48 Thomas (2005) arrives at a similar conclusion, stressing the importance of the CFSP as an intra-EU bargaining process. As EU discussions on the US-proposed Security Council resolutions mainly took place outside of the CFSP framework, the resultant lowest common denominator outcome comes as no surprise.
49 See also statement by US Ambassador-at-large for War Crime Issues, David Scheffer, before the Sixth Committee of the Fifty-third session of the General Assembly, 21 October 1998.
50 Council on Foreign Relations, 'Bellinger Says International Court Flawed But Deserving of Help in Some Cases', interview with John Bellinger, Legal Adviser to the Secretary of State, 10 July 2007. Online. Available HTTP: http://www.cfr.org/publica tion/13752 (accessed 21 December 2007).
51 Kagan, R. 'Europeans Courting Disaster', *Washington Post*, 30 June 2002.
52 U.S. Department of State, 'International Courts and Tribunals and the Rule of Law', speech by John Bellinger, Legal Adviser to the Secretary of State, Washington, DC, 11 May 2006.

References

Anderson, K. (2000) 'The Ottawa Convention Banning Landmines, the Role of International Non-Governmental Organizations and the Idea of International Civil Society', *European Journal of International Law*, 11(1): 91–120.
Arsanjani, M.H. (1999) 'The Rome Statute of the International Criminal Court', *American Journal of International Law*, 93(1): 22–43.
Bassiouni, M.C. (1998) *The Statute of the International Criminal Court: A Documented History*, New York: Transnational Publishers.
Bevers, H., Blokker, N.M. and Roording, J. (2003) 'The Netherlands and the International Criminal Court: On Statute Obligations and Hospitality', *Leiden Journal of International Law*, 16: 135–156.
Bolton, J.R. (2001) 'The Risks and Weaknesses of the International Criminal Court from America's Perspective', *Law and Contemporary Problems*, 64(1): 167–180.
Bretherton, C. and Vogler, J. (2006) *The European Union as a Global Actor*, London: Routledge.
Checkel, J.T. (2003) '"Going Native in Europe?" Theorizing Social Interaction in European Institutions', *Comparative Political Studies*, 36(February/March): 209–232.
Christiansen, T., Joergensen, K.E. and Wiener, A. (2001) *The Social Construction of Europe*, London: Sage.
Cooper, A.F., English, J. and Thakur, R. (eds) (2002) *Enhancing Global Governance: Towards a New Diplomacy?*, Tokyo/New York/Paris: United Nations University Press.
Cowhey, P.F. (1993) 'Elect Locally – Order Globally: Domestic Politics and Multilateral Cooperation', in J.G. Ruggie (ed.) *Multilateralism Matters: The Theory and Praxis of an Institutional Form*, New York: Columbia University Press, pp. 157–200.
Edgar, A.D. (2002) 'Peace, Justice, and Politics: The International Criminal Court, "New Diplomacy", and the UN System', in A.F. Cooper, J. English and R. Thakur (eds) *Enhancing Global Governance: Towards a New Diplomacy?*, Tokyo/New York/Paris: United Nations University Press, pp. 133–151.
Fehl, C. (2004) 'Explaining the International Criminal Court: A "Practice Test" for Rationalist Constructivist Approaches', *European Journal of International Relations*, 10(3): 357–394.

186 *Martijn Groenleer and David Rijks*

Finnemore, M. (1996a) *National Interests in International Society*, Ithaca: Cornell University Press.

—— (1996b) 'Norms, Culture and World Politics: Insights from Sociology's Institutionalism', *International Organization*, 47(4): 565–597.

Finnemore, M. and Sikkink, K. (1998) 'International Norm Dynamics and Political Change', *International Organization*, 52(4): 887–918.

Ginsberg, R. (2001) *The European Union in International Politics: Baptism by Fire*, Lanham, MD: Rowman & Littlefield.

Groenleer, M.L.P. and van Schaik, L.G. (2007) 'United We Stand? The European Union's International Actorness in the Cases of the International Criminal Court and the Kyoto Protocol', *Journal of Common Market Studies*, 45(5): 969–998.

Harpviken, K.B. (2002) 'The Landmines Campaign: Representations and Reflections', *Cooperation and Conflict*, 37(1): 101–108.

Jain, N. (2005) 'A Separate Law for Peacekeepers: The Clash between the Security Council and the International Criminal Court', *European Journal of International Law*, 16(2): 239–254.

Jepperson, R.L., Katzenstein, P.J. and Wendt, A. (1996) 'Norms, Identity and Culture in National Security', in P.J. Katzenstein (ed.) *The Culture of National Security*, New York: Columbia University Press, pp. 33–75.

Keck, M.E. and Sikkink, K. (1998) *Activists Beyond Borders: Advocacy Networks in International Politics*, Ithaca: Cornell University Press.

Kirsch, P. (1999) 'The Development of the Rome Statute', in R.S. Lee (ed.) *The International Criminal Court: The Making of the Rome State. Issues, Negotiations, Results*, The Hague: Kluwer Law International, pp. 451–461.

Kirsch, P. and Holmes, J. (1999) 'The Rome Conference on an International Criminal Court: The Negotiating Process', *American Journal of International Law*, 93(1): 2–12.

Laatikainen, K. and Smith, K.E. (2006) *Intersecting Multilateralisms: The European Union and the United Nations*, Basingstoke: Palgrave.

Lee, R.S. (1999a) *The International Criminal Court: The Making of the Rome State. Issues, Negotiations, Results*, The Hague: Kluwer Law International.

—— (1999b) 'Creating an International Criminal Court – Of Procedures and Compromises', in H.A.M. von Hebel, J.G. Lammers and J. Schukking (eds) *Reflections on the International Criminal Court: Essays in Honour of Adriaan Bos*, The Hague: T.M.C. Asser Press, pp. 141–154.

Lewis, J. (2005) 'The Janus Face of Brussels: Socialization and Everyday Decision Making in the European Union', *International Organization*, 59(4): 837–872.

Lucarelli, S. and Manners, I. (eds) (2005) *Values, Images and Principles in EU Foreign Policy*, London: Routledge.

Manners, I. (2002) 'Normative Power Europe: A Contradiction in Terms?', *Journal of Common Market Studies*, 40(2): 253–274.

Mayerfield, J. (2003) 'Who Shall Be the Judge? The United States, the International Criminal Court, and the Global Enforcement of Human Rights', *Human Rights Quarterly*, 94: 93–129.

Meunier, S. (2000) 'What Single Voice? European Institutions and EU–US Trade Negotiations', *International Organization*, 54(1): 103–105.

Moravcsik, A. (1995) 'Explaining International Human Rights Regimes: Liberal Theory and Western Europe', *European Journal of International Relations*, 1(2): 157–189.

Nel, P. (2002) 'Between Counter-Hegemony and Post-Hegemony: The Rome Statute and Normative Innovation in World Politics', in A.F. Cooper, J. English and R. Thakur (eds) *Enhancing Global Governance: Towards a New Diplomacy?*, Tokyo/New York/Paris: United Nations University Press, pp. 152–161.

The EU and the ICC 187

Pace, W.R. (1999) 'The Relationship Between the International Criminal Court and Non-Governmental Organizations', in H.A.M. von Hebel, J.G. Lammers and J. Schukking (eds) *Reflections on the International Criminal Court: Essays in Honour of Adriaan Bos*, The Hague: T.M.C. Asser Press, pp. 189–211.

Pace, W.R. and Thieroff, M. (1999) 'Participation of Non-Governmental Organizations', in R.S. Lee (ed.) *The International Criminal Court: The Making of the Rome Statute. Issues, Negotiations, Results*, The Hague: Kluwer Law International, pp. 391–398.

Pearson, Z. (2006) 'Non-Governmental Organizations and the International Criminal Court: Changing Landscapes of International Law', *Cornell International Law Review*, 39(2): 243–284.

Pollack, M. (2003) *The Engines of European Integration: Delegation, Agency and Agenda Setting in the EU*, Oxford: Oxford University Press.

Rijks, D. (2004) *Fortress or Façade? EU Policymaking on the International Criminal Court*, MA Thesis, Leiden University.

Risse, T., Ropp, S.C. and Sikkink, K. (eds) (1999) *The Power of Human Rights: International Norms and Domestic Change*, Cambridge: Cambridge University Press.

Scheffer, D.J. (1999) 'The United States and the International Criminal Court', *American Journal of International Law*, 93(12): 12–22.

—— (2002) 'Staying the Course with the International Criminal Court', *Cornell International Law Review*, 35: 47–100.

Sewall, S. and Kaysen, C. (2000) *The United States and the International Criminal Court: National Security and International Law*, Lanham, MD: Rowman & Littlefield Publishers, Inc.

Sjöstedt, G. (1977) *The External Role of the European Community*, Westmead: Saxon House.

Smith, K.E. (2003) *European Union Foreign Policy in a Changing World*, Cambridge: Polity Press.

—— (2006) 'Speaking With One Voice? European Union Co-ordination on Human Rights Issues at the United Nations', *Journal of Common Market Studies*, 44(1): 113–137.

Smith, M.E. (2004) *Europe's Foreign and Security Policy: The Institutionalization of Cooperation*, Cambridge: Cambridge University Press.

Stone Sweet, A., Sandholtz, W. and Fligstein, N. (2001) *The Institutionalization of Europe*, Oxford: Oxford University Press.

Strange, S. (1982) 'Cave! Hic Dragones: A Critique of Regime Analysis', *International Organization*, 36(2): 479–496.

Thomas, D.C. (2005) 'The Institutional Construction of EU Foreign Policy: CFSP and the International Criminal Court', prepared for presentation at the European Union Studies Association, Austin, Texas, 31 March to 2 April.

von Hebel, H.A.M., Lammers, J.G. and Schukking, J. (eds) (1999) *Reflections on the International Criminal Court: Essays in Honour of Adriaan Bos*, The Hague: Kluwer Law International.

Wedgwood, R. (1998) 'Fiddling in Rome: America and the International Criminal Court', *Foreign Affairs*, 77(6): 20–24.

—— (1999) 'The International Criminal Court: An American View', *European Journal of International Law*, 10(1): 93–107.

Weiss, T.G. and Gordenker, L. (1996) *NGOs, the UN and Global Governance*, Boulder, CO: Lynne Rienner Publishers.

Weller, M. (2002) 'Undoing the Global Constitution: UN Security Council Action on the International Criminal Court', *International Affairs*, 78(4): 693.

Willetts, P. (1996) *'The Conscience of the World.' The Influence of Non-Governmental Organizations in the UN System*, Washington, DC: Brookings Institution.

10 Conclusion and perspectives

Knud Erik Jørgensen

The previous chapters have explored what the European Union is doing in international organizations. The brief answer is: quite a bit (and surprisingly more than many would expect).

Within the most recent decade, the European Union's engagement in global governance institutions has changed profoundly and has generally become more sustained and consistent. The European Union has declared effective multilateralism to be a key foreign policy objective and, invests heavily in international organizations. However, a significant variation in engagement across policy fields is also part of the general pattern and, in some issue areas, continuity is more pronounced than change. Thus, it is telling that even within a field such as international political economy, which should be a heartland for a player like the European Union, the European Council Conclusions from December 1998 claim that '[i]t is imperative that the Community should play its full role in international monetary and economic policy co-operation within fora like the G-7 and the IMF', whereas a decade on the Treaty of Lisbon explicitly refers to the need 'to secure the euro's place in the international monetary system' and 'to ensure unified representation within the international financial institutions and conferences' (Treaty of Lisbon, Article 115 C). The field of defence displays similar features. Since defence policy was included directly in the European Union's policy portfolio in 1998 – after having been dealt with by the substitute organization, the Western European Union – common European capabilities in terms of institutions and military forces have been developed and this alone can rightly be characterized as a revolution in European defence. However, the overwhelmingly major part of European military forces has remained more or less as it was a decade ago. Actually, if the principle of subsidiarity was applied to the defence sector, the policy competences of EU member states should be allocated to the European level exactly because they cannot be performed efficiently at the national level.

The first chapter outlined a framework for analysis which subsequently served as guidelines for the other chapters. It was emphasized that research on US approaches to multilateral institutions can serve as a useful point of departure for our exploration of the European Union's engagement in international organizations. In the other chapters, contributors thoroughly analysed the European Union's policy towards specific international organizations, spanning the issue areas of security

Conclusion and perspectives   189

(North Atlantic Treaty Organization [NATO] and Organization for Security and Co-operation in Europe [OSCE]), international political economy (World Trade Organization [WTO], International Labour Organization [ILO], International Monetary Fund [IMF] and World Bank) and international norms and obligations (UN and International Criminal Court [ICC]). These chapters contribute important knowledge about the European Union's policies towards multilateral institutions. They contribute to our understanding and answer some of the questions, for instance, why the European Union for so long has been punching below its weight in issue areas where the European Union should be acting like fish in water.

Findings

The European Union's influence in international organizations has clearly become a political issue, sometimes addressed in a celebrative fashion and sometimes in a deploring mood. Influence is sometimes seen as an accomplishment and sometimes as merely an aspiration. When seen from a historical perspective, an increase in engagement and influence is clearly detectable and a rather steep increase characterizes the first decade of the twenty-first century. In short, considerable variation is probably the term best characterizing the current situation. Five characteristics are particularly pronounced. The European Union invests very considerable resources in international organizations, ranging from the UN, the IMF and the OSCE, to the ICC. In most cases the European Union invests more than the Union harvests in terms of influence. The Union and its member states also spend more resources on diplomatic services than any other international player – a fact that follows logically from the political priority of thoroughly duplicating diplomatic institutions. The key objective of supporting multilateral institutions – as stated in the European Security Strategy – can thus be read as simply referring to an already existing situation of supporting organizations financially. If the security strategy phrasing also refers to shaping multilateral institutions in ways we deem best, then the objective can hardly be seen as little more than an aspiration. After all, despite financial contributions and strong formal representations, the European Union has rather limited influence in a number of international organizations, including the UN, the IMF, NATO and the OSCE. This limited influence should be seen against the declared objective of effective multilateralism in general, a long-time declared interest in strengthening the European Union's position in the international financial institutions, a highly publicized priority of promoting democracy and human rights and frequent claims about having responsibility for European security. Furthermore, the European Union seems to be losing some ground in the WTO's relative gain games, not least when compared with the emerging market economies.

This rather 'not very impressive' perspective should be balanced against the following improvements in performance. The European Union's support of the UN has prompted some observers to conclude that the European Union has become the UN's best friend in the West and in order to improve working relationships several interorganizational agreements have been concluded, for instance, in the field of peacekeeping operations. Especially former Secretary General Kofi Annan

190 Knud Erik Jørgensen

developed close relations with the European Union. The European Union collectively or EU member states individually played a significant role in reforming parts of the UN, creating new institutions such as the Human Rights Council and the Peace Building Commission. While the latter has functioned without major problems, the former has become the arena in which less than cooperative EU–OIC relations are being cultivated, with the United States watching from the sidelines. In the case of the WTO, the European Union was among the founders of the organization and left a number of significant European fingerprints on its institutional design. The European Union has actively used the WTO's conflict settlement facility, indeed has been one of the most active WTO members to do so. Furthermore, the European Union has been keen to make the organization truly global in terms of membership and has actively sponsored Chinese membership. Finally, by proposing to include the Singapore issues in the Doha Round, the European Union has for the first time tried to set the international trade agenda and extend the WTO's scope of mission. It remains to be seen whether the WTO's first decade of existence also marked the heyday of the European Union's influence in the organization. Opposition to the EU and US joint hegemony has become more widespread and the same can be said about opposition to the free trade paradigm, that is, the soul of the WTO.

Concerning security organizations such as NATO and the OSCE, relations with the European Union have changed significantly. By actively developing its competence in security, the European Union has become a much more credible partner in NATO and the OSCE. Concerning NATO, the European Union has been keen to upload ideas concerning conflict resolution and peace building and NATO has concluded that it is worthwhile listening. Though trying their best not to function as a caucus within NATO, the EU-27 has developed defence capabilities which would allow the country grouping to act like a caucus. The European Union's duplication of NATO assets is thus comparable to the United States' duplication of NATO defence capabilities. When the former US secretary of state Colin Powell in response to the 2003 Tervuren military HQs project claimed that 'we do not need more headquarters', at least some European NATO members asked, 'Who said "we"?' The European Union has been co-responsible for institutionalizing the Conference on Security and Cooperation in Europe (CSCE) process in the mid-1990s, that is, the very creation of the OSCE. Subsequently the European Union has used the OSCE to achieve milieu goals in the European environment rather than go after narrowly defined instrumental goals. The development of the Union's neighbourhood policy implies that the Union has defined its preferences concerning economic and political developments in, for instance, the Caucasus, while in parallel supporting the OSCE's activities in the same area. Concerning the ICC, EU member states realized during the founding Rome conference in 1998 that they actually shared interests in establishing the ICC – even if they had not actively attempted to build a consensus view. Subsequently, the European Union has been a staunch defender of the ICC, even during times when the international court has been under attack from a less than supportive US Administration.

Taking all these contradictory patterns of engagement into consideration, a rather complex picture of EU instrumentality emerges and both successes and

Conclusion and perspectives 191

failures are parts of the fabric. Perhaps the most perplexing finding is the degree to which the European Union has been incapable of playing a major role in key issue areas within international political economy, while at the same time emerging as a major player within (European) security and defence, not least concerning peace support operations and engagement in de-escalating potential or actual conflicts. Paradoxically, the European Union's first ever military mission was launched in parallel to the serious political row over Iraq. Despite setbacks, lack of success in some fields and challenging future scenarios, the dominant trend in the complex picture is that the European Union is getting increasingly engaged and influential in the world of international organizations.

However, relations between the European Union and international organizations have not been a one-way street of influence. Generally speaking, international organizations have influenced EU institutions and policy-making processes, and in some cases actually rather significantly. The UN has unsurprisingly insisted on a global perspective on world politics and the European Union, being preoccupied by reinventing Europe by means of a single market, European law, institutional reform and the process of enlargement, has slowly got used to more global outlooks. Indeed, some policy fields have been global for quite some time, whereas others only begin to face such challenges. The European Union's traditional priority of cultivating most favoured relations with the African–Caribbean–Pacific group of state countries within the broader category of developing countries has gradually been left behind and replaced by universal criteria for engagement in development issues. The European Union has also been influenced – negatively – by the UN's structures of governance, prioritizing (EU member) states first and permanent observers last, causing the difficult situation of the European Community, represented by the European Commission. In this fashion, the UN and the European Union represent two different worlds: a world of (united) nations and a world of post-modern statehood. These two worlds do not mingle well and it takes a good deal of informal arrangements and diplomatic flexibility to make the relationship beneficial to both parties.

In the case of IMF influence, both EU institutions and policies can be said to have been influenced. Institutions because the governance structures of the IMF make EU institutional changes very difficult. Larger EU member states simply prefer to keep their individual IMF chairs rather than move to, for instance, a supervised delegation model in which their power decreases, at least nominally. In terms of policy, the so-called Washington consensus constitutes a policy paradigm that remains unchallenged by the European Union, indeed the European Union often models its own policies on the Washington consensus.

When it comes to the WTO, the impact has been significant. Thus, the WTO has consistently challenged the Common Agricultural Policy, that is, one of the traditional cornerstones of European integration. Second, processes of globalization have been sponsored by the WTO, in turn influencing the global environment in which the European Union is situated. Third, because support of multilateral institutions by powerful players such as the European Union implies a degree of (self-imposed) constraint *vis-à-vis* weaker players. Fourth, external influence by

192 *Knud Erik Jørgensen*

other governments is often channelled through the WTO, as so splendidly heuristically demonstrated in the banana case. Finally, the very existence of the WTO helps free traders within the European Union strengthen their position *vis-à-vis* trade protectionists and, depending on the changing configurations of EU domestic power, policies are shaped accordingly.

NATO has had a nothing less than profound impact on the European Union, the ESDP institutions being largely modelled on NATO templates (obviously except the civilian crisis management institutions) and with the transfer of Javier Solana from NATO to the European Union as a most useful background. Several peace support operations have been defined by NATO which also took the first turns (for instance, SFOR and IFOR), only to be substituted by peace supporting military forces under EU command. The increasingly global commitment of the two security players has emerged in parallel and cannot be attributed to either NATO or the European Union. The relationship between the CSCE/OSCE and the European Union has been long and mutually beneficial. Thus, it was by involvement in the CSCE process during the 1970s and 1980s that the European Community was gradually recognized by other actors as a player within the field of European security. Furthermore, it was European states which insisted on keeping the CSCE process alive, also when it was most difficult during the so-called second Cold War of the 1980s. The European Union's involvement implied that the CSCE/OSCE became somehow present within the European Union, represented by those officials on whose desks security issues were placed. The involvement in tasking the OSCE implied in turn that the European Union started to ask how possibly OSCE missions could be supported by the European Union. It remains to be seen whether the ICC will have a similar influence on EU institutions or policies.

The fact that international organizations are *governmental* institutions is reflected in their governance structures, making it difficult for non-governmental institutions to fully demonstrate their potential. Hence, the state-centric nature of the multilateral system influences the European Union by enhancing the role of the rotating presidency and limiting the role of the European Commission. A similar pattern characterizes policy-making processes. By contrast, some international organizations consider the European Union a whole complementary to its constituent parts – the EU member states. Thus, the Organisation for Economic Co-operation and Development (OECD) reviews the European Union's economic performance and the IMF treats the Eurozone as a whole. Furthermore, some international organizations – the WTO and the Food and Agriculture Organization of the United Nations – have accepted the European Community as a full member.

In summary, international organizations have significantly influenced EU institutions, policies and policy-making processes. Variation across time and policy fields has been considerable and the direction of change has not been uni-directional. In some cases, the European Union has been catching up for some time – adapting to or complying with global governance institutions, only to overtake some international organizations. Despite variations, the changing relationship between European and global governance institutions is nothing but remarkable. In turn, this is a particular good reason to identify the most important explanatory factors.

Conclusion and perspectives   193

Findings concerning explanatory factors – external, internal and constitutive – are characterized by highly interesting patterns. In stark contrast to findings concerning changing US instrumentalities, we cannot rule out the role of external factors. Thus, changes in the international distribution of power contribute to explain why relations between the European Union, the UN and NATO, respectively, have been able to change in the first place. Changing polarities thus work as a permissive or enabling factor which also explains, at least to some degree, why the change from the security regime CSCE to the institutionalized organization, the OSCE, was possible and desirable. In a sense the CSCE was a Cold War sideshow because the militarily more important issues were handled within the context of the CFE and START negotiations, that is, processes of negotiation in which the European Union played no role at all.

Changing polarity is less capable of explaining why the EU-27 has been keen to create and nourish both the Kyoto Protocol and the ICC in spite of fierce US opposition. Actually, the ICC case demonstrates how external challenges sometimes breed unity rather than diversity. In the introductory chapter I referred to a scenario in which the European Union and the United States are losing ground; in the case of the European Union we can speak about newly acquired ground. The scenario is directly informed by a distribution of power argument and actually, though probably unknowingly, it fits neatly with Kenneth Waltz's (2000) argument about an emerging multipolar international system. In short, though the European Union officially despises power, distribution of power explanations seems to be here to stay and highly relevant for explaining certain dimensions of the European Union's relations with international organizations.

However, domestic factors should clearly not be dismissed as irrelevant in explanations of changing EU instrumentality *vis-à-vis* international organizations. Strong domestic forces – ranging from public opinion, political parties and shared images of world order – contribute to explaining the European Union's commitment to the UN. Similarly, strong interest groups – farmers, industrialists and service providers – have high stakes in EU policies within and towards the WTO and therefore do their best to influence these policies. Something similar characterizes the ILO, the key difference being that employers and employees are directly represented in the organization and that the stakes in most cases are lower. Non-Governmental Organizations (NGOs) have a direct interest in most international policies, ranging from development, environment and the promotion of human rights, to democracy and justice. However, having an interest in an issue area is obviously not the same as influencing the making of EU policies. The potential NGO impact foremost applies to the UN, the WTO and the ICC, whereas it applies considerably less to the cases of the IMF, NATO, OSCE and the ILO. For a composite unit such as the European Union, the 'divisions within the executive branch' factor has unsurprisingly been important in most cases. Though many ingenious and several less ingenious arrangements characterize this area, it is striking just how important the factor is in explanations of the changing instrumentality characterizing most cases.

In some cases, it has been useful to relax the sharp and exclusive distinction between external and internal factors. Thus, the launch of the 2001 'Everything but

194 *Knud Erik Jørgensen*

Arms' initiative can be seen as addressing both external and internal concerns. The initiative influenced simultaneously the position of both domestic and international actors in trade and agriculture. Similarly, the frequent calls for IO reform and performance improvement reflect domestic constituency politics but also the actual (external) performance of international organizations, the balance between the two varying depending on the individual organization in question. In some cases, it is the mutual rather than one-directional impact that characterizes the European Union's relations with international organizations. Also a possible change of the European Union's representation in the IMF will have both external and internal ramifications. Externally, the European Union will likely gain in terms of influence and internally a redistribution of power will take place, with especially France, the United Kingdom and Germany as the relative losers of the game and, hence, their reluctance to implement a decade-old European Council decision.

In summary, if the book is considered a feasibility study, then it clearly demonstrates that there is considerable substance in the topic and more than sufficient to merit future research projects engaging in further explorations. The following section focuses on such wider perspectives.

Perspectives

The research community engaged in research on relations between the European Union and international institutions is growing in terms of numbers and is getting better organized. Hence, let us briefly reflect on the wider perspectives that follow from the findings in this volume. Essentially we have analysed changes (and continuities) over a period of up to two decades. This change issue could be taken further. Does the arrival of a new Secretary General of the UN, Ban Ki-moon, lead to a redefinition of EU–UN relations? Furthermore, it is clear that the Doha Round is in trouble, yet how much does it take to kill it and which role does the European Union intend to play in this context? Do different European Commissions take different views on the European Union's role *vis-à-vis* global governance institutions? Finally, many international organizations face institutional reform, that is, political efforts which potentially produce change. Such an environment of changing configurations of change and continuity seems ideal for a new international player declaring that effective multilateralism is among its key objectives and possessing the soft power it takes to turn objectives into reality.

The present volume has deliberately focused on selected aspects of relations between the European Union and international institutions. We have focused on some policy fields, being cultivated by some international organizations, and we believe that these selected aspects are among the important ones. Other cases and aspects have been left outside the scope of the volume, for instance culture (UN Educational, Scientific and Cultural Organization), communication (International Telegraph Union), political economy (OECD) and environmental issues (Kyoto Protocol). Such aspects and cases deserve to be thoroughly analysed in the future. Furthermore, we have focused on international organizations. However, the European Union's engagement in international regimes presents itself as a very promising

Conclusion and perspectives 195

research agenda. Thus, Clara Portela starts an article in the following way: 'Only a few years ago, the idea that the European Union (EU) could become a significant actor in the nuclear non-proliferation regime would have met with great scepticism' (Portela 2004; but see also Krause 2007). Like other fields of study, research on the European Union and international regimes is highly compartmentalized and the density of case studies is considerable – very few, if any, have so far dared to synthesize case-specific findings in comprehensive studies of regime dynamics. Something similar characterizes reflections on linkages between regimes and organizations. Though this book focuses on the European Union's relations with international organizations, it seems likely that the analytical framework also can be applied in studies of the European Union's policy towards international regimes.

Research on EU policies towards multilateral institutions often emphasizes issues of formal representation. Despite the fact that voting seldom takes place, shares of votes and debates on possible redistribution of votes remain often discussed issues in research. Perhaps this obsession with formal representation reflects both the legalistic administrative culture of the Union and the strong position of legal studies in major parts of Europe. Even political science approaches tend to emphasize formal dimensions, for instance, when employing principal–agent or rational choice models (Hawkins *et al.* 2006). In any case, it has been demonstrated that, in the case of the IMF and the World Bank, formal dimensions matter less than the administrative-scientific culture of these institutions (Woods 2003, 2006). Does it therefore make a difference that the managing director of the IMF always is a European and the World Bank director always an American, or are outcomes more influenced by the (economic) science paradigms that are embedded in these institutions? Furthermore, while formal representation and actual performance do not demonstrate neat correlations, the European Union's actual performance within international institutions has so far not been the target of structured, focused research. Similarly, research on dimensions of power could define an enlarged agenda by means of taking a point of departure in broader conceptions of power (see Barnett and Duvall 2005).

Both the book's specific studies and general findings invite further research not just on individual cases but also conducted as comparative studies. The number of specific cases is perhaps not unlimited but with the existence of hundreds of international organizations – small or large, important or insignificant – there is still quite some work to do. However, it is important to emphasize that we do not just need more studies of individual international organizations. We also need research on specific aspects, for instance the European Union's performance in international organizations, the European Union's support of international organizations in the context of the current crisis of multilateralism, or on dilemmas in the national foreign policy of EU member states, triggered by the European Union's increased engagement in the multilateral system. Turning to comparative studies, it is clear that they can be designed in a number of ways. Some would include two or more international organizations or compare the European Union to other important international players, such as the United States, Russia, China, Japan or India. Even organizations like the Organisation of the Islamic Conference (OIC)

196 *Knud Erik Jørgensen*

seem relevant in this perspective, as Karen Smith has pointed out in a study on the UN Human Rights Council (Smith 2008). Yet, a comparative perspective could also imply a more sophisticated research design than the one applied in this book, which has focused on just one analytical perspective. A comparative research design would include more than just one analytical perspective on the same case(s), partly in order to generate findings from several perspectives and partly to specify each perspective's relative strengths and weaknesses.

Instead of global governance or legal-institutional approaches, the framework has been inspired by the rich literature on the United States' policy towards multilateral institutions. Perhaps a surprise to some but it clearly makes sense to use such state-centric studies as a source of inspiration for analysing the European Union's changing relations with international organizations. Such a choice entails a number of clear advantages, for instance that the approaches have been tested in previous studies and they are potentially connected to major international relations theories. They focus on issues of instrumentality. These strengths can be said also to be their weaknesses. First, though being useful as points of departure, it is necessary to consider the degree to which it is necessary to adapt existing analytical frameworks for research on EU policy towards international organizations. Second, observer bias has consequences for the understanding of multilateral institutions. On the one hand, many of these institutions surely are marked by US instrumental action but, on the other hand, that is only part of the full story. Essentially we do not know the whole story until we have compared with the role multilateral institutions play for other states or for players such as the European Union. For the Union, promotion of multilateralism is often presented as both a means and an end in its own right and, hence, a key component of world order understood as the domestication or legalization of world politics.

References

Barnett, M. and Duvall, R. (eds) (2005) *Power in Global Governance*, Cambridge: Cambridge University Press.

Barnett, M. and Finnemore, M. (2004) *Rules for the World: International Organizations in Global Politics*, Ithaca: Cornell University Press.

Baroncelli, E. (2008) 'On the EU foreign economic policy role in multilateral contexts: Perceptual dynamics and policy responses in the World Bank', paper presented at the conference 'The European Union in International Affairs', Brussels, Palais d'Egmont, 24–26 April.

European Council (2003) 'A secure Europe in a better world', *European Security Strategy*, Paris: Institute for Security Studies.

Foot, R., MacFarlane, S.N. and Mastanduno, M. (eds) (2003) *US Hegemony and International Organizations*, Oxford: Oxford University Press.

Hawkins, D.G., Lake, D.A., Nielson, D.L. and Tierney, M.J. (eds) (2006) *Delegation and Agency in International Organizations*, Cambridge: Cambridge University Press.

Krause, J. (2007) 'Enlightenment and nuclear order', *International Affairs*, 83: 483–499.

Portela, C. (2004) 'The EU and the NPT: Testing the New European Nonproliferation Strategy', *Disarmament Diplomacy Issue 78*, July/August. Online. Available HTTP: http://www.acronym.org.uk (accessed 1 September 2008).

Rittberger, V. and Zangl, B. (2006) *International Organization. Polity, Politics and Policies*, Basingstoke: Palgrave.

Smith, K. (2008) 'Speaking with one voice but having little impact: The EU at the UN's Human Rights Council', paper presented at the conference 'The European Union in International Affairs', Brussels, Palais d'Egmont, 24–26 April.

Waltz, K.W. (2000) 'Structural realism after the Cold War', *International Security*, 25: 5–41.

Woods, N. (2003) 'The United States and the International Financial Institutions: Power and influence within the World Bank and the IMF', in R. Foot, S.N. MacFarlane and M. Mastanduno (eds) *US Hegemony and International Organizations*, Oxford: Oxford University Press, pp. 92–114.

Woods, N. (2006) *The Globalizers: The IMF, the World Bank and their Borrowers*, Ithaca: Cornell University Press.

Index

Afghanistan 46, 55, 111–12, 118–19
African Union 48, 107, 112–13, 122
Agriculture, agricultural 26, 30, 84–5, 88, 92–4, 191–2, 194; *see also* trade
Althea 103, 107, 109, 116, 119, 121, 125, 140; *see also* military missions
American Service members Protection Act (ASPA) 171, 179–80
Asia 1, 24, 28, 69, 70, 112; Central 133–6, 140–1, 144, 146; East 34

balance of power 8, 9, 13, 33, 43, 102
Balkans 9, 37, 102, 109–12, 135–44
bargaining 91, 150–1, 156–60
Berlin Plus Agreement 101–9, 114–22
bilateral, bilateralism 8, 12, 26, 28, 46, 84–6, 91, 95, 144, 169
bilateral agreement(s) 12, 91, 171–2, 176–81
bilateral trade 28, 80, 84, 87, 91
Blair House 85–6, 92
Bretton Woods 21–4, 28–9, 69
burden sharing 47, 106, 114, 141
Bush administration 13, 16, 45, 49, 113–14, 171–3, 181

Caucasus 8–9, 133, 135, 140–4, 190
China 21, 24, 36, 39, 54–5, 64–5, 80, 87–91, 94–5, 170–1, 180, 195
Chinese 13, 27–8, 51, 87, 96, 190
civil society 82, 93, 174, 179
Civilian Headline Goals 155
Climate 43–4, 47, 57
COJUR 169, 172, 176–8
Cold War 9, 12, 16, 38, 103, 110–12, 120–1, 124, 131, 134, 192–3; post-Cold War 12, 102–6, 111–12, 119, 121–3

Commission on Human Rights 52–3, 153; *see also* Human Rights Council
Common Foreign and Security Policy (CFSP) 42, 51, 103, 116, 134, 143, 168–70, 176, 182
Commonwealth of Independent States (CIS) 143–4
Concordia 101–2, 106–7, 117, 121; *see also* military missions
Conference on Security and Cooperation in Europe (CSCE) 7, 134–5, 190, 192–3
conflict prevention 37, 117, 138–40, 145
constructivist approaches 39–40, 46, 92, 119
Council of Ministers 81, 152–8
crimes against humanity *see* genocide
crisis management 101–2, 105–9, 111–13, 117–25, 138, 140, 144–5, 192
crisis prevention 67, 72

delegation model 31, 33–4, 191
development: aid program 71; regional 24, 78, 84; sustainable 67
Diplomatic Conference 169, 174–5
Doha 95; Doha round 12, 26, 80–1, 86, 190, 194
Domestic: factors 10, 12, 44, 92, 193; institutions 10–11; values 10
donors 48–9
dysfunctional governance 30

Ecofin 61, 66–7, 76
Economic and Social Council 37, 39, 41, 153, 158
economic weight 21, 64, 74
economies of scale 32, 62

Index 199

effective multilateralism 1–3, 13, 16, 40, 56, 101–3, 109, 112, 117, 119, 122–5, 133, 188–9, 194

emerging market economies 21, 61, 69, 74, 78, 90, 189

EU presidency 22, 47, 66, 73, 136–8, 141, 143–5

EUFOR 107–8, 113–14; *see also* military missions

European: Bank for Reconstruction and Commerce 24; Central Bank (ECB) 11, 22, 27, 31, 66–8, 76–8; Commission 80, 132, 134, 136–42, 145, 181, 191–4; Community 2, 6, 41–2, 81–2, 103, 114, 133–5, 144, 191–2; Court of Justice 152, 154, 157; exchange rate 24–5, 27–9, 61, 66–7; executive branch (of government) 11, 76, 193; Neighbourhood Policy (ENP) 140, 142; Rapid Reaction Force 105, 119; Security and Defence Identity (ESDI) 104–5, 111; Security and Defence Policy (ESDP) 105, 107–24, 192; Security Strategy 5, 13, 37, 45–6, 101, 189

FAO 6, 41

finance ministers, ministers of finance 21–3, 61, 64–78, 162

financial support 55, 71–2, 136

first order 158, 163; *see also* principal agent framework

fishing, fisheries 42, 154–6, 159

foreign policy: EU foreign policy 3, 5, 9, 56, 135, 167–8, 180–1; strategy 109, 123; US foreign policy 5, 8, 25, 84

G7 22–4, 28, 31, 33

G77 48, 53–5

GATT 80, 83–9

General Assembly 48, 50–2, 59–60, 118, 167, 169

genocide 43, 126, 167, 170, 172; crimes against humanity 167, 170, 172

geopolitical 70–1, 103, 180

global governance 1, 3–4, 11, 16–17, 25, 32, 80, 132, 188, 192, 194, 196,

globalization 9, 14, 81, 90–5, 132, 159, 191

Guiding Principles (ICC) 172, 177, 179–80

hegemon, hegemony 28–9, 34, 86, 89, 91, 136, 190

Helsinki 105, 112, 134–5, 147; Helsinki Accord 134

Human Rights Council (HRC) 13, 37–9, 46, 52–4, 190, 196; *see also* Commission on Human Rights

humanitarian aid 37, 44, 71

IFOR 105, 111, 192

ILO 10, 149–66, 189, 193

IMEC 151, 153, 161–4

IMF 6–7, 21–36, 61–79, 81, 87, 188

Immunity 171, 173–4, 176–7, 181

Institutional: design 7, 87, 102, 116–18, 120–3, 190; power 24, 29; reform 7, 85, 88, 134, 191, 194

Institutionalist 39–40

Integration 22, 25, 30, 40–1, 69, 86, 88–90, 95, 109–10, 132, 134; European 10, 46, 66, 89

Interdependencies 80, 150–1, 154–5, 159, 164

interest groups 10, 16, 32, 193

international: commitments 12, 47, 136; community 68–9; cooperation 4, 11, 56; criminal justice 173, 175, 181; cultural environment 12, 14; development 12; distribution of power 12, 193; finance 25, 28, 33; influence 35; labour conference 149, 151–64; law 169, 175, 178–9, 181; monetary systems 27, 188; political economy 89, 188–9, 191; social structures 13

International Atomic Energy Agency (IAEA) 9, 37, 39, 46–7

International Criminal Court (ICC) 38, 45, 47, 167–82, 189–90, 192–3

Iraq war 44–5, 111–13

Joint Declaration (EU–OSCE) 137, 144

Kyoto Protocol 25, 38, 45, 47, 193–4

Like Minded Group (LMG) 169, 174–5

Lisbon 42, 91, 158; Treaty of 61, 76–7, 188

Index

Maastricht Treaty 42, 48
Maritime: strategy 119; transportantion;
   152, 154, 159, 165
market liberalization 84, 89
migration, migrant workers 161
military missions 103, 107–8, 114,
   116–17, 121
millennium development goals 44
multilateral: cooperation 12, 34, 122;
   institutions 1, 3–5, 10–12, 14–16, 167,
   188–9, 191, 195–6; trade 11–12, 26, 80,
   84, 86
multipolarity 12

NATO 9, 13, 43–4, 101–31, 135–8, 140,
   142, 189–90, 192–3
NATO Response Force (NRF) 109,
   119, 122
neoliberalism 84
neo-mercantilism 83–4, 89
NGO 10, 53, 81–2, 92–3, 95, 172,
   175–81, 193
Nice Treaty 33, 105, 159
Non-Aligned Movement (NAM) 51–3
normative power theory 40
Nuremberg tribunal 174

observer status 41, 76, 96
Ohrid agreement 139
OSCE 6–9, 131–48, 189–90, 192–3

Peacebuilding Commission (PBC) 51–2
peacekeeping, peacekeepers 37, 41, 44–8,
   135, 172–3, 177, 181, 189
Permanent Council 134, 136–7, 144–5
policy: implications 3–4, 22, 34, 143, 168;
   makers 9, 29–30, 108, 180; oriented,
   orientation 29, 88–9, 149
political: action 11, 15; and security
   committee 107, 138, 172
power: distribution of power 12, 16, 22,
   34, 193–4; international power 25;
   redistribution of power 15, 33, 194; soft
   power 25, 131, 141–2, 146, 194
Preparatory Committee 169, 178
principal agent framework 151, 163–4
private sector 28, 67–8, 70
protectionism 84, 86, 90–2

quotas 21, 23, 61, 72, 74, 78, 83, 91

Rapid Reaction Force 105, 108, 119;
   see also European RRF
Realism 38, 89–90, 92; neo- 12
Realist 39, 43–4, 47, 91–2; neo- 12;
   structural 84
regional: block 26; development 24, 78,
   84; organizations 142
regionalism 26–7
Rome: conference 168–9, 173–5, 178,
   190; statute 168, 170–6, 181–2;
   Treaty, Treaty of Rome 9, 83
Russia, Russian 13, 22, 44–5, 52,
   54, 64, 87–90, 136, 142–6,
   170–1, 195

SCIMF 66–7, 76
second order 151, 158, 161, 163–4;
   see also principal agent framework
Security Council (SC) 7, 15,
   37–52, 112, 169, 172–81;
   reform 7, 50
SFOR 116, 192
Single Market 29, 84, 87–8, 91, 191
social dialogue 156, 159
social market economy 161
soft policy 161, 164
Solana, Javier 9, 11, 46, 115–17,
   121, 124, 182, 192
sovereignty 37, 76
St Malo 102, 104, 113–14, 117, 123
state centric approach 5, 8, 11–12, 15,
   192, 196
structuration theory 14, 83
Sudan 44, 107, 112, 122
supranational 81, 150
surveillance 22, 25, 66–7, 69, 72,
   78, 158

The Hague 167, 174, 178, 180
Trade: agreements 12, 27, 80, 91;
   agricultural trade 30, 83–4, 86;
   barriers, Trade Barrier
   Regulation (TBR) 94; diplomacy,
   diplomats 81–95; global trade 80,
   86–7; international trade 9, 25–6,
   30, 64, 81–2, 95, 190; negotiations
   26, 84; policy 42, 80, 82, 89, 91–5,
   150; transatlantic trade 93–4
transparency 53, 72, 83, 88, 106, 122,
   132, 161

tripartite 152, 153, 156
troika 138–9, 145, 179
Turkey 47, 62–3, 105, 107
two-level game 81–2, 85, 89, 92–3

Ukraine 47, 62–3, 87–8, 139, 142
UN charter 38
UNESCO 8–9
United Nations 1, 3, 37–60, 108, 110–13, 122, 139, 191–2
UNPROFOR 9, 43
Uruguay round 85, 88

voluntary contributions 48
voting share 64–5, 74–5

war crimes 167, 170, 172, 175
war on terror 112–13, 120
Washington 67, 78, 86, 94, 136, 172–3, 176–7, 181, 191
Weapons of Mass Destruction (WMD) 9, 46, 143
Western European Union (WEU) 104–6, 114–16
working group for social affairs 152–4
World Bank (WB) 6–8, 23, 28, 46, 64, 67–8, 71, 76, 81, 189, 195
World Economic Outlook 67, 69
WTO 6–10, 13, 23, 25–6, 55, 80–99, 118, 189–93

eBooks – at www.eBookstore.tandf.co.uk

A library at your fingertips!

eBooks are electronic versions of printed books. You can store them on your PC/laptop or browse them online.

They have advantages for anyone needing rapid access to a wide variety of published, copyright information.

eBooks can help your research by enabling you to bookmark chapters, annotate text and use instant searches to find specific words or phrases. Several eBook files would fit on even a small laptop or PDA.

NEW: Save money by eSubscribing: cheap, online access to any eBook for as long as you need it.

Annual subscription packages

We now offer special low-cost bulk subscriptions to packages of eBooks in certain subject areas. These are available to libraries or to individuals.

For more information please contact webmaster.ebooks@tandf.co.uk

We're continually developing the eBook concept, so keep up to date by visiting the website.

www.eBookstore.tandf.co.uk